Pr

"Helen Brown's remarkable memoir took me on a journey that threatened to break my heart, and right when I thought I couldn't possibly bear to read another word, I realized that she didn't break my heart at all—she opened it."
—**Beth Hoffman,** *New York Times* bestselling author of *Saving CeeCee Honeycutt*

"Possibly the next *Marley & Me, Cleo,* by Helen Brown, is an honest and un-mawkish true story of ordinary people rebuilding their lives after a tragedy, with the help of a kitten. Even non cat-lovers will be moved."
—*Good Housekeeping*

"Heartwarming, fun, and romantic. *Marley & Me* fans will love it."
—*Closer*

"This is an absolute must gift for yourself or a cat-loving friend."
—*Cat World*

"Helen Brown's Cleo is not just a tender story about a cat and a family facing the world again after a family bereavement. It's also an epic, genuinely moving, funny, and ultimately, uplifting. Don't be surprised to find yourself smiling through tears after reading it."
—**Witi Ihimaera,** author of *The Whale Rider*

Cleo

The Cat Who
Mended a Family

HELEN BROWN

CITADEL PRESS
Kensington Publishing Corp.
www.kensingtonbooks.com

CITADEL PRESS BOOKS are published by
Kensington Publishing Corp.
119 West 40th Street
New York, NY 10018

This is the American edition of the hardcover published in Great Britain by
Hodder & Stoughton.

All Kensington titles, imprints, and distributed lines are available at special quantity
discounts for bulk purchases for sales promotions, premiums, fund-raising, educational, or
institutional use. Special book excerpts or customized printings can also be created to fit
specific needs. For details, write or phone the office of the Kensington special sales manager:
Kensington Publishing Corp., 119 West 40th Street, New York, NY 10018, attn: Special Sales
Department; phone 1-800-221-2647.

CITADEL PRESS and the Citadel logo are Reg. U.S. Pat. & TM Off.

First printing: September 2010

10 9 8 7 6 5 4 3 2 1

Printed in the United States of America

Library of Congress Control Number: 2010924998

ISBN-13: 978-0-8065-3303-2
ISBN-10: 0-8065-3303-X

To those who say
they aren't cat people
but deep down
know they are.

Contents

Cleo

Choice

A cat chooses its owner, not the other way around.

"We're not getting a kitten," I said, negotiating our station wagon around a bend the shape of a pretzel. "We're just going to look at them."

The road to Lena's house was complicated by its undulations, not to mention the steepness. It snaked over what would qualify as mountains in most parts of the world. There wasn't much beyond Lena's house except a few sheep farms and a stony beach.

"You said we could get a kitten," Sam whined from the backseat before turning to his younger brother for support. "Didn't she?"

The backseat was usually the boys' battleground. Between two brothers aged nearly nine and six the dynamic was predictable. Sam would set Rob up with a surreptitious jab that would be rewarded with a kick, demanding retaliation with a thump, escalating into recriminations and tears—"He punched me!" "That's 'cos he pinched me first." But this time they were on the same side, and my usual role of judge and relationship counselor had been supplanted by a simpler one—the Enemy.

"Yeah, it's not fair," Rob chimed in. "You said."

Helen Brown

"What I said was we *might* get a kitten one day. One big dog is enough for any family. What would Rata do? She'd hate having a cat in the house."

"No, she wouldn't. Golden retrievers like cats," Sam replied. "I read it in my pet book."

There was no point recalling the number of times we'd seen Rata disappear into undergrowth in pursuit of an unfortunate member of the feline species. Since Sam had given up trying to become a superhero and thrown his Batman mask to the back of his wardrobe, he'd morphed into an obsessive reader brimming with facts to destroy any argument I could dredge up.

I didn't want a cat. I probably wasn't even a cat person. My husband, Steve, certainly wasn't. If only Lena hadn't smiled so brightly that day at our neighborhood playgroup when she'd asked: "Would you like a kitten?" If only she hadn't said it so loudly—and in front of the kids.

"Wow! We're getting a kitten!" Sam had yelled before I had a chance to answer.

"Wow! Wow!" Rob had echoed, jumping up and down in his sneakers with the holes I'd been trying to ignore.

Even before we'd met Lena I'd been in awe of her. A willowy beauty with an eclectic fashion style, she'd migrated from Holland in her late teens to become a highly regarded painter. Her portraits invariably contained political comment about race, sex or religion. An artist in the deepest sense, she also chose to live independently from men with her three children. Personally, I wouldn't have been surprised if Lena had summoned her offspring from some parallel universe only she and Pablo Picasso had access codes to. I wasn't about to make a fuss about a kitten in front of her.

✦

Raising a pair of boys was proving to be more demanding than I'd imagined back when I was a schoolgirl watching baby-shampoo ads on television. If there'd been an Olympic medal for teenage-mother naivety, I'd have won gold. Married and pregnant at nineteen, I'd smiled at the notion of babies waking up at night. Those were *other* people's babies. Reality struck with Sam's birth. I'd tried to grow up fast. Midnight phone calls to Mum three hundred kilometers away hadn't always been helpful ("He must be teething, dear"). Fortunately, older, more experienced mothers had taken pity on me. With kindness and great patience they'd guided me through Motherhood 101. I'd eventually learned to accept that sleep is a luxury and a mother is only ever as happy as her saddest child. So in those closing days of 1982 I was doing okay. They were gorgeous boys, and put it this way: I hadn't been to the supermarket wearing a nightgown under my coat for several months.

We were living in Wellington, a city famous for two things—bad weather and earthquakes. We'd just managed to purchase a house with the potential to expose us to both: a bungalow halfway down a zigzag on a cliff directly above a major fault line.

Minor earthquakes were so common we hardly noticed when walls trembled and plates rattled. But people said Wellington was overdue for a massive quake like the one of 1855, when great tracts of land disappeared into the sea and were flung up in other places.

It certainly seemed like our bungalow clung to the hill as if it was prepared for something terrible to happen. There was a faded fairytale appeal to its pitched roof, dark-beamed cladding and shutters. Mock Tudor meets Arts and Crafts, it wasn't shabby chic; it was just plain shabby. My efforts to create a cottage garden had resulted in an apology of forget-me-nots along the front path.

Quaint as it was, clearly the house had been built with a family of alpine goats in mind. There was no garage, not even a street frontage. The only way to reach it was to park the car up at road level, high above our roofline, and bundle groceries and children's gear into our arms. Gravity would take care of the rest, sucking us down several zigs and zags to our gate.

We were young, so it was no problem on sunny days when the harbor was blue and as flat as a dinner plate. Whenever a southerly gale roared up from Antarctica, however, tearing at our coat buttons and flinging rain in our faces, we wished we'd bought a more sensible house.

But we loved living a twenty-minute walk from town. Equipped with ropes and rock-climbing shoes we could have made it in five. When we headed into the city, an invisible force would send us plummeting down the lower end of the zigzag. Hurtling through scrub and flax bushes, we'd pause for a glimpse. A circle of amethyst hills, stark and steep, rose above us. I was amazed we could be part of such beauty.

The path then pulled us across an old wooden footbridge spanning the main road. From there we could either take steps down to the bus stop or continue our perpendicular journey to the Houses of Parliament and central railway station. The slog home from the city was another matter. It took twice as long and demanded the lungs of a mountaineer.

The zigzag had a sharply divided social structure. There was a Right Side, on which substantial two-story houses nestled in gardens with aspirations to Tuscany. And the Wrong Side, where bungalows sprinkled themselves like afterthoughts along the edge of the cliff. Wrong Side people tended to have weed collections rather than gardens.

The prestige of jobs declined in direct correlation to the zigzag's slope. On the top right-hand side Mr. Butler's house sat like a castle. Grey and two-story, it oozed superiority not only over the neighborhood but the city in general.

Below Mr. Butler's, a two-story house opened out over the harbor, looking as if it would hardly be bothered by mere social comparisons. With eaves graceful as seagull's wings, it seemed ready to take off in the next decent gale to a far more glamorous world. Rick Desilva ran a record company. People said that before they were married, his wife, Ginny, had been a fashion model, New Zealand's answer to Jean Shrimpton. Shielded behind a thicket of vegetation that no doubt could be dried and smoked, they had a reputation for parties.

There was a ridiculous rumor that Elton John had been seen staggering out of their house drunk as a dog, though in reality it was just someone who looked like him. Their son, Jason, was at the same school as our boys. They were perched on the lip of a gully about half a mile farther up the hill, but we kept our distance. The Desilvas had a sports car. Steve said they were too racy. I had no energy to argue.

Our side of the zigzag specialized in recluses and people who were renting for a while before moving somewhere less exposed, with better access and not so close to the fault line. Mrs. Sommerville, a retired high school teacher, was one of the few longtime residents of the Wrong Side. She inhabited a tidy weatherboard house one down from us. A lifetime with adolescents had done nothing for her looks. She wore a permanent expression of someone who'd just received an insult.

Mrs. Sommerville had already appeared on our doorstep with complaints about our dog terrorizing her cat, Tomkin, a large tabby cat with a matching sour face. Even though I tried to avoid her, I bumped into her most days, giving her the opportunity to point out skid marks where boys had been zooming down the zigzag illegally on skateboards, or the latest graffiti on her letterbox. Mrs. Sommerville's pathological dislike of boys included our sons, who were suspects of every crime. Steve said I was imagining things. While she loathed boys, Mrs. Sommerville knew how to turn the charm on for men.

•

I worked at home, writing a weekly column for Wellington's morning newspaper, *The Dominion*. Steve worked one week home, one week away, as radio officer on one of the ferries that plowed between the North and South Islands. We'd met at a ship's party when I was fifteen. A grand old man of twenty, he was the most exotic creature I'd ever encountered. Compared to the farmers who steered us around country dance halls near New Plymouth where I grew up, he was from another world.

His face was peachy white and he had baby-soft hands. I'd been mesmerized by his blue eyes, which glowed under their long lashes. Unlike the farmers, he hadn't been frightened of conversation. I'd assumed that being English, he was probably related to one of the Beatles, if not the Rolling Stones.

I'd loved the way his tawny hair draped across his collar, just like Paul McCartney's. He'd smelled of diesel oil and salt, the perfume of the wider world that was impatient for me to join it.

We'd written to each other for three years. I'd sprinted through school and a journalism course (straight Cs), then flown to England. Steve was literally the man of my dreams—I'd met him in person for only two weeks during the three years we'd been letter writing—and reality had no hope of matching up. His parents were probably unimpressed with his big-boned girlfriend from the colonies.

We'd married in the Guildford registry office a month after my eighteenth birthday. Only five people had been brave enough to turn up for the ceremony. The officiant was so bored he forgot to mention the ring. My new husband slipped it on my finger afterwards outside in the porch. It was raining. Distraught back in New Zealand, my parents investigated the possibilities of annulment, but they were powerless.

About two weeks after the wedding I'd stared at the toilet seat in our rented flat and thought it needed polishing. That was when I knew getting married had been a mistake. Yet we'd upset so many people by insisting on it I couldn't back out. Short of running away and causing more pain, the only solution I could think of was to create a family. Steve reluctantly obliged. Honest from the start, he'd made it clear that babies weren't really his thing.

We returned to New Zealand, where I'd labored through a December night too frightened to ask the nurse to turn the light on in case it was breaking hospital rules. Somewhere through a drug-induced haze I'd heard the doctor singing "Morning Has Broken." Minutes later she'd lifted baby Sam from my body.

Before he'd even taken his first breath he turned his head and stared into my face with his huge blue eyes. I thought I'd explode with love. My body ached to hold this brand-new human with his downy hair glowing under the delivery room lights. Sam was wrapped in a blanket—blue in case I forgot what sex he was—and lowered into my arms. Kissing his forehead, I was overcome by the sensation that I'd never be safely inside my own skin again. I uncurled his tiny fist. His lifeline was strong and incredibly long.

Even though it was supposed to be our first meeting, Sam and I recognized each other immediately. It felt like a reunion of ancient souls who'd never spent long apart.

Becoming parents hadn't brought Steve and me closer together. In fact, it had the opposite effect. Two and a half years after Sam's birth Rob slid into the world.

Lack of sleep and jangled nerves had made our differences more apparent. Steve sprouted a beard, a look that was becoming fashionable, and retreated behind it. Returning from a week at sea, he was tired and irritable.

He became annoyed with what he perceived as my extravagance over the boys' clothes and upkeep. I bought a secondhand sewing machine that emitted electric shocks and I taught myself to cut their hair. I grew louder, larger and more untidy.

The times we weren't sure how much longer we could stay together were interspersed with phases of holding on and hoping things might improve for the sake of the boys. Even though we were drifting apart like icebergs on opposing ocean currents, there was absolutely no doubt we both loved them.

◆

"Now, boys," I said, pulling up outside Lena's house and heaving the handbrake high as it would go. "Don't get your hopes up. We're just going to look."

They scrambled out of the car and were halfway down the path to Lena's house before I'd closed the driver's door. Watching their blond hair catch the sunlight, I sighed and wondered if there'd ever be a time I wouldn't be struggling to catch up with them.

Lena had opened the door by the time I got there, and the boys were already inside. I apologized for their bad manners. Lena smiled and welcomed me into the enviable tranquillity of her home, which overlooked the playing field where I often took the boys to run off excess energy.

"We've just come to look at the . . ." I said as she escorted me into her living room. "Oh, kittens! Aren't they adorable?"

In a corner, under some bookshelves, a sleek bronze cat lay on her side. She gazed at me through amber eyes that belonged not to a cat but a member of the aristocracy. Nestled into her abdomen were four appendages. Two were coated with a thin layer of bronze hair. Two were darker. Perhaps once their fur had grown they'd turn out to be black. I'd seen recently born kittens before, but never ones as tiny as these. One of the darker kittens was painfully small.

The boys were on their knees in awe of this nativity scene. They seemed to know to keep a respectful distance.

"They've only just opened their eyes," Lena said, scooping one of the bronze kittens from the comfort of its twenty-four-hour diner. The creature barely fitted inside her hand. "They'll be ready to go to new homes in a couple of months."

The kitten squirmed and emitted a noise that sounded more like a yip than a meow. Its mother glanced up anxiously. Lena returned the infant to the fur-lined warmth of its family to be assiduously licked. The mother used her tongue like a giant mop, swiping parallel lines across her baby's body, then over its head for good measure.

"Can we get one, please, PLEASE?" Sam begged, looking up at me with that expression parents struggle to resist.

"*Please?*" his brother echoed. "We won't throw mud on Mrs. Sommerville's roof anymore."

"You've been throwing mud on Mrs. Sommerville's roof?!"

"Idiot!" Sam said, rolling his eyes and jabbing Rob with his elbow.

But the kittens . . . and there was something about the mother. She was so self-assured and elegant. I'd never seen a cat like her. She was smaller than an average cat, but her ears were unusually large. They rose like a pair of matching pyramids from her triangular face. Darker stripes on her forehead whispered of a jungle heritage. Short hair, too. My mother always said short-haired cats were clean.

"She's a wonderful mother, pure Abyssinian," Lena explained. "I tried to keep an eye on her, but she escaped into the bamboos for a couple of nights a while back. We don't know who the father is. A wild tom, I guess."

Abyssinian. I hadn't heard of that breed. Not that my knowledge of pedigreed cats was encyclopedic. I'd once known a Siamese called Lap Chow, the pampered familiar of my ancient piano teacher, Mrs. McDonald. Our three-way relationship was doomed from the start. The only thing that hurt more than Mrs. McDonald's ruler whacking my fingers as they fumbled over the keys was Lap Chow's hypodermic-needle claws sinking into my ankles. Between the two of them they did a good job creating a lifelong prejudice against music lessons and pedigreed cats.

"Some people say Abyssinians are descended from the cats the ancient Egyptians worshipped," Lena continued.

It certainly wasn't difficult to imagine this feline priestess presiding over a temple. The combination of alley cat and royalty had allure. If the kittens manifested the best attributes of both parents (classy yet hardy), they could turn out to be something special. If, on the other hand, less desirable elements of royalty and rough trade (fussy and feral) came to the fore in the offspring, we could be in for a roller-coaster ride.

"There's only one kitten left," Lena added. "The smaller black one."

Of course people had gone for the larger, healthier-looking kittens first. The bronze ones probably had more appeal, as they had a better chance of turning out looking purebred like their mother. I'd already decided I preferred the black ones, though not necessarily the runt with its bulging eyes and patchy tufts of fur.

"But the little one seems to have a lot of spirit," Lena said. "She needs it to survive. We thought we were going to lose her during the first couple of days, but she managed to hold on."

"It's a girl?" I said, already stupid with infatuation and incapable of using cat breeder's language.

"Yes. Would you like to hold her?"

Fearing I'd crush the fragile thing, I declined. Lena lowered the tiny bundle of life into Sam's hands instead. He lifted the kitten and stroked his cheek with her fur. He'd always had a thing about fur. I'd never seen him so careful and tender.

"You know it's my birthday soon . . ." he said. I could guess what was coming next. "Don't give me a party or a big present. There's only one thing I want for my birthday. This kitten."

"When's your birthday?" Lena asked.

"Sixteenth of December," said Sam. "But I can change it to any time."

"I don't like kittens to leave their mother until they're quite independent," she said. "I'm afraid this one won't be ready until mid February."

"That's okay," said Sam, gazing into the slits of its eyes. "I can wait."

The boys knew the best thing to do now was to shut up and look angelic. Maybe nurturing a kitten would wean them off war games and tune them into feminine sensibilities. As for Rata, we'd do our best to protect the kitten from such a monstrous dog.

Further debate was pointless. How could I turn down a creature so determined to seize life? Besides, she was Sam's birthday present.

"We'll take her," I said, somehow unable to stop smiling.

A Name

There's only one correct name for a cat—Your Majesty.

"It's not fair!" Rob wailed. "He's getting a kitten *and* a digital Superman watch for his birthday!"

Lifting the banana cake out of the oven, I burnt the side of my hand and suppressed a curse. The pain was searing, but there was no point yelling. Not with an electric sander drilling my eardrums and the boys on the brink of World War III. I plonked the cake on a cooling rack and glanced out at the harbor.

The risk of living on the fault line was neutralized by the sea view framed by hills stabbing the sky. Who cared if the bungalow had been "renovated" twenty years earlier by a madman who used wood one grade up from cardboard? Wandering over its ivory-colored shag-pile carpet, ignoring the lurid wallpapers, we'd echoed the estate agent's mantra: "Character . . . Potential." Besides, Optimist was my middle name. If the town was hit by a serious earthquake the house would almost certainly plummet off the cliff into the sea, but we'd probably be somewhere else that day. Yes, we'd just happen to be inside one of those downtown skyscrapers built on gigantic rollers specifically designed to endure the earth's groans.

Steve and I were both hoping our differences would dissolve in the bungalow's magical outlook. A marriage between

two people from opposite sides of the world and whose personalities were as likely to blend as oil and water could surely
be crafted into survival here. Besides, Steve was willing to
renovate the 1960s renovations, as long as it didn't cost too
much. His latest project, to strip back the paint on all the
doors and skirting boards to expose the natural wood grain,
was deafening.

"Can you turn that noise down, please?" I shouted down
the hall.

"I can't turn it down!" Steve yelled back. "There's only one
volume. It's an *electric* sander."

"Sam has to wait eight more weeks for the kitten," I explained
to Rob, running my hand under the cold tap and wondering
why it wasn't doing any good. "Besides, if you ask nicely I'm
sure you can have a digital Superman watch when it's your
birthday."

"Sam doesn't even play Superman anymore," Rob said. "He
just reads books about history and stuff."

He was right. Sam's new phase didn't include comic book
heroes. A Superman watch wasn't Sam anymore. Nevertheless,
when he'd opened the parcel that morning he'd smiled and
been gracious.

"I hate my watch," Rob said. "It should go in a museum.
Nobody has a watch that ticks anymore."

"That's not true," I said. "There's nothing wrong with your
watch."

The sander's shrieking mercifully stopped. Steve appeared
coated in paint dust and wearing a mask and a bath cap.

"You look funny, Daddy," Rob said. "Like a big white Smurf."

"It's no good," Steve sighed. "That paint's glued to the
wood. I'll have to take the doors off. There's a place in town
that'll soak them in acid baths. It's the only way we'll get rid
of that paint."

"You're removing all our doors?" I asked. "Even the bathroom's?"

"Only for a week or two."

Lured by the smell of banana cake, Sam wandered into the kitchen. Rata trailed behind, clicking her toenails over the vinyl. If boy and dog were ever twin souls those two were it. She'd arrived, a milk-colored puppy, when Sam was just two years old. They'd grown up together, comrades in arms whenever the fridge needed raiding or Christmas presents unearthing two weeks early from under our bed.

I couldn't remember exactly when Rata decided she was the senior partner and assumed the mantle of guardianship. Perhaps Rob's birth, two and a half years after Sam's, had something to do with it. With Rob's arrival, Rata took on nanny duties. The retriever would stretch in front of the fireplace, her tongue lolling nonchalantly on the carpet; Rob used her as a pillow while he sucked on his bottle of milk. The drawbacks of living with such an animal—layers of silvery hairs over our carpet and furniture, a pervasive doggy smell that I imagined made visitors balk—were a miniscule price. Rata had a heart bigger than the Pacific Ocean. I hoped that heart could encompass a small furry stranger.

"Have you thought of a name for the kitten yet, Sam?" I asked.

"She could be Sooty or Blackie," Rob volunteered.

Sam fixed his younger brother with the look of a tiger about to lunge at a chicken.

"I think E.T. would be a good name," Sam said.

"Noooo!" Rob wailed. "That's a horrible name!"

Rob hadn't fully recovered from the movie *E.T.* His terror of Steven Spielberg's alien had provided Sam with a wealth of fresh material to freak Rob out. Ever since Sam told him the gas meter on the zigzag was E.T.'s cousin, Rob refused to walk past it without clutching my hand.

"Why not?" Sam said. "The kitten looks a bit like an E.T. with hardly any hair and those bulging eyes. But not as scary as the E.T. I saw in our bathroom last night. He's still there, but don't look at him, Rob. If he sees you looking he'll eat you up and it's worse than being eaten by an alligator because he's got no teeth . . ."

"Sam, stop it," I warned. But it was too late. Rob was already running out of the kitchen with fingers planted in his ears.

"He makes green slime run out of his nose so he can dissolve your bones and suck you up!" Sam yelled after him.

"Not funny," I growled.

Sam slid onto a kitchen chair and examined his cake. Apart from the times he was teasing his brother, Sam had transmuted into an introspective soul, so unlike the wild warrior he used to be. I occasionally worried what went on inside his head. Mixing icing in a saucepan, I asked if he'd like to help decorate the cake. He said yes—just a few jellybeans would do.

Sam had kept his word about a modest birthday and invited only one friend, Daniel, from around the corner. He claimed to be sick of "those big parties where everyone goes crazy." I had to agree. Those tribes of boys who trashed the house and tied sheets together to leap out of windows surely needed medication, or more of it.

At the last minute I'd felt guilty and tried to persuade him to ask more boys. But he said he was happy with just his best friend, Rob, and Rata. The only thing he insisted on was to be allowed to light his own candles. It seemed a small enough request.

I spread newspaper on the kitchen table and spooned the pale icing onto the cake. The texture was about right for once, smooth and easy to shape. To prove I was a half-creative mother, I added cocoa powder to the dregs of the icing in the pot, stirred in some boiling water and trickled a large, wonky "9" on top of the cake. Sam pressed the jellybeans into the sticky surface.

As he glanced up at me his sapphire eyes darkened. He suddenly appeared ancient and wise. I'd seen that look several times recently. It unnerved me, especially when he said things that seemed to emanate from a soul who'd been on earth countless times before and was aware he was merely passing through.

"It's a good time to be alive," he said, sneaking a black jellybean under the table to Rata.

"It's a *great* time to be alive," I corrected.

"I'm jealous of Granddad. He was alive when the first cars were made and they started flying planes. He saw towns get electricity and movie theaters. That must've been exciting."

"Yes, but when you get to be an old man you'll have seen even bigger changes. Things we can't imagine now. You'll be able to say to your grandchildren, 'I had one of the first digital Superman watches ever.'"

He glanced down at his wrist and arranged his lips in a diplomatic smile. I wanted to take him by the shoulders, hold him close so I could savor the delectable smell of his skin.

"I was just joking about calling the kitten E.T.," he confided, scraping a teaspoon around the pot to collect what was left of the chocolate icing and shoveling it into his mouth. "Her mother looks like an Egyptian queen. I think we should call her Cleopatra. Cleo for short."

"Cleo," I said, running a hand through his hair and wondering if children ever understand the painful depth of their parents' love. "That's a great name."

"I'm giving Rata a lot of attention, so she doesn't get jealous of the kitten. I brushed her coat twice yesterday. We've talked a lot about it. She's going to like Cleo."

Rata put her head in his lap and gazed up at him with liquid eyes.

"She seems to understand every word you're saying," I said.

"Animals know a lot more than people do. Dogs can tell when there's going to be an earthquake. Birds can fly halfway around the world to find their nest. If people listened to animals more often they wouldn't make so many mistakes."

Sam's connection with animals had become apparent when he was a baby. Our outings were devoted to animal spotting more than anything else. Enthroned in his pushchair, he'd wave chubby arms at dogs and cats wherever we went. One day, he pointed at a seagull circling above our heads and said his first word—"Dird!"

Animals were a tactile experience for Sam, too. He adored the feel of fur and feathers. Mum gave him an old goatskin rug that was black and white and shiny with age. Sam had dragged it into his bed to sleep on its comforting smoothness every night.

He was born with a wild sense of humor, a tool to test boundaries. When he was small I feigned shock at his use of rude words. He retaliated by following me around humming "Bum, bum, bumble bee." Never afraid of flamboyance, he'd flung himself fully dressed into a bath of water and insisted on wearing a monkey mask with matching feet for the duration of his eighth birthday. Life was too magnificent not to be made fun of. I understood where he was coming from. Teachers were either amused or appalled by him, though none of them complained when, at the age of eight, he scored a reading age of thirteen. While he wasn't disruptive at school, he enjoyed making bold personal statements, like excusing himself from class if he thought I might be in the school grounds, or asking to have his hair cropped close to the scalp when other boys were diligently growing theirs long.

I knew and loved every part of his body, especially the so-called imperfections: the scar above his left eyebrow where as a toddler he'd collided with the edge of the coffee table; his square hands with their chewed fingernails; the wart in the middle of the palm of his right hand. I adored the chip in his front tooth (tricycle accident), the flecks that made his eyes seem so wise sometimes, his feet (often grubby) and his nuggetty legs toasted by the sun. Without these he'd have been a flawless boy, a cherub too perfect for planet Earth. His scratches, bruises and scars formed a secret code only the two of us knew the history and formation of. Knowing Sam the animal lover and clown, I wasn't sure what to make of his serious approach to his ninth birthday. Maybe he wanted to prove how much he'd grown up.

The knocker rapped against the front door. Sam and Rata trotted down the hall to answer it.

Daniel seemed to understand it was an understated birthday. The three boys sat around the kitchen table with Rata strategically positioned underneath to collect her share of the feast. I snapped a few photos while the birthday boy lit his nine candles. The atmosphere was rich with feeling, yet strangely somber.

Weeks later, when the photos came back from the processor they were so dark it was hard to make out the images. Even though the kitchen had been flooded with sunlight that afternoon, Sam's image was cloaked in shadow, with a halo of gold light around the edges. Maybe I was a lousy photographer. Or perhaps it was one of those supernatural tricks some people believe cameras are capable of performing.

Loss

Unlike humans, cats are accustomed to loss.

Most days are so similar they're forgotten almost before the sun sets on them. Thousands of days dissolve into each other, evolving into months and years. We slide through time expecting each day to be as predictable as the one before. Lulled into routines involving the same breakfast cereals, school runs and familiar faces, we're anesthetized into believing our lives will go on unchanged forever.

The twenty-first of January 1983 started out that way. There were no hints this date would slam down on us and slice our lives permanently in two.

After breakfast the boys wrestled in their pajamas on the living room floor, with Rata refereeing while Steve unscrewed the bathroom door from its frame. The last door headed for the acid dipper in town, it was also the most political. Nobody wanted to pee in public.

Doors are heavier than they look. It took the four of us, aided by cheerful tripping up from Rata, to carry the thing up the zigzag and stow it in the station wagon. It was January—summer holiday time on this hemisphere—and the boys were bronzed, their hair almost white from the sun. Unlike me, they were keen to meet the mysterious acid dipper. After Steve had tied the bathroom door to the car, the boys slid into what was left of the backseat.

On the way into town, Steve dropped me at my friend Jessie's place in a suburb wedged between the hills. Climbing out of the car, I turned and invited Sam to take my place in the front passenger seat. Smiling, I told him I'd see him after lunch. His blue eyes beamed into mine as he slid into the front. We had no reason to believe that "after lunch" would never happen.

Jessie was on the mend after a week in bed with the flu. Like a Victorian heroine in her white nightgown, she stretched on the covers and made the most of her semi-invalid status. We drank soup, talked and laughed about our kids. Her boys were older than ours, well into high school and turning into artistic rebels. I imagined Sam and Rob would be getting up to similar antics in the not-too-distant future.

Somewhere a phone rang. Jessie's husband, Peter, answered. I was vaguely aware of his voice in the background. His tone was clipped, then jagged. He seemed to be receiving some kind of bad news. Wondering if he'd lost an elderly relative, I arranged my face in what I hoped was a sympathetic shape as he entered the bedroom. He looked pale and on edge, like someone being devoured by a drama he wanted no part of. He glanced at Jessie, then at me. His eyes were black as onyx. The phone call, he said, was for me.

There'd obviously been some kind of mistake. Who'd ring me at Jessie's house? Hardly anyone knew I was there in the first place. Confused, I walked into the hallway and lifted the receiver.

"It's terrible," I heard Steve's voice say. "Sam's dead."

His voice reverberated across space into every cell of my body. His tone was measured, almost normal. "Sam" and "dead" were words that didn't belong together. I assumed he was talking about some other Sam, an old man, a distant cousin he'd previously forgotten to mention.

I heard myself scream into the telephone receiver. Steve's voice arrived like rounds of artillery fire in my ear. Sam and Rob had found a wounded pigeon under the clothesline. Sam had insisted on taking it to the vet. Having seen the Disney film *The Secret of NIMH* the day before, he was feeling even more attuned than usual to the suffering of animals.

Steve had been making a lemon meringue pie in preparation for lunch. He'd told the boys if they wanted to take the bird to the vet, they'd have to do it themselves. They'd lowered the bird into a shoebox and carried it down the zigzag. Lennel Road was a main route into town from the outer suburbs. In a less car-obsessed age, a town planner had decided to wedge in a bus stop for people wanting to travel up the hill out of town. The road narrowed so dramatically at the footbridge that there was only room for a footpath on one side of the road. Any pedestrian wanting to go farther down the hill into town had no choice but to cross the road at the bus stop. It was a perilous crossing with no signs to make traffic slow down.

As the boys arrived at the bus stop at the bottom of the steps, a bus pulled in on its way up the hill. Rob told Sam he thought they should wait until the bus had moved on before they tried to cross. But Sam was impatient to save the bird. Determined to reach the vet's rooms down the hill as quickly as possible, he told Rob to be quiet, and ran out from behind the stationary bus. He'd been hit by a car coming down the hill.

The words were like pieces from different jigsaws that didn't fit together. A nightmare voice that wasn't mine yelled down the phone, demanding to know if Rob was okay. Steve said Rob was fine, though he'd seen the accident and was badly shaken. A shudder of relief jolted through me.

When people receive ghastly news, some say a sensation of disbelief sets in. Perhaps it was the simple harshness of Steve's language, but his words hammered through me straight-away. My mind collapsed into different compartments. From a position high on Jessie's hall ceiling I watched myself wailing and screaming below. My head felt about to burst. I wanted to smash it against the glass panels of Jessie's front door to stop the pain.

At the same time, I registered the incongruity of the situation. The purpose of my visit had been to cheer Jessie up. Now here she was, standing in her white nightgown, trying to soothe me. Having trained as a nurse, Jessie switched into practical mode. She rang the hospital's accident and emergency ward. When she asked if Sam was D.O.A. the logical part of my brain deciphered the abbreviation. I'd heard it as a cadet reporter late at night on the police round. Dead On Arrival. Leaden with resignation, she put the phone down.

I wept and raged, but couldn't encompass the grief. No collection of human tissue was resilient enough to endure such pain. My life was over. Time squeezed up like an accordion. We waited for Steve and Rob to arrive. Refusing offers of tea and alcohol I watched light filter through a window and listened to the bellowing from the back of my throat. Part of my mind was curious about the noise my body made, and the way it seemed to go on like a chant, for infinity.

I wanted to compose myself for Rob's arrival. The poor kid had seen enough. But my mind and body refused to obey instructions. I'd become a roaring animal. We waited maybe twenty minutes for Steve and Rob to appear in Jessie's hallway. It felt more like twenty years.

They materialized like a pair of ghosts, a sad man, hunched over as if he'd been shot in the stomach, holding the hand of a traumatized child. I'd seen that body language before in photos of refugees and war victims. Steve's face was blank as a wall, his eyes empty like a marble statue's. Rob seemed to have shrunk into himself. I looked into the boy's face, so passive and contained. Falling to my knees, I wrapped my arms around our surviving son, and wondered what nightmares were whirling inside his head. He'd just seen his brother run over and killed. How could he ever recover?

Clutching my son, I sobbed. My body shook. The intensity of my grip must've been frightening. He wriggled and withdrew from my embrace. Trying to regain composure, I asked Rob what had happened. He explained how he'd tried to stop Sam crossing the road, to wait on the footpath until the bus had gone, but Sam wouldn't listen. His last words to Rob were "Be quiet."

Sam had looked like a cowboy lying on the road, Rob said, with red string coming out of his mouth. It took a while for me to understand what he'd meant by red string. His young mind had interpreted the scene as a Western movie. Sam had become John Wayne, flat on his back after a gunfight, with stage makeup trickling down his chin. It was my first glimpse of how differently a child perceives death.

As we staggered numbly towards the car, Rob asked if he could have Sam's Superman watch. I was shocked, but he was only six years old.

The road unfurled beneath us like licorice. Houses peeled away at drunken angles. I hated this town with its hills and twisted streets. Everything about it was harsh and ugly, on the brink of destruction. I didn't want to go back to the house. Couldn't face the zigzag and the sight of Sam's possessions. But there was nowhere else for us to drive to.

When Steve asked if I wanted to see the footbridge I hammered my head against the car window and screamed. I never wanted to go anywhere near that thing. He drove the long way home so we wouldn't have to pass under its shadow. People might still be there, shaking their heads, looking for stains on the tarmac.

Accusations shot like flames from the back of my throat. I yelled at Steve, demanding to know why he hadn't driven the boys to the vet. He'd been busy with the lemon meringue pie, he replied. Wild as a she-wolf, I accused him of caring more about lemon meringue pie than his sons. A cooler part of my mind knew that my behavior was cruel and irrational.

Absorbing my recriminations without the retaliation they deserved, Steve pointed out that the vet was only a short walk down the hill. He reminded me the boys knew the road rules, and there was no stopping Sam when he got an idea in his head. "We both know what Sam is like—*was* like—with animals." Steve's change of tense was an obscenity.

Like an octopus, my mind scrambled for possibilities. Maybe there'd been a mistake and Sam wasn't dead. Steve refused to be dragged into my fantasies. He'd spoken to the ambulance driver, who'd told him he was sorry but our son had passed away.

Passed away? The words unleashed a fresh onslaught of fury. Back in journalism school our tutors had drummed into us that dead meant dead, not passed away, passed over or sleeping in God's arms. How could an ambulance driver who saw death every day use such euphemistic language?

Ignoring my raving, Steve continued to repeat what the ambulance driver had said. If by some miracle Sam had managed to survive such a severe head injury his only triumph would have been to spend the rest of his life a vegetable. My subconscious snared that snippet of information.

Dead. Lifeless. Gone. Such final words. If our son really was dead, then someone had killed him. My mind boiled, desperate for someone to blame. A murderer who deserved punishment. I created a Hollywood villain inside my head, a man full of hate with a history of crime.

"It was a woman," Steve said, "a woman in a blue Ford Escort. She'd been driving back to work after lunch. There was hardly any damage to her car. Just a cracked headlight."

A cracked headlight for my child's life? I'd kill her.

Staggering down the zigzag to the house I couldn't believe I'd never again feel Sam's weight on my lap, his arms around my neck. Never was such a finite word. Rata greeted us at the door, her head to one side, gazing up at us, questioning. I flung myself on her neck and wept. Her head drooped, her tail curved under her hind legs and she tumbled to the floor. Sam's words echoed in my head. Animals understand . . .

Hands trembling on the receiver, I made the worst phone call of my life. Mum's voice sounded nonchalant when she answered. There was no way to soften the news. Her cherished grandson was gone. I was the ultimate failure as a parent. I could hear her intake of breath. Her voice deepened. The tiny part of me that remained an observer was surprised by her calm response. She belonged to a more seasoned, tougher generation that through the horrors of World War II had developed strategies to deal with outrageous loss. She brought my yelps and wails to a halt and said she was on her way.

I fastened the Superman watch around Rob's wrist and flung myself on Sam's unmade bed, its sheets and blankets still in the shape of his living body. I drank the smell of his clothes, heard his voice in my head. Steve led me to the living room and coaxed a glass of brandy between my lips. Hot alcohol shot through my veins.

An hour or so later, two policemen, young and embarrassed, arrived on the doorstep. They said the pigeon was still alive and asked what we wanted done with it. What had gone wrong with life's logic? How could a bird have more right to survival than our boy? Steve told them to take the pigeon to the vet as Sam had wanted. The police also needed someone to go to the morgue and identify the body. Steve steeled himself and went.

He arrived home ashen-faced. Sam still looked the same, he said. Beautiful. Nobody would have known anything had happened, except for the gash in the side of his forehead. Just a tiny gash. He'd meant to cut a lock from Sam's hair, but had forgotten the scissors. I yearned for the lock of hair, anything that was part of Sam, but Steve was stretched like a rubber band about to snap. I could hardly insist he go back to the morgue.

✦

Mum appeared at the door. She seemed weighted with triple quantities of sadness. On top of her own grief I could tell she was carrying concern for the rest of us. She would have been tired, too, after a five-hour drive. I expected her to burst into tears, but she squared her shoulders and raised her head. I'd seen actors do the same thing before stepping onstage.

"I saw the most beautiful sunset just now," she said. "Glorious streaks of reds and golds. I thought Sam must be part of it."

My ravaged mind interpreted her words as callousness. How could she surrender her grandchild to a *sunset*?

A funeral director turned up while she was unpacking. Harbor lights twinkled malevolently behind him as he sat in the corner of the living room asking for Sam's measurements— height and breadth. *Didn't he have a nine-year-old son of his own to go by?* White coffins, he said, were favored for children. *There were fashion trends in death?* I couldn't face a church service. Not when there was so much business to discuss with God over this. Someone had recommended the new university chaplain. A short ceremony conducted by him at the graveside would do. The funeral director made no effort to hide his dis-approval. While I was stunned by his coldness at the time, I now realize he probably had no idea what to say so was clinging to the framework of his professional training.

Soon after the funeral director strode into the night, the university chaplain stepped cautiously over the shag pile. He was young, barely out of school, and nervous. He told us he'd never buried a child before. We said we were in the same position. When he asked what we'd like I wanted to scream: "Isn't it obvious? We want our son back!" But he was faced with a daunting task. There was enough sanity left in me to feel sorry for him. I offered to write a poem for him to read at the graveside.

Our family doctor arrived and scribbled a prescription for sleeping pills. Over a mug of coffee she mused that maybe it was a good thing from Sam's perspective, because the adult world was so hard to survive in.

Steve mentioned he'd taken the Superman watch away from Rob—he hadn't felt comfortable passing it on so quickly.

I protested but he assured me Rob understood. Steve had put the watch away in a box inside his desk.

Rata collapsed across the boys' bedroom doorway. We tried to coax Rob into his old bed, but he refused to sleep in the room he'd shared with Sam. His eyes flashing with terror, he said a dragon lived in there. Steve carried his mattress into our bedroom and placed it in a corner under the window. Like shipwrecked sailors we drifted into our first night without Sam. I thought falling asleep would be impossible, but unconsciousness dropped like the blade of a guillotine, delivering me into merciful nothingness.

Leaving what our world had become was the easy part. Returning to it was almost unbearable. Opening my eyes next morning, I heard a thrush call, its "took took" echoing across the hills. For an instant I imagined life was normal. I'd just woken from a nightmare of grotesque proportions. With sickening horror, the events of the previous day exploded in my mind and sent me plummeting into despair.

It was no easier for Steve. A few days after the accident I awoke under a waterfall of his tears. He'd never cried in front of me before. I should have reached out and embraced him then, but I was half-awake, unprepared. Distraught, momentarily confused, I simply asked him to stop. I didn't imagine the request would be taken literally and he'd never express sorrow in front of me again.

Our house choked with flowers. As days passed I became weary of their sickening fragility. Water in their vases turned rancid in the summer heat, filling the air with the stench of stagnant ponds. In every room stalks drooped, petals dropped like tears on the floor.

Steve decided flowers upset me. Maybe he was right. He took to hiding freshly delivered sheaths of chrysanthemums, lilies and carnations, deathly in their perfection, under garden shrubs to keep them out of sight. It's impossible to judge whose behavior was more strange—the grieving woman who went hysterical at the sight of floral deliveries or the husband who hid them under bushes.

The front door stayed permanently open as scores of people, many of them strangers, streamed down the hallway over the carpet I'd never liked. Some oozed platitudes or quotations from the Bible till I wished they'd go away. The only words that resonated with me were Shakespeare's—"time is out of joint." Other visitors appeared angry—among them a doctor who said he'd seen the accident. It affected him personally, he said. He had two sons of his own. His anger was irrelevant. Doctors seemed to excel at injecting negative interpretations into the atmosphere.

A few (women, mostly) claimed to be suffering similar levels of anguish. Spurting tears and demanding comfort, they thrust their sobbing faces at me. Their words were tactless: "I wouldn't survive if it happened to me"; "At least it'll give Rob a chance to flourish. He was always in his big brother's shadow." I assumed they were self-indulgent, possibly even crazy, though I was no longer capable of judging the dividing line between sanity and madness.

A distorted remnant of what was left of me, a hysterical joker, wanted to screech with laughter at their pale faces and quivering lips. When they said they'd "felt the same" after their father/ dog/grandmother died I wanted to slap them. How could the predictable death of an old person compare with this?

Still others brooded silently out the window over the harbor. Immune to human suffering, the bay sparkled, ridiculously turquoise. I found no comfort in its beauty, loathed its shimmering indifference.

A Maori friend from journalism school, Phil Whaanga, turned up unannounced and simply put his arms around me. We'd never been particularly close, but there was more comfort in his embrace than the thousands of words I'd been forced to listen to. From a culture less afraid of death than our own, Phil didn't feel a need to examine aloud the freakishness of what had happened. I was grateful to him.

Mostly I sat on the sofa, nursing the scar where my hand had been burnt making Sam's birthday cake. It was impossible to accept the scar was still part of the living world while he was not.

Adding to the disjointedness of our situation was the lack of our bathroom door. Our bathroom was like our hearts, torn open for public viewing. Visiting mourners had no way of relieving themselves in private. Neither did we. Steve pinned a shower curtain over the door frame, but its flimsy floralness stopped well above floor level, exposing visitors up to their knees. I hadn't realized what a substantial, noble piece of furniture a door can be. But then there were a lot of things I hadn't thought about before.

◆

Several days after the funeral I assured Mum we'd be okay. She nodded uncertainly and climbed into her Japanese hatchback. Steve's mother phoned from England. I sighed when she said she'd been in a theater audience to see the famous medium Doris Stokes. Apparently Doris had called her up onstage and said she had a message from Sam. Doris told her Sam wanted us to know he was all right. I'd nodded impatiently when Steve passed this on. Every spiritual medium says the same thing. Doris went on to describe a strange new setup Sam was in. Like boarding school, but more fun. Just as I was about to make derogatory comments about English mediums and their tendency to re-create images involving pubs, tearooms and scenes that were quintessentially British, there was one more thing. Steve's mother said she had no idea what Doris was talking about, but perhaps it made sense to us. Sam said it was okay. Rob could keep his watch.

The Intruder

A cat doesn't go where it's invited. It appears where it's needed.

Forever. Sam was gone forever. How long was that going to be? Was it some kind of infinity? The symbol for infinity is a figure eight. If I waited long enough in some universal bus shelter would Sam spiral back to me?

Never. I'd never see him again. Not unless I believed in heaven, reincarnation or the boarding school of Doris Stokes. I couldn't imagine Sam at boarding school, even one run by angels. He'd find out what the rules were and break them straightaway so he could be expelled and sent home.

If any of those other realities, present or future, existed I had no access to them. Nevertheless, I liked to think I'd inherited some of my dad's connection to the nonphysical world. One of his favorite quotes from Shakespeare was: "There are more things in heaven and earth, Horatio, than are dreamt of in your philosophy."

Dad often spoke of the near-death experience he'd had as a young man on an operating table. He'd shot up a tunnel of sparkling light to meet some wonderful people at the top. He was overjoyed to be there, but then a voice told him gently, "I'm sorry. You have to go back."

Hurtling down that tunnel back to the ordinary world was, he said, the biggest disappointment of his life. The experience left him open-minded about ghosts, nature spirits, Ouija boards, any form of spirituality that wasn't what he called "churchianity." He'd met too many people who'd claimed to be Christian while demonstrating none of Jesus' more admirable traits.

Dad certainly was an unusual person. With his delphinium blue eyes he had a habit of looking not so much through people as around them. He often gave the impression of carrying out a conversation simultaneously with the person and their invisible companions.

Some people are happy to die on a golf course. Dad managed his equivalent during the interval of a concert he'd taken Mum and me to when the boys were still small. Having just heard his favorite Bruch violin concerto, he turned to me and said, "God, the acoustics in here are great." His head suddenly drooped over his chest and he let out a cry of pain. I put my arm on his shoulder and asked if he was okay. He raised his head, gazed at a point above the stage and smiled ecstastically. This time whoever was at the top of the tunnel was saying, "Come on up!" and Dad couldn't wait to get there.

While it was a shock for us, it was a perfect death for Dad. He'd been ready and willing. Longing for him to return seemed nothing short of selfish. But Sam was another matter. I searched for signs Sam might still be with us. If a curtain trembled there was always a breeze to account for it. On the wall I saw a shadow that resembled Sam's head, but it was simply the branches of a tree fern waving outside.

The only message we found were the words "Dumb Bell" scribbled in green felt pen in his handwriting high on a bedroom wall that Steve had started wallpapering. Sam would've had to climb a ladder to get up there to accomplish his graffiti. It was typical of our son to dispel expectations with a joke. If he was telling us anything it was he thought we were idiots for wallowing in our misery.

Never. Sam would never grow up and savor the ecstasy of falling in love, the joy of seeing his own children born. Forever. He was lost to the world forever, remembered as a golden boy who never had the chance to become a man. The only way to stop the words spinning through my head was to go to the picture window—one that couldn't be taken to the paint strippers because it was attached to the house—and attack it with a small crimson paint scraper. *Never, forever, never,* until my wrist ached and my fingers were bleeding and on the brink of bursting into flames. The view through the picture window of city, hills and harbor felt malignant, but it was the frame that needed scraping. With each stroke I stripped another layer of pain. Maybe when the wood was finally bare and smooth my heart would be healed. One time (was it daylight or dark?) Steve led me gently away from the window that had no solution. My pointless, obsessive behavior was disturbing.

On the few occasions I ventured out into the world—the impersonal stage set of shops and offices—I had no qualms burdening strangers with the facts of my recent tragedy. "My son died," I'd confided to the woman behind the post office counter. "Yes, he was run over three weeks ago. He was only nine." The woman had turned pale all of a sudden, narrower and taller. She seemed to want to dissolve into the poster advertising a new series of pictorial stamps. Collector's items, an excellent gift for friends overseas, convenient to post. Glancing nervously towards the door, she'd said she was sorry. Her tone was flat and quiet. Sorry about what? That I'd used her as a receptacle for shocking information or that I'd walked into her post office in the first place?

A fleeting wave of shame had washed over me. What business had I ruining the day of a normal person who was simply trying to earn a living? She'd had every reason to think I was mad, lying, or both.

I told the bank teller, too. His reaction was similar. What was this need to expose my wounds, so horribly raw, to strangers? The satisfaction of witnessing their shock and discomfort had been minimal. I must have had some kind of need to redefine my place in the world, to wear a label for strangers to read and, ultimately, force myself into accepting the unacceptable. Perhaps there was logic in olden-day mourners wearing black for a year. It would be a signal that the wearer was at best unstable.

While I resented roosting at home to be the target of compassionate visitors, I was in no shape for the outside world, either. Walking down the main street searching for new clothes for our surviving son, children's designer clothes of a quality so fine he'd be protected and sheltered *forever*, I became suddenly lost and disoriented. Awash in a tide of faces, all of them unfamiliar and disengaged, I fought an urge to cry out. Glossy shop windows leaned forward, threatening to crush me on the pavement. My knees weakened. An acquaintance spotted me and guided me back to the car. Humiliated by my need, I thanked her and sent her away.

Gulping breaths in front of the steering wheel, I knew exactly how I must've looked. A human skull with hairs protruding from its scalp. Glancing in the rearview mirror, I was astonished to see a twenty-eight-year-old woman, unaccountably young, with red eyes.

We tried to resume normal life, whatever that was. A couple of weeks after the funeral, wearied from my weeping and yelling, on top of the burden of his own secret grief, Steve packed his bag and headed off like a sleepwalker for a week at sea. I hoped he might find serenity in the routines and order of shipboard life.

A few days later I heard the knocker pound against the front door. Sheltering in the shadows at the end of the hallway, I contemplated the figure behind the frosted-glass panel. While the silhouette appeared feminine, its shape wasn't familiar. It seemed tall for a woman, the hair short and shaggy.

Rob glanced up from the kitchen table, where he was building a space station with his new Lego set. In past weeks he'd been showered with toys and clothes, all blindingly bright in their shiny wrapping. Rata, once a reliable guard dog, maintained her prostrate position in the doorway of the boys' old bedroom and pricked an ear. Ever since the accident she'd been immobile, inconsolable, and would barely lift her head. Whenever anyone tried to comfort her, she rolled a mournful eye.

"Let's not answer it," I said. "They'll go away in a minute."

Another visitor was the last thing we needed. Exhausted and numb to the core, I wasn't capable of conversation. The story would have to be told *again*. He—or she—would gaze at me with whirlpool eyes while I explained how our two beloved sons went down the road and only one came home. Retelling the story, reciting it like plainsong in an empty cathedral, wearied me. I didn't want their tears, was tired of their cancer-ward voices.

Alternatively, perhaps our visitor was one of the people who'd brought food. Countless plates laden with sandwiches, muffins, roasted chicken, food for uncertain appetites had appeared on the doorstep over the past three weeks. I was grateful to those cooks for their practicality and restraint. Their anonymous gifts were a welcome relief from emotional confrontation. Even though food was of no interest to me the meals seemed to disappear.

A guilt-inducing pile of empty plates was growing taller on our kitchen counter. I had no idea who had brought them. Perhaps the visitor was one of those benefactors, with sufficient courage to revisit a house of sorrow and reclaim her plate.

No, I wouldn't open the door to whoever was hovering be-hind the frosted glass. He or she could leave the food, flowers

or sympathy card oozing saccharine prose on the mat and retreat to a life without pain.

As I stepped backwards to the safety of the kitchen, the
figure tapped on the glass. Rata leapt to her feet and let out a
simultaneous bark. It was the first time we'd heard her emit
anything other than a whine since Sam's death.

"Good girl!" I said, stroking the lovable rug of her back as
she lunged towards the front door, her tail wagging.

The head behind the glass shifted expectantly. Whoever
it was had heard both the bark and my response. There was
no choice now. Refusing to open the door would be plain old-
fashioned rudeness.

Looping Rata's collar through my fingers, I turned the latch.
Sunlight stabbed my brain. The graceful figure belonged to
Lena. Attached to her long elegant arm was her son, Jake, who
was the same age as Rob.

Most people had kept their children away. All except one
or two of Rob's closest friends had maintained their distance.
Understandably. The death of a grandparent is enormous
enough for a child to encompass, let alone the annihilation of
someone their own age. Who knows what effect the sudden
departure of someone from their own generation could have on
their unformed nervous systems? And there's no proof tragedy
isn't contagious.

I wasn't confident about my reactions to other people's
children yet, either. When names were mentioned, especially
boys Sam's age, vengeful rage would boil inside. *What right has
your son to be alive when mine is not?*

Lena's son stared up at me unblinkingly, then at Rata joyously
bursting to escape my grip on her collar. Jake peered around
me into the hallway. Perhaps this was going to be a half-normal
visit after all, refreshingly free of the old "I'm so terribly sorry.
Please let me know if there's *anything* I can do."

"Would you like to see Rob?" I asked the child, in case Lena wanted to express the platitudes I'd learned to expect. "He's building a city on the moon."

Jake stood still, a smile flickering on his lips.

"You could use the toilet if you like," I blabbered, trying to stop Rata's flailing tongue drowning him in saliva. "Except it's not very private at the moment, I'm afraid. They said they'd need two weeks to strip the door, but it's taking forever. We're in a bit of a mess . . ."

Lena bent like a willow over her shoulder bag, a huge patchwork sack, flamboyant and colorful enough to have been made by the artist herself. Reaching into the bag, she excavated a small creature with large triangular ears. It was black and not so much furry as sprinkled with occasional hairs. Perhaps she'd stitched together some kind of toy to comfort a boy grieving for his lost brother.

I was alarmed when the tiny thing's head moved. Its eyes bulged like a pair of glass beads. A set of impossibly dainty feet draped themselves through Lena's fingers. I was reminded of those photos of premature babies whose miniature scale is demonstrated alongside an adult human hand. An organism so helpless it would surely have difficulty supporting its own life.

"We've brought the kitten," said Lena, smiling steadily.

The kitten? What kitten?

"Sam's kitten!" said Rob, running down the hall and squeezing around me.

Rata barked loudly and sprang free of my grip. Jumping on her haunches, she almost knocked Lena over. The kitten recoiled into Lena's breast. Our dog must have seemed a monster to the little thing. The two animals obviously loathed each other.

"Down, girl!" I growled. "She's not used to cats." Grabbing the dog firmly by the collar again, I led her inside and back down the hallway.

"Don't worry, old thing," I said, rubbing a hand through her coat. "We'll sort this out."

Rata seemed to understand that being jailed in the kitchen was a temporary inconvenience. The kitten, Sam's kitten, didn't belong in our house. It had arrived like E.T. in a spaceship (disguised as Lena's patchwork bag). The kitten was from another time. We were different people when Sam was with us and our lives were whole. Now that we were broken, frayed remnants of our former selves there was no place for a kitten. Not with us.

I couldn't possibly cope with a baby animal and all its needs. Not when I'd already proved myself a failure as a parent of one human child, aged nine. How could I nurture such a tiny, vulnerable creature? Besides, poor Rata had suffered enough. She certainly didn't need her life messed up any more than it was already by a natural-born enemy.

Lena would have to take the intruder back. She'd understand. Finding a family better equipped than ours to look after the kitten would be no problem for her. It was a presentable enough animal, and she was a brilliant saleswoman. Heading back to the front door, I prepared my speech. Lena would feel let down, but her disappointment would be nothing compared to what we'd been through.

As I reached the front doorstep I saw Lena haloed in sunlight, lowering the kitten into Rob's hands.

"She's yours now," Lena said softly.

"I'm sorry, Lena . . ." I was about to launch into my speech.

But then I saw Rob's face. As he gazed tenderly down at the kitten, and ran a chubby finger over her back I saw something I thought had vanished from the earth forever. Rob's smile.

"Welcome home, Cleo," he said.

Trust

A cat is always in the right place at exactly the right time.

As Rob disappeared inside with his new kitten, Lena turned to go. Seized with panic, I grabbed her elbow.

"There's something you should know," I blabbed. "I'm not really a cat person. I mean our family *had* cats when we were growing up, but they were more like wildcats. They just lived under the house and we fed them occasionally. Mum grew up on a farm, you see, and she never really *got* cats. She let a couple of them come inside and we semi-tamed them, but they weren't friendly . . ."

Lena's face clouded. She needed to hear this. Not telling her would've been worse than filling out a customs form and ticking "Haven't been on a farm in the past thirty days" when in fact you've been helping cousin Jeff milk his dairy herd for the last two weeks.

"One of them, Sylvester, used to poop in Mum's shoes, which was horrible for her, because she sometimes forgot to look before she put her shoes on. She'd scream the house down. She said Sylvester was temperamental because he was part Persian, with the long hair, you know. Black and white, he was. The thing is, Lena, I'm pretty sure we're more dog people."

Lena turned her head like an exotic lily and surveyed the scrub that was our garden. Casting her eye over the mountainous piles of dung Rata had bombarded the front lawn with, she sighed.

"This is a very special kitten," Lena said. "And if you don't like cats . . ."

"It's not that I don't *like* cats," I continued. "It's just I don't really know how to look after them. I haven't read any books about kitten rearing or anything."

"They're very easy to care for," she said in kindergarten teacher tones. "Much easier than dogs. She'll be no trouble. Just keep her inside for a day or two to settle. Give me a call if you have any problems. And if you change your mind you can give her back to me."

"But . . ." Lena didn't seem to realize I'd made my mind up already. I didn't want the kitten.

"All she needs is a little love."

Love. Such a simple, four-letter word to roll off the tongue. So much easier for the facial muscles to arrange themselves around than "lasagna," "leisure suit" or "leave me alone forever, please." My heart had been ripped out and pulverized. How could it possibly squeeze out a drip of anything resembling the L word for a creature I'd forgotten we'd ever agreed to own and wasn't in the slightest way equipped to look after?

Besides, a cat, assuming by some miracle it survived long enough in our company to grow into one, is an arduous, practically never-ending responsibility.

I'd gone down enough in Lena's estimation without tactfully asking how long a cat of this breed might live. From what I could remember, the ones I'd grown up with, even the semi-tame ones, were lucky to spend more than six years in our company. Most of them met sudden fates usually described in solemn, no-nonsense terms by our parents: "poisoned," "run over" or "run away." Further questioning was not encouraged. "Who did it?" or "Where?" were invariably answered with "Who knows?"

Even if this kitten by some miracle managed to reach the grand old age of nine, that would take Rob through to the age of fifteen, a million years into the future. Considering the battering our endocrine systems were taking, I doubted any of us could realistically expect to survive that long.

Lena smiled thinly and disappeared with Jake down the path. Poor Lena. I should have been more diplomatic. Abandoning her kitten to self-confessed dog people, she must have felt wretched. Nevertheless, she *had* offered to take the kitten back. Maybe I could let Rob play with it for a day or two, then we could return it to the embrace of a cat-loving household.

Rata moaned loudly from behind the kitchen door.

"Don't worry!" I called to the old dog. "We'll sort this out."

Rob was curled up in a corner of the living room, cradling the tiny creature in his arms. To have called it beautiful or even pretty would have made Elton John's spectacle frames the understatement of the eighties. It was a scrap of life wrapped in a dishcloth. A toy you'd take back to the department store to exchange for one with more stuffing. I refused to think of it as something with a name, but if it did have one, "Cleopatra" would be far too long and elaborate. Something that miniscule wasn't hefty enough to handle a name with more than one syllable. It wasn't going to be staying with us long, so for now "it" would suffice.

Sam's observation had been spot-on. With the prominent head and neck narrower than a vacuum cleaner hose, the animal was more like E.T. than a kitten. To the non–cat person the lack of fur offered too much information about feline anatomy. I tried not to notice the folds of semitranslucent skin draped over its rib cage. The skin was a deep charcoal shade, which mercifully concealed some of the detailed rippling of movement under the surface. If I looked any closer it might've been possible to see the throb of a tiny heart. It was safer to avert the eyes.

How anything could be born with so much spare skin was a mystery. The flaps under its arms (front legs?) were generous enough to double as wings. A saggy pouch hung under its abdomen. There was enough spare skin to make at least two other animals the same size. The struggle to survive as the runt had obviously been touch-and-go. No doubt older brothers and sisters had pushed their puny sibling off their mother in order to fill their own bellies.

The kitten would need to do an awful lot of eating and growing to fill those empty pouches. Even then it stood no chance of looking presentable. A larger, filled-out version of the kitten had freak potential. I took a step backwards. It was definitely one of those things that looked better from a distance. At least the color was consistent. The kitten couldn't have been blacker. From the claws and pads of its feet to its whiskers it was black. Even the pins of its claws were black. Its eyes were the only things that broke the rule. They were shimmering green mirrors that hardly belonged to a cat. Surely they'd been stolen from a creature from another world. As Rob stroked her forehead with his finger, the kitten gazed adoringly up at him. My heart lurched. All of a sudden the kitten wasn't ugly anymore. Sun caught her fur. Affection beamed from her eyes. She radiated a kind of silvery light. The room filled with beauty, the pure essence of all new beings. They looked so perfect together, like a scene from a 1950s advertisement.

"Sam was right," he said, beckoning me forward and lowering her into my reluctant hands. "Animals *can* talk. Listen to her. She's growling."

Maybe it was the warmth of her miniscule weight, the fragility of her limbs or the softness of her fur, but my chest suddenly filled with a fluttery sensation as I lifted her into my hands. "That's not growling," I said, running my finger along the delicate beads of her spine. "It's purring."

Gazing into the innocent furry face overshadowed by gigantic ears I felt momentarily overwhelmed. Even though we'd lost Sam, and I sometimes felt my existence was finished, this scrap of feline life had summoned up the cheek to burst in on our world with no apologies. Not only that, curled in my hands, she was apparently expecting things to turn out perfectly. She was tiny, helpless. And had no choice but to trust us.

Cleo stretched a lazy paw and yawned, revealing a lollipop-pink mouth palisaded with dangerous-looking teeth. The astounding eyes gazed into mine with an expression that hardly matched the vulnerability of her size. Her unwavering stare said it all. As far as she was concerned this was a meeting of equals.

"Touch her ears," Rob said. "They're soft."

Cleo didn't object to having her ears rubbed. In fact she dipped her head and nudged firmly into my hand to intensify the contact. Delicate as antique silk, her ears slipped between my fingers.

A reward was the last thing I expected. It was delivered in the form of a sandpapery swipe from her tongue. Cleo's lick on the back of my hand was startling, like a lover's first kiss. Part of me wanted to envelop her and never let go. The other part, so wounded, was wary of the tsunami of affection washing over me. To love is ultimately to lose. The unwritten contract that arrives with every pet is they're probably going to die before you do. The more devoted you are to them the more sorrow their departure will inflict. Opening my heart to Cleo would've been the equivalent of placing an already bruised organ on an airport tarmac and inviting planes to land on it.

"Let's see how she walks," I said, lowering the kitten to the floor. We watched her paddle like a clockwork toy through the carpet. The shag pile was the equivalent of tall grass for her. Using the worm of her tail as a rudder she paced jerkily towards the rubber plant.

I'd never been a fan of the rubber plant. We'd inherited it from the owners of our previous house. I gradually understood why they'd left it behind. With its big waxy leaves it had an indestructible, vaguely humorless presence. Like an unwelcome guest at a dinner party, it eavesdropped on every conversation and contributed little in return except, perhaps, when it was in the mood, oxygen. We'd been hoping to leave the thing behind when we moved to the zigzag, but the removal men had mistakenly packed it into their truck with our furniture.

When I transplanted the rubber plant into an ugly orange plastic tub its confidence surged. It sprouted dark-green branches the size of Frisbees and sent feelers trailing creepily around picture frames and across curtain rails. Technically more a tree these days, the darned thing had ambitions to engulf the entire suburb. I'd tried cutting it back with a pair of hedge clippers, but that only encouraged it to swamp the sideboard.

About a meter away from the plant's orange tub Cleo paused. Her ears and whiskers pointed forwards. Her nose twitched as if she was sampling some dangerous perfume. She crouched and, with the stealthy determination of a lion stalking an antelope, eyed her prey—a pendulous leaf dangling from one of the lower branches. Quivering on her haunches, she waited for the moment the leaf would be least suspecting. Satisfied her prey was foolishly absorbed in leafy thoughts, she attacked furiously, claws exposed, teeth perforating the startled victim's skin.

Then something strange happened. It began with a noise, unfamiliar at first, a soft gurgle followed by vague hiccuping. Our mouths widened, the soft tissue at the back of our throats went into spasm, but not for crying this time. Laughter. Rob and I were *laughing*. For the first time in weeks we reveled in the simplest, most complex healing technique known to humanity. Grief had pulled me so deeply into its dungeon I'd forgotten about laughing. It took a boy, his kitten and a rubber plant to engage me in a function essential to human sanity. The horror of past weeks dissolved, padlocks of pain were unlocked momentarily. We laughed.

In the Cleo versus rubber-plant leaf war, there was no doubt who was winning. The leaf was twice Cleo's size and firmly attached to the plant's trunk. Every time she tried to grip the vegetation between her claws it slipped away and bounced insolently skyward again.

"She's a gutsy little thing," I said.

The kitten suddenly stopped and collapsed on her haunches. She looked up at us and emitted a dictatorial mew. No interpreter was needed. Cleo was tired of entertaining us. She demanded to be scooped up for more cuddles. A mournful howl from the kitchen reverberated through the wall, reminding us it was time for Cleo to meet the lady of the house.

I instructed Rob to let Rata out of the kitchen while I held on to Cleo. But what if the dog lunged at the kitten and tried to eat it? Adult muscle strength would be needed to restrain the dog. The only option was to instruct Rob to hold the kitten carefully while I brought Rata in.

Overjoyed to be released from kitchen confinement, Rata showered me with saliva. She was seemingly oblivious of my prison-warden's grip on her collar.

"Now girl, there's someone we'd like you to meet," I said, sounding like a dentist introducing a first timer to the drill. "There's nothing to worry about, but you'll have to be very gentle."

The golden retriever knew exactly where we were going. Like a jet boat with a water-skier in tow, she dragged me into the living room. Rob stood by the window anxiously clutching Cleo close to his chin. Rata took one glimpse of the kitten and tightened every muscle under her collar. Cleo's eyes widened to become a pair of glittering jewels. The kitten puffed her patchy tufts of fur out to double her size, though she was still hardly big enough to intimidate a chihuahua. She arched her back and flattened her ears. Just when I thought things couldn't get worse, Rata barked, puncturing the air like gunshots. The poor little kitten was going to die of terror.

Any normal animal outclassed in size would have recoiled into Rob's arms, but Cleo was no common beast. Glowering down from her human fortress, she shrank her pupils to pinpoints and lasered out enough malevolence to intimidate the entire canine empire. She then peeled back her mouth, exposed two parallel rows of fangs—and hissed.

Rob, Rata and I froze. Frighteningly primeval, Cleo's hiss was something a python would emit before swallowing a rabbit, a hiss worthy of Cleopatra herself. It was an imperial hiss, one not to be argued with.

Rata fumbled under her collar and collapsed on her haunches. Shocked at the kitten's ferocity, the retriever hung her head and studied the floor. The old dog seemed disappointed, confused.

Then it struck me. I'd been misreading Rata's signals all along. Her jumping at Lena by the front door had been a welcome, not an attack. The growl just now had been one of friendly excitement, the bark an invitation to play. Rata's feelings had been wounded not only by me misinterpreting her intentions but by a stroppy kitten not much bigger than her front paw.

"It's okay," I said. "Bring Cleo over here."

Nursing Cleo in his arms, Rob walked cautiously to our side of the room. Rata gazed up at the kitten with an expression so soft and kind it could have been stolen from Mother Teresa. Nevertheless, I maintained the grip on her collar.

"See? Rata doesn't hate the kitten. She's just not sure how to make friends. Put Cleo down and see what she thinks. I won't let Rata go."

Rob took several steps backwards and lowered Cleo to the floor. The kitten stood on all fours and blinked at her monumental housemate. Rata tilted her head, pricked her ears and whined tenderly as Cleo advanced steadily towards her. When the kitten finally reached Rata's front paws, Cleo stopped and glimpsed up at the monstrous dog face towering above her. She then turned around twice, curled up like a caterpillar and snuggled between Rata's giant feet.

Our retriever trembled with delight at being recognized for the super nanny she was. Not since the boys were babies had I seen her so bursting with maternal instinct. In the way she'd been utterly protective with our children, I knew Rata would be equally trustworthy with the kitten.

Ours weren't the only hearts that had been mashed to pulp. Whatever dog-deciphering system Rata had access to, there was no doubt she knew what had happened to Sam. In some ways Rata's grief had been more consummate than ours. Without the release of language and tears, she could only lie on the floor and will the hours away. Pats and tender words from us seemed to provide only momentary comfort. But the kitten had rekindled something in the old dog. Perhaps Rata's heart was resilient enough to open up one last time.

As I let go of her collar her tongue unfurled like a ceremonial flag. Without a twitch of uncertainty, the young intruder succumbed to being lovingly slurped over from tail to nose and back again.

"Where's Cleo sleeping tonight?" Rob asked.

"We'll set up a bed for her in the laundry. I'll fill a hot-water bottle to keep her warm."

"We can't do that! She'll be missing her brothers and sisters. She'll have nightmares. I want her to sleep with me."

Rob hadn't mentioned the words "missing" and "brother" in the same sentence since 21 January. Nevertheless, the Superman watch stayed glued to his wrist. During daylight hours Rob gave a surprisingly good impression of a child enjoying a trauma-free life. Nights were a different matter. Tortured by dreams of being chased by a monster in a car, he slept fitfully on the mattress in a corner of our bedroom.

"There isn't room for all three of us *and* a kitten in our bedroom," I said. "Besides, Cleo's probably going to make a fuss the first few nights while she's settling in."

"I don't care," he said. "She can sleep with me in my old bedroom."

The bedroom Rob and Sam had shared still sat empty. We'd bundled up Sam's clothes and toys and dumped them in a school charity recycle bin on an afternoon so surreal in its hideousness I'd felt like a figure in a painting by Hieronymus Bosch. After that we'd done the expected thing and set about giving the room a makeover. Steve painted the walls sunshine yellow. I sewed some Smurf curtains and pinned up a Mickey Mouse poster. Steve nailed together a kit-set bed and stained it red. I bought bright new covers.

But for all its primary-colored dazzle the revamp hadn't made a cat's hair of difference to Rob. I'd envisaged him sleeping in the corner of our bedroom until his twenty-first birthday and beyond.

"You're ready to move back into your bedroom, Rob?"

"Somebody has to look after Cleo at night."

Ensconced in his new/old bedroom that night, Rob looked almost as disoriented as his new kitten. The smell of fresh paint spiked our nostrils. The bedcover had an almost neon glow. The new sheets were crisp and cold.

Adding to the uncomfortable sense of newness was the acid-dipped bathroom door that had been delivered and fitted back in its frame that afternoon. Even though the house was piecing itself together around us, we in no way shared its confidence for the future.

Certain favorite bedtime stories had to be avoided these days. *Green Eggs and Ham* was out because of the character Sam I Am. I couldn't face *The Digging-est Dog* because it featured a boy named Sam Brown who was devoted to his dog. With Cleo curled between us we settled for *One Fish Two Fish*, so familiar and comforting in its rhythms I could recite it pretty much from memory.

As we reached the last page, I could sense Rob's anxiety swelling like a wave on the horizon. "Are you sure there are no monsters in here?" he asked, glancing anxiously under the bed.

"Absolutely." It didn't seem the right time to tell him where the worst monsters hide. They conceal themselves cleverly inside our heads and wait for the moments we're at our most vulnerable—bedtime, or when we're sick or anxious.

"Will you check for me?"

"I looked under the bed before."

"Can you look again?"

"Okay," I said, bending to reexamine the battalion of fluff balls in hiding from the vacuum cleaner.

"What about behind the curtains?"

Picking up Cleo—why did I make excuses to hold her all the time?—I peeled back a corner of the curtains. For the first time I detected a glint of hope in the city's sparkling lights. Or was it? More likely, they were playing a cruel trick, laughing at us for even wondering if tonight might be a little easier.

"No monsters," I said, tugging the curtains firmly shut. "Now, good night, darling boy." I stroked his hair and kissed his forehead, savoring the delectable smell of his skin. Strange how every child is born with a distinctive aroma, complex, intoxicating and immediately recognizable to the mother. I wondered if he had any inkling how much my life depended on his at that moment. Without the example of his courage and his need for me the lure of brandy and several bottles of sleeping pills would have been too strong.

"Did you look in the wardrobe?"

"Nothing but soccer balls and raincoats in there."

"Can I have Cleo now?"

The kitten. Rob's kitten officially. As I lowered the furry bundle into the crook of his left arm Rob sighed and raised his thumb to his lips. He and Cleo had a lot in common. When a wife loses a husband she becomes a widow. Children are called orphans when their parents die. As far as I knew there was no word for someone grieving for a sister or brother. If there was such a word it would have described both boy and kitten. Since birth their lives had overflowed with clumsy hugs, play fights, the noise and physical warmth of their siblings. Now brutally brotherless, they were both lost and frightened. Yet they were so brave and full of life. The only option for them was to snuggle into the night together and trust that tomorrow would sort itself out.

I switched the light out and ran the day's events across a screen of darkness in my mind. The relentless ache of living without Sam permeated everything. Nevertheless, I realized with a sense of guilt, almost, that the past twenty-four hours hadn't been entirely bleak.

Steve would still need to be convinced, of course, but Cleo, as kittens went, was proving remarkably civilized.

Awakening

A kitten knows joy is more important than self-pity.

"Oooow! Help!"

I woke with my hair pinned painfully to the pillow. A wild beast was attacking my scalp, clawing my hair and making dangerous chomping noises. It had to be a tiger or a lion escaped from a television wildlife show. Whatever it was had mistaken me for an antelope that needed eating. Emitting a stifling odor of fish breath, it obviously had a taste for marine mammals as well.

"It's only Cleo," Rob giggled.

Cleo? How could a kitten morph into a woman-eating panther in a matter of hours?

"Get it off!" I yelled.

"She's not an 'it,'" he said, disentangling the kitten from my hair and placing her gently on the floor. Her legs barely touched the carpet before she sprang back on the bed for a fresh lunge at my hair. I wailed in agony. The kitten's purr of satisfaction reverberated through my eardrum. Is this the last sound a cat's prey hears?

The moment I disengaged the animal from my head and set her on the floor, she bounced up on the bed again. How anything that small could leap several times her height was beyond me. She was like an Olympic pole-vaulter minus the pole.

Maybe she'd had springs surgically implanted in her hind legs. I sighed and plonked her back on the floor. Eyes gleaming like neon signs, ears huge as moth wings, she bounced up again. She seemed to think it was a game. The animal had no respect for the fact we were engulfed in a grieving process so overwhelming we had little chance of recovering.

"Noooo!" I whimpered, using the pillow as a shield. Cleo was jubilant and hugely pleased with herself. Anyone would think she was the first creature on earth to invent the hair-attack-jumping-back-on-the-bed game. Come to think of it, she probably was. The pillow offered no protection: Cleo simply burrowed under it. I put her on the floor *again*. She jumped up. Down. Up. Down. Up. This dance routine was going to last all morning if I didn't do something.

If Steve had been home I might've been able to employ him as a human shield. But he hadn't officially agreed to having a kitten in the house, let alone one that ate humans. Cleo was just an *idea* of a kitten to him. Over the phone I'd described to him her every curve. "You're going to love her!" I'd said. Even with my best marketing job, he sounded less than keen. I wasn't looking forward to his reaction when he arrived home from sea. He was as likely to warm to Cleo as the Pope was to Buddhism.

Rolling reluctantly out of bed I slid into my dressing gown. As I stomped semiconscious towards the kitchen, I experienced a tugging sensation. Looking down I saw Cleo hanging from the belt of my gown like Tarzan from a vine.

"Naughty kitty!" I said, peeling her off my belt and putting her on the floor. The moment I tried to reclaim the belt and loop it around my waist she sprang at my thighs, dug her claws into my flesh and, with her tail swinging wildly, snared the belt between her teeth. I wailed painfully for the second time that morning.

Removing the kitten from my thigh inflicted more pain than the world's worst Brazilian wax. Obviously there was only one way to deal with this young cat: firmness. I wrapped the belt around my waist, tied a knot and proceeded forwards with all the dignity it was possible to muster. Cleo raced ahead and flicked swiftly between my ankles, before suddenly skidding to a halt. In a single slow-motion movement I tripped over the hump of her spine and sailed through the air, only just managing to grab hold of a wall hanging to stop myself landing on top of her.

Clinging to the macramé tassels, I froze in a position worthy of an advanced yogi and apologized. The kitten rolled on her back, raised a bent paw and fixed me with a wounded expression. I felt terrible for hurting her.

Just as I bent to pick her up, the furry ball exploded to life, sprang to its feet and lunged away from me. Relieved, I followed—until she bounced to a halt and tripped me up again. And *again*!

Cleo seemed to have decided I was a ridiculous animal, with my bird's-nest hair and insistence on prancing about on two legs. Her mission was to trim my coat and get me down on all fours so I could savor the exuberance of being a cat.

But I didn't need a crazy kitten. The animal had no right to dance through our grieving chambers as if life was some kind of joke. If Sam were here, I thought, he'd know how to calm her down. I could almost see him bending over her, hand outstretched, lips damp and tender . . .

I hurried to the bathroom, the only place I could weep in private, and closed the door. Rob didn't need to witness any more adult distress than he'd already seen. If only events had unfolded differently that day. If Sam hadn't found the pigeon, if Steve hadn't been making lemon meringue pie, if I hadn't been out for lunch, if that woman hadn't been driving back to work . . . *That woman.* It was all her fault. I wondered if she had children of her own and any idea the anguish we were going through. My mind had turned her into a monster.

A series of jagged sobs erupted. Trying to repress the noise, I leaned my forehead against the cool blue tiles and clutched my stomach. My chest muscles ached. The capacity of human tear ducts continued to amaze me. How many buckets could one pair of eyes fill? Just when I thought I'd exceeded the lifetime quota, another tanker load would discharge down my cheeks. Crying had become just another bodily function, like breathing, something that happened without conscious effort.

As I bent over the toilet bowl, part of my consciousness peeled away to float on the bathroom ceiling. It looked down with benevolence at the howling woman doubled over with hurt and hatred. This other me who examined things from a distance didn't take things so personally. It was spooky and detached. Maybe it had been there since birth and I'd spent the rest of my life crowding it out with emotions, obligations and conforming to what was expected.

At the same time it frightened me. What if I was tempted to float away with it for eternity, smiling down on human drama like an amused zookeeper? The idea of shedding my body and escaping pain was suddenly attractive. I slid the cabinet drawer open and held the bottle of sleeping pills to the light. Each pill glowed like a promise through the brown glass. There were plenty left. They didn't smell too bad. Washed down with enough brandy they'd be tolerable. I unscrewed the lid.

The bathroom door opened a crack. Dammit. I hadn't closed it properly. The shower curtain rippled. Assuming Rob had opened the front door and set a draft going through the house, I leaned forwards to shut the door. It continued to nudge itself open. Glancing down I saw a black paw run down the gap. Cleo pushed her way in, padded over the tiles and mewed for me to pick her up. Sighing, I put the pills back in the drawer and closed it quietly. To arrange a permanent exit would be the ultimate act of indulgence. Cleo's impertinent arrival in the bathroom was a reminder of my responsibilities. I had no right to opt out when a boy and a kitten needed continuity in their lives, and someone to nurture them through to adulthood. Gathering Cleo in my hands, I sobbed into her fur. She didn't seem to mind being a handkerchief. Purring, she nuzzled my neck and gazed at me with such affection I was taken aback. Not since the boys were babies had a living creature offered so much undiluted love. Once I'd regained composure I lowered her to the floor. She skipped away and I went to find Rob.

The house had gone through a metamorphosis overnight. The hallway resembled the aftermath of a battle. Empty supermarket bags were scattered over the shag pile. Among them lay a selection of unmatched socks. Rob's blue and white sports sock lay shriveled alongside one of Steve's. A rainbow-striped bed sock curled around a fallen deodorant bottle. With its cap resembling Napoleon's hat, the deodorant bottle looked like a deceased general who, knowing he'd lost the campaign, had taken a bullet and tumbled on his side.

In the family room rugs were rumpled and mysteriously askew. Lampshades hung crooked like jaunty headwear. Chairs and tables had rearranged themselves at subtly different angles. Photos had toppled on the window ledge. A rubbish basket lay on its side spewing apple cores and chewing gum wrappers.

The kitchen blinds had collapsed at half-mast and wouldn't budge up or down. Closer inspection revealed the curtain cords had been either surgically severed or chomped through.

Assuming we'd been burgled, I hurried to the living room. To my surprise the stereo and its speakers still lurked inside their ugly veneer cabinets. The television hadn't budged, either, though the flock of sympathy cards had taken wing during the night and fluttered to the floor.

The rubber plant lay toppled on its side, its pendulous leaves stretching over the sofa and coffee table. Dirt from its tub avalanched over the carpet. The landslide was decorated with three small, bullet-shaped turds.

I'd never been house proud, but this was too much. Our kitten had undergone a personality change after dark. She was nothing short of a feline werewolf.

The day ahead stretched towards a horizon littered with socks, fallen rubber plants, supermarket bags and acupunctured ankles.

"*Where's Cleo?*" I roared, scooping up a blanket I'd lovingly stitched together for Rob. The blanket had taken months to knit. As I clutched the manifestation of mother's love to my chest, three half-eaten tassels dropped to the floor.

Rata tilted a lazy ear from her sleeping post in the doorway. Rob shrugged. On the tree fern outside a bird was practicing scales. A ship's horn moaned out on the harbor. Inside, the house was eerily silent. Except for strange tinkling noises coming from the kitchen.

I marched over the linoleum to declare war on a creature one-tenth my size. The clock emitted bored ticks from its watch post above the kitchen sink. The tap, like a drummer with no sense of rhythm, wept into the plug hole. Otherwise, silence. Our furry delinquent had gone bush.

For no logical reason, I reached for the oven door. Just as well we weren't expecting a visit from Martha Stewart. Grease stains trickled like frozen tears down its glass front. I'd get around to cleaning them off someday, in the next year or two, or whenever there was a day on the calendar marked "World Oven-Cleaning Day." A pair of roasting dishes glowered back at me from the gloom.

I was about to check out the pot cupboard when we heard the unmistakable sound of plates shattering. Rob lowered the dishwasher door. Cleo was having too much fun crashing around last night's dinner plates to take notice of us. She ignored my yells to get out. When Rob reached into the dishwasher Cleo shot out and slithered between his legs, then scampered away before either of us could lay hands on her slippery fur.

I'd heard people say kittens were playful and could be almost as demanding as new babies. *Almost?* Babies stay in their bassinets, for heaven's sake. They don't go out of their way to attack your hair or send you flying through the air with the prospect of spending the rest of your days in a wheelchair. This kitten's behavior was beyond any normality curve—human, animal or vegetable. She was uncontrollable, destructive, possibly psychotic and a sock fetishist to boot. In less than twenty-four hours she'd changed from helpless, charming aristocrat to crazed feral.

We chased after her down the hall, leaping over socks and supermarket bags, but Cleo was nowhere to be seen. We stopped and listened. All that could be heard was the sound of our labored breathing.

I peered through the crack of Rob's door. Curled on his pillow was the personification of kittenly cuteness. She mewed affectionately, stretched, and gave the prettiest yawn. Cleo had morphed back into the creature we'd fallen in love with.

Rob moved towards her. Cleo's eyes snapped wide open. Glaring, she pinned her ears back and lashed the pillowcase with her tail. Before either of us could get any closer she sprang to her feet and flitted mischievously across the room. Rob flung himself to the floor, trying to pin her down in a rugby tackle. She slithered through his grasp, leapt on top of his bookshelf and scrambled out of reach up the Smurf curtains, using her claws for crampons.

Swinging from Smurfland, the kitten was deaf to my concerns for the interior decor. Nevertheless, a glimpse towards the ceiling confirmed she couldn't climb any higher. Descending meekly into our arms, however, wasn't an option. In less than a breath, she dropped onto my shoulder, a mere springboard from which she then plunged to the floor.

Back on the carpet, she leapt in wild circles around the room, bouncing off the window ledge, the bed, the bookshelf. This was not a kitten. It was a dynamo with enough energy to power a discotheque. Even watching her was exhausting.

It wasn't going to last. We weren't cat people. Our house no longer belonged to us. Cleo had invaded and turned us into prisoners. Even though she was tiny, her personality filled every corner of every room. If she wasn't stealing socks from the laundry basket or chewing the covers of precious books she was hiding in a shopping basket waiting to ambush us.

Admittedly, the trouble she was causing had provided diversion from our pain. Every moment spent worrying what part of the house she was destroying was one not steeped in grief. But I was a barely functioning human being and in no condition to deal with the undiluted force of nature that was Cleo.

The only thing more unnerving than her presence was her sudden, inexplicable absence. "Where's Cleo?" I muttered after resurrecting the rubber plant and disposing of the turds. The house was too quiet. Rob found her eating potato peelings inside the kitchen cupboard that contained our rubbish bin.

I'd once read somewhere that cats sleep seventeen hours a day. Presumably kittens needed more than that. Going by the damage to our surroundings, Cleo must've slept a total of three hours in the past twenty-four. Some other kitten in a blissfully calm household had surely stolen Cleo's designated downtime and grabbed it for itself. It'd be pigging out on hours of extra sleep, dozing on a cushion in a patch of sunlight somewhere, not causing any trouble. Its stress-free, thoroughly spoiled owner would look at its plump, snoring form and wonder at its passive nature.

I couldn't stand another minute of that kitten. I persuaded Rob to leave the house with me for an hour or two. The only terms he'd agree to was a visit to a pet shop that sold stuff for kittens.

We crept around the abandoned supermarket bags toward the front door. I turned the lock smoothly to avoid loud clicks that might draw attention to our escape. Just as I shuffled Rob out ahead of me, the supermarket bag closest to the door suddenly inflated to twice its size, exploded to life and emitted a terrifying yowl. A miniature panther pounced from its depths and dug its teeth in my ankles.

I tried to shake her off. The kitten was several notches below us on the Darwinian scale. She had no right—let alone the brains and technology—to detain us. Nevertheless, she was having a damn good try.

Rob picked up a sock and shook it. Cleo was immediately mesmerized. Ferocity: 10. Attention span: 0. She leapt and danced after the hosiery. When Rob threw it to the other end of the hall she scurried after it.

We slid out the front door as Cleo's tail disappeared into the shadows. *She's only a cat, for heaven's sake!* my mother's voice lectured inside my head. But I hadn't felt so guilty since I'd tried leaving the boys at a day-care center that was clearly run by a direct descendent of Adolf Hitler.

We headed along the path to the zigzag. A force tugged me back towards the house. I turned to see our kitten peering out of Rob's window. If a representative of Hallmark Cards had wandered up the zigzag he'd have signed her up for a lifetime of schmaltzy photo shoots. Nestled in a basket or garden pot, dangling from a Christmas stocking, she'd have been irresistible.

Back in the bathroom she'd rescued me from one of my bleakest moments. I was grateful to her for that. She was beautiful, wonderful. And impossible to live with.

Taming the Beast

A cat tames people when they are ready.

Cats and people are unlikely allies. If they were logical, humans, with practically the entire animal kingdom to choose from, would opt to tame creatures more like themselves for pets. Monkeys would be an obvious choice. Furry, intelligent and largely vegetarian, monkeys can learn tricks. But people don't warm to primates on the whole. In a monkey's eyes they recognize their own cunning gleaming back.

Instead, humans prefer creatures closely related to their fiercest enemies—lions and tigers and wolves, who'd rather gnaw their bones than sit at their feet and amuse.

The pet shop mostly catered for this preference. Out of habit or instinct, I headed for the dog section. An Aladdin's cave of squeaky balls and rubber bones, it was Rata heaven. Rob steered me to the other side of the shop and pointed out a cushiony thing he thought would be an excellent bed for Cleo. The leopard-skin cover certainly reflected something of Cleo's personality.

A shop assistant homed in on us and recommended a sack of dried kitten food. (*Special food for kittens? I could almost hear my mother wail. Has the world gone mad?! We'll have women running the country next.*) The shop assistant said our kitten would love a soft toy stuffed with catnip, adding that it made them extra playful. Imagining Cleo on the feline equivalent of LSD, I said no thanks.

On our way to the counter she talked us into buying a bag of kitty litter and a plastic tray to put it in. I didn't want a kitten. Steve was almost certain to throw a fit when he came home and saw what Cleo was capable of. What were we doing purchasing all these accessories? Rob stood on tiptoes and slid the cat bed across the counter's glass top.

She was a talented saleswoman. Beaming down at him, she asked for his kitten's name. His face turned pink with pride as he said the word. And, he added, she was the best kitten in the whole world.

◆

Life was complicated. I drove the long way home, winding down the gully past the Botanic Gardens, where the boys and I used to feed ducks. Visiting the ducks was always a good way to defuse their energy when they'd been cooped up inside after days of bad weather. Feathered or furred, animals always had a way of reaching into their frazzled, overactive souls and calming them down. The sight of a brown duck gliding over silvery water tuned all three of us into a wider world where problems didn't seem so insurmountable. We invariably left the duck pond feeling calmer. In spring we'd count the ducklings, always one or two fewer than the week before. But it was impossible to mourn for long, not when the tulips were out. The boys would run, their hair fiery gold in the sunlight, through rows of dazzling reds, pinks and yellows.

I asked Rob if he wanted to see the ducks but he was keen to get back to Cleo. I couldn't face them, anyway. And I wouldn't be visiting the tulips this year, either. They would have to flower by themselves. Every corner of Wellington housed gut-wrenching reminders of our previous life. The town was one big mausoleum.

But home was no longer a shabby retreat from the world. Within twenty-four hours the kitten had taken charge and transformed it into the House of Cleo, invading every centimeter of my personal space, coiling between my ankles, scrabbling up the back of my chair if I sat down for a coffee, following me to the bathroom and pouncing on my lap the instant I settled on the toilet seat. Socks, supermarket bags and all the collateral damage from the night before still had to be cleaned up. If I wanted to avoid making explanations to Steve I'd need to find someone in the Yellow Pages to fix the curtain cords. And who knew what additional acts of vandalism she'd pulled off while we were out?

Maybe we didn't need to go home. We could just keep driving till we hit the motorway that slithered around the harbor and headed north. The house, cat, shaky marriage and friends with their harrowing outbursts of sympathy could all be left behind. We'd go and live with Mum in New Plymouth, the provincial town I grew up in—for about two weeks until Mum and I drove each other nuts. The town and I didn't seem to fit together anymore, anyway. Whenever I went back for funerals or birthdays, people invariably asked two questions: "How's the writing?" and "When are you leaving?" The second was always easier to answer than the first. I never classified what I did as "writing." It was more about sharing stories with people whose lives were equally imperfect, and having a few laughs together. Readers of my column were like friends, with the added bonus of almost never turning up in the flesh. They had been amazingly kind lately. I'd grown so accustomed to sharing intimate aspects of our lives with them through my weekly installments it seemed appropriate to tell them about Sam's death. The only alternatives were to continue writing diverting tales about domestic life as though nothing had happened (impossible), or retire. As I sat in bed, dripping tears into my portable typewriter, and recounted the events of that dreadful day, I had no idea I was tapping into a great source of healing. Letters and cards arrived in the hundreds, demonstrating the enormous generosity of strangers. Their letters, a few from people who'd also lost children, offered more strength than almost anything else. I carried a carefully typed sheet of paper around in my handbag. It was from an Indian couple whose two-year-old had wandered into a national park and was never seen again. Ten years after the event they said they were still sad, but surviving. They were living proof that parents who lose children in dreadful ways—they're *always* dreadful—can survive.

An even bolder option would be to keep heading north till we reached the flashy lights of Auckland, a bigger city, where I'd get a job on a newspaper or magazine. Except only a lunatic would hire a grief-raddled, worn-out solo mum.

I nudged the car against the earthen bank draped with ferns at the top of the zigzag. The city spread below us in cubes of grey, windows glinting in the sun. In one of those office towers would be the woman who'd taken Sam's life on her way back to work from her lunch break. I wondered what she looked like, and what she was doing. Sliding a file out of a cabinet, on the phone to someone? Wellington was such a small place we were bound to have some acquaintances in common. Nobody had given a hint they knew her. Perhaps they sensed her life would be in danger if I set eyes on her. She'd have to appear at the court inquest soon and confess she was drunk or driving too fast. Her punishment would come in good time.

Beyond the office blocks and over the hills past Lena's house was the cemetery where Sam's body lay. Beyond that, on Makara Beach, families would be making the most of what was left of the summer. Mothers would be spreading rugs over the stones, pouring orange cordial and telling their children the waves weren't as cold as they looked. Boys would be charging into the surf, their skin goose-pimpled and gleaming in the waves. Some of them would be Sam's friends. I didn't want to see them or their mothers again.

A southerly breeze spiked my nostrils. Not so long ago I'd relished the thought of living in our house on the fault line, fixing the place up, along with our marriage. Suddenly it seemed too hard.

Rob scrambled out of the car, eager to show Cleo her new bed. Laden with kitty litter and the plastic tray I followed him down towards the house. I tried to prepare mentally for whatever fresh hell the-house-that-now-belonged-to-a-cat had to offer. At least it was still standing, its painted beams peeling in the sun. There was no sign of the kitten.

When I turned the key a tiny panther gamboled down the hall towards us, her tail waving like a banner. She emitted squeaks of welcome, each ending in a higher tone: *Where have you been? Why did you take so long? Did you bring me anything?* She sprang up on her hind legs, plunged her chin into our hands and flossed her teeth on our fingernails. The throb of her purr told us all was forgiven. We'd turned the sky blue again and glued the sun back in the sky simply by returning. I was entranced once more. How could I have considered sending her away? We needed her almost as much as she needed us.

But when Rob thrust the leopard-skin bed at her, Cleo arched her back and fluffed her tail out like a bottlebrush. She hissed violently. The cat bed was as threatening as the leopard it imitated. She pounced and savaged it, thumping it with her hind legs before swiftly withdrawing under the sofa. The enemy had no time to retaliate.

Cleo refused to emerge until her foe had retired to the laundry. We didn't realize at the time, but it was the beginning of lifelong "issues" with bedding. Once it was gone she shot out from under the sofa to skid on a supermarket bag before climbing inside it. After catching her breath inside its plastic belly she ambushed the phone cord and scuttled to the safety of the kitchen pot cupboard.

Our cat was wired tighter than a violin. Every shadow, ball of dust, shopping list, discarded ribbon and household implement was a potential attacker. Noises alarmed her. She jumped at the squeak of a door. A distant bird's song spiked every hair on her body.

No sock in the house was safe. She abducted them from bedrooms, empty shoes and the laundry basket, carefully separating each one from its twin so it was vulnerable to assault. The sock was then dragged through the house by its toe, tossed in the air, caught between two sets of claws and tortured mercilessly until it feigned death.

I was developing a headache. Cleaning up the day's mess was pointless. It only gave the kitten scope to invent some new form of household devastation.

"Don't you *dare!*" I said when Cleo sprang on the hall table and patted a tall vase of foxgloves with a tentative paw. Looking up at me she shook her whiskers and shrunk into her coat. I was serious. She lowered her paw and jumped obediently back on to the floor. I'm not proud to say I felt a glow of satisfaction. Having a close to wild animal respond to my commands was exhilarating. Megalomaniac teachers must experience similar power surges. Pleased with my venture into authoritarianism I glided into the kitchen to put the kettle on. But like every dictator I was delusional.

The house shook with a resounding thud. I charged back into the hall. Foxglove stems were sailing through the air, closely followed by the vase, from which billowed a spout of water. Surfing the waterfall was a four-legged figure, spread-eagled in an attempt to stay upright.

The vase crashed to the ground. Foxgloves scattered in elegant angles down the hallway. I watched as the kitten was engulfed. Caught in a flower-vase pipeline, she had no choice but to ride it out.

Like most natural disasters, it was over almost as quickly as it started. A house that seconds earlier had resembled a normal, if scruffy, family home was now worthy of relief funds from the UN. Sploshing through the tide, Cleo shook each paw after each step as if the water caused personal offense. Ears flattened, tail drooped, she wouldn't have won first prize in any beauty contest. Or even best and fairest.

I yelled at Rob to get some towels. Together we tried to bring the house back to dry land. I soaked up the carpet damage while Rob toweled the animal dry. It was the first time I'd seen her anything close to humble.

Healer

*A cat loves with all its heart, but not so fervently that there's
nothing left over for itself.*

Steve was back from his week at sea just in time to experience
the mayhem our new kitten had caused. While he cleaned and
tidied the house, I stood at the kitchen bench watching a seagull
glide on the updraft from the cliff. The bird and I were at the
same eye level. It swiveled the slash of its beak towards me. We
exchanged glares.

Not so long ago I'd liked birds, empathized with their
struggle. Around the age of eight or nine I'd found a baby
thrush on the front lawn. It couldn't fly. Our cat Sylvester was
bound to get it if I didn't do something. I scooped the ball of
feathers up in my hands. It didn't seem to mind resting its
reptilian feet on my fingers. Its beak and claws were too big for
its body. It was not yet a functioning bird. I had no choice but
to take it inside. A shoebox was lined with cotton wool. Holes
were punched in the lid with a knitting needle. The thrush took
eager gulps of sugared water from an eyedropper. Certain the
bird would die overnight, I closed the lid. The box chirruped.
Not a call of alarm. Just a chirrup. The box sat on my dressing
table all night. I dreaded what I'd find next morning. But when
I scrambled out of bed and opened the lid, the bird was sitting
upright. Its eyes shone black and expectant. I closed the lid and

took the box outside to the front lawn. When I opened the lid the thrush hopped onto the grass. It wobbled uncertainly, then with a thrilling whirr of wings flew up onto a branch. It perched there for a while, pretending I didn't exist. I called, but it hurtled across the valley to the pines. I thought it might fly back to thank me. Of course it never did.

The seagull peeled away, swooped down over the ferry terminal and across the harbor. Five weeks had passed since our older son, inside his white coffin, had been lowered into the hills behind Lena's house. We'd visited the grave a couple of times. I found no comfort on the windswept summit of Makara Cemetery, with its soldier lines of plaques. The first few times we went it took a while to work out where Sam's grave was in that mosaic of misery. Steve pointed out it was in line with the toilet block. I could almost hear Sam laughing about that. He'd always had a lavatory sense of humor. In typical incongruity he'd been buried between two people who'd lived well into their eighties. Kneeling above him, my tears irrigating the grass, I searched for something of his essence. There was nothing of him in the gnarled bushes bent permanently against the wind. Clouds wrapped themselves in improbable shapes. Sheep bleated. Sam didn't belong in that empty place.

I felt like an actor wearing someone else's clothes. On the outside we resembled the same people we'd been a month or so earlier. I drove the same car, went to the same supermarket, but my internal organs felt like they'd been rearranged and scrubbed with steel wool. Shock, probably. I no longer trusted the goodness of being alive. Hatred and fury flared easily. I was angry at the people who lay alongside Sam. They had no right to live so long.

Even though the new school year had started we'd decided to keep Rob home for a couple of weeks. He hardly ever mentioned Sam but he still wore the Superman watch every day. Maybe he thought the action figure on his wrist was a hotline to his big brother. Rob needed a superhero more than any boy I could think of. If only Superman could jump through his bedroom window with Sam laughing in his arms.

I began to wonder if the point of superheroes isn't so much the extraordinary feats they perform as the fact they have other lives as uncool males struggling for acceptance. Most boys relate to Clark Kent, geeky and rejected by the woman he loves. Like Clark Kent, every boy has an inner hero. His only hope of knowing a real live Superman is to become one, a goal that sets most young men up for disappointment. As they grow older the search for Superman continues. Sports heroes, rock stars, billionaires. Yet the real hero isn't so far away. He lies within.

Reluctant as I was to admit it, I was getting help from Cleo. She seemed to know when I was bottoming out, whatever time of day or night it was. A paw would slide down the crack of a door, she'd leap on our bed or sit nearby, not demanding anything. Purring patiently, she'd simply wait until I surfaced.

Even her destructive behavior seemed to have purpose. It dragged us into dealing with the here and now. During the few moments I was yelling at her about curtain cords or toppled photo frames, I wasn't eating my insides out over Sam. Infuriating, impish and bursting with affection, Cleo pulsed with exuberance. From the point of her tail to the tips of her whiskers she was one hundred percent alive. There was more Sam in her than there was under the whistling skies of Makara.

But Steve didn't seem to see it that way. Even though I'd explained how Sam had picked her out, I had the feeling Steve associated the kitten with the life we'd had before Sam died, not this surreal existence we were trying to eke out now. Adopting a pet without his consent was hardly a functional family thing to do. Besides, he came from a long line of dog people.

+

Steve unpacked his seabag under Cleo's watchful gaze. She appeared to be making an inventory of his clothes, and which might be portable. His eyes slid sideways at her. I could tell he was thinking only one word. Mess.

One of the many differences in our personalities was attitude to mess. I was, and still am, comfortable with quite a lot of disorder. Amazingly creative ideas can spring from piles of old paper and clothes you forgot you ever had. At least, that's what I tell myself when I can't be bothered sifting through them, which is almost always.

Steve, on the other hand, could have been mistaken for a graduate from the Zen school of the obsessively tidy. As a teenage bride, I'd strived to satisfy his craving for immaculate surroundings. Whenever he was due home from a week at sea, I'd rush around the house dusting skirting boards, straightening curtains and arranging rug tassels in parallel lines. I was a slow learner. It took years to realize that no matter how perfect I thought the house looked it made no difference to Steve's perception. Oblivious to my efforts, he moved like a robot through the same routine every time he arrived home from sea: unleash vacuum cleaner, wipe countertops, even if I'd cleaned them half an hour earlier, and unpack seabag. Vacuuming had been out of the question today, due to the saturated shag pile. He had to content himself with picking up socks and supermarket bags.

Just as I launched into a spiel about how much Rob adored the kitten, Cleo dived into Steve's bag and emerged with the toe of a black sock between her teeth. Scurrying away, she tossed it above her head and jumped in the air. She caught it between her front paws with panache, before rocketing away full tilt, the sock trailing between her legs. One of her back legs stepped on it, bringing her to such a sudden halt she somersaulted through the air and landed on her back. I sucked a breath. The poor creature had surely damaged her spine. We'd have to take her to the vet's. She'd writhe in agony. There'd be no cure. Unperturbed, Cleo wriggled to her feet, picked up the sock again and sprinted away.

Unimpressed, Steve trudged out of the room in search of his sock. It generally took us two days to adjust to Steve's routine after he'd been away. With the additional tension of an unwelcome kitten, domestic harmony was more problematic.

I'd read somewhere that seventy-five percent of marriages fail after the death of a child. I wasn't prepared to buy into that. Defying statistics was one of my specialities. But I was beginning to understand why so many relationships crumble.

Steve's pain was no less than mine, but it was different, more internal. I grieved in wild expressionist brushstrokes, sobbing, wailing, accusing, wanting to be held. His sorrow was more orderly and restrained. Words, when he said them, were as carefully considered as dewdrops on an orange in a Dutch master's still life.

While Steve had been able to undertake the tasks expected of a man—identifying the body, the police interview and, tomorrow, an appearance at the court inquest—his ability to convey what was going on behind the fortress of his face had shut down. I was to blame for some of that. I should never have asked him to stop crying that morning after the accident. His gaze slithered everywhere these days, from curtains to carpet to rubber plant. Never into my eyes. When he'd asked if I'd go along to the inquest with him I'd refused. The thought of reliving it all in front of strangers was too much. If I'd had the courage to agree I'd have been a better wife. We were both at our most needy, yet neither had reserves to soothe the other.

Rob called us to the living room, where he was crouching over Cleo, dangling Steve's sock. He tossed the sock across the room. Cleo chased it, caught it neatly between her teeth, trotted back to Rob and dropped it at his feet. She then sat neatly beside Rob and waited, staring up at him expectantly.

"See? She can fetch!"

"Only dogs can fetch," said Steve, swooping his sock off the floor.

"No, you try it," said Rob.

Hesitantly, Steve flung the sock into the air. Cleo barrelled away and retrieved it, depositing it at my feet this time.

The kitten ensured we were all awarded equal time throwing the sock. She wanted it to be a family game.

"Cleo can play sock-er!" said Rob.

Her enthusiasm was limitless. The three of us were soon mesmerized by the wiry figure dancing to and fro after her sock victim. When it rolled under the sofa's underskirts I was almost relieved. No way would she be able to slide into the two-inch gap between the sofa and the floor.

But I'd underestimated Cleo's yogi-like flexibility. Without hesitation she flattened her haunches and wriggled under the sofa. It was like watching birth in reverse.

The silence that followed was unnerving. She was stuck under there. Seconds later, a single black paw appeared from behind the high back of the sofa. It was swiftly accompanied by another paw. With leverage from two sets of claws a face appeared, much narrower than the last time we'd seen it, the eyes half-closed, the ears reduced to mere flaps flattened against its skull. Clamped victoriously between its thin lips was the sock.

✦

The sun glinted like a giant tiger eye as it sank behind the hills. The sky was turning pink with exhaustion. Slipping on a cashmere cardigan, I chopped chicken breasts. Risotto was bland enough not to offend anyone's tastebuds.

Cleo lifted her nose and, like a connoisseur analyzing the aromas of a rare Bordeaux, half-closed her eyes. Following my ankles as I moved about the kitchen, she emitted a series of squeaks. Not the mews of a cat begging for food, but the demands of a priestess impatient to have offerings laid at her feet.

Gathering her up, I snuggled her against my chest and sat down with her on a kitchen chair. She strained wistfully towards the chicken but soon became intrigued by my precious cashmere cardigan. Simple sheep's wool was of no interest to Cleo. Fiber removed from domestic goats and then painstakingly dehaired was another matter. She chomped the wool around the middle button.

I disentangled her and lowered her firmly to the ground. Cleo sprang back on my lap. Like a famished lion she dug her teeth into my cardigan. I tried to dislodge her. A sudden pain in my thumb as she sank a fang through my flesh. Not only had she ruined my cardigan but she'd drilled a hole in me.

Crying out, I stemmed the river of blood with a paper towel. When Steve saw my injury he was unimpressed: Cleo was doing a good job fulfilling his prejudices against kittens.

When we sat down to the meal the furrow between Steve's eyebrows deepened as Cleo demonstrated how unwilling she was to understand the words "Don't jump on the table." She attacked all three of our plates, not to mention the place mats, salt and pepper shakers and cutlery.

Heat pulsed up the back of my neck. My thumb throbbed. The effort of selling a kitten to a reluctant husband was taking its toll. I grabbed her and shut her firmly in the laundry.

"She hates it in there," Rob whined.

"She can't ruin our lives!" I shouted to drown out the yowls from behind the laundry door. Something about her jagged cries tipped me over a precipice. It wasn't just the kitten, the thumb and the husband. The inquest was the next morning. Steve would come face-to-face with that woman. Policemen would prove her guilt. She would go to jail. I would finally have to accept Sam was dead.

Cleo's yelps intensified. My body started shaking. Breaths came in shallow gasps. "I can't stand it anymore! She'll just have to go back to Lena!"

Rob stared into his risotto and swallowed back tears. "You're. So. Mean."

Scraping back my chair, I reeled to my feet and ran to the bedroom. Sobbing loudly into the pillow, I knew Rob was right. I *was* mean. And out of control. A bad mother, hopeless wife, a failed human being in general. I longed for sleep to drop its blanket over me.

Instead, a boy's hand touched my shoulder. "She loves you, Mummy," he whispered. "Listen . . ."

A bulk of fur nestled into my neck. The rhythmical growl of her purr roared in my ear. It was the deep primeval sound of waves rolling in on the black sand beaches of my childhood, the noise a baby hears when it's in the womb. Wise and eternal, it could be the earth's lullaby or the voice of God.

A cat's purr is said to have a profound effect on the human body. Tests have proved purring reduces people's stress, lowers blood pressure and helps mend muscles and bones. The healing powers of cats are increasingly acknowledged by the many hospitals and nursing homes that employ resident cat doctors. Regular doses of purring have the potential to repair heart tissue as well. Listening to her throaty melody, my chest filled with liquid honey.

Cleo nudged her head under my chin, stared at me with maternal concern and to my amazement planted her damp nose on my cheek. It was an unmistakable kitten kiss. Nestling into my neck, she stretched a delicate front leg across my face. I took the paw between my fingers, caressed it and watched the claws gently open and close. No threat of attack this time. The pads of her foot were softer than my fingertips, and sensitive enough to feel the earth's subtle tremors (or so I'd heard). As we lay "holding hands," our souls reached across the divide of species and shared a connection beyond words.

I awoke several hours later with Cleo wedged between the sheets, her head resting on the pillow beside me. She felt entitled to be there. Her motionless form, the peaks of her ears against the white cotton, the restful comfort of her breathing made me wonder if we hadn't slept that way, human and feline, side by side, since Earth's first dawn.

Goddess

A cat is a priestess in a fur coat.

"You do like Cleo, don't you?" Rob asked over breakfast next morning.

I opened the kitchen window. Another seagull screeched across the agate-blue harbor. The half-eaten curtain cord swayed in the breeze. Steve had already put on his tie and left for the magistrate's court.

"Yes," I sighed.

"Good, because she likes you."

"Of course she does," I said, smiling weakly.

"No, Mummy. She *really* does!" he said. "She told me last night."

"That's nice, dear," I said. "Finish your toast."

"She told me other stuff, too."

Rob was a sensitive boy. He'd suffered more trauma than any young child should endure. We hadn't discussed the inquest with him, but he'd probably picked up on the vibes. Now he was dreaming up ideas of the kitten talking to him.

"She said she comes from a long line of cat healers," he continued.

The poor kid's imagination was off its leash.

"You mean in a *dream?*" I asked, fearing for his grip on reality.

"It didn't feel like a dream. She said she's going to help me find friends."

There'd always been a psychic streak in the family, but talking to a kitten was too much. If word got out at school that he was having conversations with his kitten he'd be a target for bullies and all sorts of misery.

"I'm sure she is," I said, putting my arm around his shoulder and kissing his ear. "But let's keep it a secret for now."

"You won't give Cleo back to Lena, will you?" he asked.

I crouched beside him, rested my hands on his shoulders and examined his face, so serious. His body was rigid with tension. "No, Rob. We're keeping her."

His shoulders dropped. Relief rippled through him. He put his head down. His hair moved like wheat. His arms wriggled in a subtle dance of joy. Even though he wasn't looking at me I could tell he was smiling.

✦

Humans were slow to understand how essential cats were to their survival. One of the attractions of giving up nomadic wandering in favor of farming permanent settlements was the reduced risk of attack from large predators. People spent several generations congratulating themselves on this achievement without realizing a more devastating enemy was thriving in their walls, basements and grain stores. The humble rodent was responsible for far greater devastation than its carnivore cousins. A hoard of mice could destroy a year's crop, leaving an entire village diseased and starving.

Wildcats circled the settlements, drooling at the prospect of mousey banquets. Occasionally some were bold or desperate enough to venture into the villages to hunt rats, mice and snakes. People gradually began to realize the cats weren't doing any harm. In fact, they were useful pest controllers.

They started to appreciate the creature's qualities. They noticed its elegance, admired its aloofness and its refusal to submit to human superiority like a cow or dog. The ancient Egyptians were the first to be impressed by the fact that a cat did not necessarily come when it was called.

Felines were decked out in gold jewelry and allowed to share food from their owners' plates. Punishment for killing one of these creatures was death. Cats often had more elaborate funerals than people. When a family feline passed away its body was displayed outside the home and the entire household shaved their eyebrows as a sign of mourning—behavior that in today's suburban neighborhood would result in phone calls to local authorities.

As well as saving millions of lives by killing rodents, our soft-footed friends have helped heal countless hearts. Sitting quietly at the ends of beds, they've waited for human tears to ebb. Curled on the laps of the sick and elderly, they've offered comfort impossible to find elsewhere. Having served our physical and emotional health for thousands of years, they deserve recognition. The Egyptians were right. A cat is a sacred being.

◆

The kitchen clock dragged itself through the morning. The hearing was taking longer than expected. I assumed there was time-consuming evidence against the woman, previous convictions for dangerous driving—*anything* to explain what had happened.

A mug of coffee. And another. The harbor was a turquoise Frisbee just as it had been the day Sam died. Malevolent in its perfection. While I willed the second hand to circumnavigate the clock, Cleo introduced Rob to an old paper bag she'd stolen from the cupboard under the kitchen sink. She seemed to love the crackling sound it made as she rolled on it. When Rob held the paper bag open, Cleo bounded away from him across the kitchen and skidded to a halt. Turning, she crouched low and focused on the paper cave Rob had created. With pupils dilated, her eyes were almost entirely black apart from their thin green rims. Shifting her balance, she lifted her right front paw and positioned herself for the assault. The preparation was so painstaking and time consuming her audience was in danger of losing interest. Just as we were about to give up entirely and turn our attention to an unopened packet of chocolate-chip cookies, a black dart flew across the vinyl and shot into the crinkled depths of the paper bag.

"Look, Mummy," he said, lifting the bag that was now satisfyingly round and weighty.

I moved to rescue the kitten from her paper prison, but the bag emitted happy purrs.

Steve returned close to noon, hollow-eyed and semi-transparent in the hallway. His tie, half-undone, hung limp over his chest.

The pity I felt for him was immediately obliterated by hungry rage. "What does she look like?" I asked, surprised at the harshness in my voice.

"Why are you angry, Mummy?" I hadn't noticed Rob following me down the hall with the purring paper bag in his hands.

"I'm not angry." My tone was dry and cold.

"Daddy, look what Cleo can do!" As Rob offered him the paper bag, Cleo's head emerged mischievously from its mouth.

"Not now," I snapped. "Take her into the kitchen, will you?"

Sensing the jagged atmosphere, Rob left obediently. If only, I wished, one day there could be a time when our son might be able to understand and forgive.

"Well?"

"I dunno," he sighed, rubbing his eyes wearily. "Ordinary . . ."

I probed as much out of him as I could. Her hair was brown, possibly fair. Her build was on the heavy side. She worked for the Health Department. She was wearing a coat, probably navy blue. He couldn't remember if she wore glasses. They hadn't really looked at each other across the courtroom. She seemed sad, but offered no apology.

I needed more, much more. The shape of her nose, the placement of moles, her smell . . . I wanted to devour every detail about her.

"How old is she?"

"Mid thirties, maybe."

"Is she going to jail?"

Gazing over my left shoulder, he shook his head slowly.

"They must be prosecuting her for *something*. A fine, at least?"

A fly performed a lazy figure eight above his head.

"They can't." His voice was calm and kind, as if he was speaking to a lunatic. "It was an accident."

What did he mean *accident*?

"There was no way she could've seen him running out from behind the bus. It wasn't her fault. She didn't do anything wrong."

My brain spun to a halt. He might as well have been saying the sky was green. If Sam's death really had been an accident and the woman wasn't at fault, there was no one to blame. I had no right to hate her. I might even be expected to forgive her.

My heart was tight and hard. Forgiveness was for the gods.

Resuscitation

Cats are willing to take into account the fact that people are slow learners.

The moment my old school friend Rosie heard we had a kitten there was no stopping her. I put her off the first time she phoned. That was like a bowl of sardines to a starving stray. A couple of days after the inquest she broke through the invisible barricades around our house. Notorious for her ebullience and lack of tact, Rosie wasn't everyone's favorite person. Steve suddenly remembered an important appointment he had in town.

"Poor itty-bitty baby Cleo," she crooned, examining Cleo through giant red spectacles. "Fancy having to come and live wid a whole lot of humans who aren't cat people."

"I didn't say we're not cat people, Rosie."

"So you can honestly say you *are* a cat person?" she asked, peering at me over her crimson horizons.

"Yes. Maybe . . . I'm not sure."

"Then you're definitely *not* a cat person," she said. "You'd know if you were. It's like being a Christian or a Muslim. You just *know* when you are one."

Rosie didn't have a Church of England background like mine, where you could mumble the Lord's Prayer, sing "There

Is a Green Hill Far Away" and slurp tepid tea while avoiding conversation with the vicar before going home free from any sense of allegiance.

Rosie was a cat lover extraordinaire. She'd adopted six strays she'd named Scruffy, Ruffy, Beethoven, Sibelius, Madonna and Doris, though it was impossible to guess which one belonged to its name. Adopted wasn't exactly the right word. More accurately, Rosie had invited a sextet of four-legged thugs to invade and decimate her property. Ungrateful to the core, the fur balls shredded her curtains and splintered her furniture while sprinkling her house with the unmistakable stench of ammonia. When they weren't indulging in gang warfare and raiding rubbish tins they were murdering local wildlife. Whenever humans dared venture through Rosie's gate, six sinister shapes skulked under her bed. None of which, she said, stopped them having *fabulous personalities* and being *unbelievably cute* and *adorable*.

There was nothing Rosie didn't know about cats. Her radar was bound to suss out a member of the kittyhood that had been condemned to life with us on the zigzag.

"She's not exactly the *prettiest* kitten, is she?" Rosie continued. "I've seen more fur on a golf ball. She looks like she's been in prison camp. And those eyes. They're so . . . bulgy."

"Nobody's perfect," I said, riding an unexpected surge of loyalty. "She's a work in progress."

"Hmmm," said Rosie doubtfully. "Part Abyssinian, eh? Famed for their love of water and high places." Rosie used every opportunity to show off her knowledge. "Even taking into account that she's related to the short-haired Asian cats that are lightly built and therefore able to tolerate warm climates more easily than their more sturdy European cousins, she's pretty skinny. What are you feeding her?"

"Cat food," I sighed.

"Yes, but what *sort* of cat food?"

"I don't know. Stuff from the pet shop."

"Vitamin supplements?" she asked in courtroom tones.

"Of course," I lied, changing the subject. "Do you want to see her play sock-er?"

I held a sock above Cleo's nose. Cleo pretended she'd never seen such a thing before.

Rosie shook her head. "Cats don't play fetch," she said. Her ginger curls tumbled forwards as she reached into her red handbag. I felt a twinge of remorse. Even though she could be irritating, she deserved a thousand brownie points for turning up. So many of our friends had found excuses to withdraw.

Rosie hadn't changed her manner since Sam's death. Her behavior was mercifully dictatorial and cheerful as ever. What's more, she wasn't speaking to me in that hushed, now familiar, tone that implied the house had some kind of curse over it.

"You'll need these," she said, thrusting a pair of dog-eared books at me. *Kittens and How to Raise Them* and *Your Cat and Its Health*. "Oh, and I thought this might be helpful."

Bossy, crazy, sweet Rosie. For all her quirks and her conviction I had Cleo's worst interests at heart, her deep-down goodness was undeniable. Why else would she present me with *On Death and Dying* by Elisabeth Kübler-Ross offhandedly along with the kitten books?

I knew about the five states of grief Kübler-Ross put together to help people deal with grief. There was a lot I recognized.

1. Denial. Definitely during those initial shocking moments after the phone call at Jessie's house. A big chunk of me continued to be in denial. On street corners and in shopping malls, I still saw Sam running and laughing. They were all blond-haired impostors. Something in the dungeon of my subconscious clung to the ambulance man's words that Sam would have been a "vegetable" if he'd survived. Several nights a week I dreamt everyone had decided to hide from me the fact that Sam was still alive. Suddenly aware of their lies, I'd sprint through a labyrinth of hospital corridors to find him attached to machines in a darkened room. He'd then turn his head and fix me with those blue eyes, just as he had when he was born. I'd wake up, heart thumping, pillow saturated.

2. *Anger.* It would've been helpful if, after a few weeks of Denial, I'd faded recognizably into Anger. Every cell in my body raged at pigeons scattered like pieces of torn paper in the sky, women driving Ford Escorts, in fact, women drivers in general, and Sam's school friends who had the effrontery to still be living. If only I could be assured the Anger stage would pass. Trouble was I was angry *and* in denial all at once. And yes, there had been a few pathetic . . .

3. *Bargaining Sessions.* Sometimes, in the bathroom or behind the steering wheel, I conducted one-sided negotiations with God asking Him (or, if Rosie was to be believed, Her) to please wind the clock back, so the events of 21 January would unfold five seconds earlier, so the car rolled down the hill before Sam's foot touched the curb, the pigeon was delivered safely to the vet and we all sat down around the kitchen table for Steve's lemon meringue pie. What was a little time shuffling for someone (or something) as omnipotent as the Great Creator? In return I'd do anything He (or She) required, including join a nunnery, take up women's rugby and pretend to enjoy sleeping in tents. All of which would save me from . . .

4. *Depression.* The wardrobe of sorrow houses many outfits. For casual daywear there's plain old self-pity, which sufferers sometimes flippantly refer to as depression. Postnatal depression is slightly dressier. For full-blown formal occasions (complete with attendant psychiatrists and pills) there's clinical depression, suicidal sadness and, ultimately, insanity.

My uncles returning scrambled as eggs from World War I were said to be depressed, possibly crazy. One of them was incarcerated in a mental home. A maiden aunt didn't speak for years after my grandparents insisted she put an end to her affair with the local postmistress. With the compassion and understanding typical of rural 1930s New Zealand, the wider family called her Creeping Jesus. As far as I could understand, my aunt and uncles had logical reasons to be depressed.

Even though all these variations of sorrow are shoved into the same closet, they seem to have as much in common as flax skirts and Dior gowns.

The word depression wasn't big enough to describe the ocean of melancholy I'd slipped into. There was no shoreline. The sea had no floor. Some days I fought to stay afloat. On others I was suspended lifeless, like a broken willow branch, drifting in its infinity. For Kübler-Ross to label this mere "depression" and a "stage" was outrageous folly. And then, to imply there would be a final stage of—

5. *Acceptance.* No way was I *ever* going to say it's okay for a beautiful nine-year-old boy to die. Kübler-Ross missed a few other stages while she was at it, including guilt, self-hatred, hysteria, loss of hope, paranoia, unacceptable confessions in public, a powerful urge to open the car door and hurl oneself onto the motorway.

I thanked Rosie for the books and flicked through *Your Cat and Its Health.*

"You will read it properly, won't you?" she said.

"Look Rosie, we might not meet your standards, but we'll do our best. We're not going to kill her, at least I hope not . . ."

"Never mind, baby Cleo," Rosie said, putting on that silly voice again and burying the kitten between the steamed puddings of her breasts. "Itty-bitty kitty can come and live with Auntie Rosie any time."

Cleo writhed between Rosie's sweltering mounds. Then, in a split second that seemed to be happening in slow motion, she flattened her ears, rolled back her lips, hissed and swiped a fully armored claw at Rosie's face.

"Ohmyyyygoooodddd!" wailed Rosie.

"I'm so sorry!" I said, dabbing the blood on her cheek with a paper tissue that had been doubling as a table napkin. "I'm sure she didn't mean . . ."

Clutching the tissue to her cheek, Rosie glared down at her assailant.

"This kitten . . . *your* kitten . . . has fleas!" declared Rosie, rearranging her spectacles.

"Really?" I said, scratching an ankle. Steve and Rob had complained of being "itchy" over the past few days. I'd dismissed their complaints as neuroticism. It now dawned on me I was itchy, too. An archipelago of miniature volcanoes encircled both ankles and stretched up my legs.

"Yes, look," she said, parting the sparse forest of Cleo's underbelly. "Dozens, possibly even hundreds . . ."

The sight resembled one of those shots taken by helicopter over Manhattan. Oblivious to us staring down at them, an entire city of fleas bustled through avenues of Cleo's hair. So engrossed were they in their flea workday, so confident that whatever they were doing was the most important job on earth right now, not one paused to glance up at a pair of horrified human giants.

"That's a serious infestation," said Rosie, awe verging on admiration in her voice.

"How do we get rid of them? Do I get some powder from the pet shop?"

"Too late for that," pronounced Rosie. "What this kitten needs is a *bath.*"

When I pointed out cats have a natural loathing of water, and that immersing a kitten would surely be close to animal cruelty, she shrugged. "Well, if you don't want to take responsibility for your kitten's health . . ."

Rosie had me cornered. If I didn't obey her she'd report me to some kind of committee of animal protection feminists.

They'd plant burning crosses on our front lawn and glue posters around the neighborhood.

"But we don't have a kitten bath," I said, almost certain I'd never seen such a household item, not even in a pet shop. "Or kitten shampoo."

"The bathroom vanity will do," she said. "And mild human shampoo is fine. Now, find me a hand towel, please."

The closest thing we had to a hand towel was a faded blue rag that had enjoyed a previous life as a beach towel until the boys and Rata tore it apart during a tug-of-war. With the efficiency of an Egyptian embalmer wrapping up a cat mummy, Rosie wound the cloth around Cleo's shoulders. With her legs (and claws) tucked against her body, Cleo was defenseless. Her startled, furry face emerged from one end of the towel. The other end was wedged deep in the folds of Rosie's T-shirt. I desperately wanted to rescue Cleo. But, immune from any more scratch attacks, Rosie had taken control.

She instructed me to fill the basin with warm water, then tested the temperature with her free elbow. When the depth and temperature were ideal, Rosie swiftly unwound the cloth and passed Cleo to me.

"I thought *you* were going to do this?" I said, wrestling with legs and tail, which were moving in opposite directions simultaneously.

"You're the mother," Rosie replied, taking a step back towards the safely of the towel rail.

Our kitten relaxed in my arms. I took it as a huge compliment. Staring down from her dry vantage point, Cleo was fascinated by the water, and expectantly watched it glistening in the basin, as if it might house a school of goldfish. I unwound, too. Maybe Cleo had inherited the famous Abyssinian love of water and was going to enjoy her bath.

Inhaling deeply, I lowered her into the water. Swift handling combined with respect for feline pride would be required. Cleo seemed to understand the procedure. She kept still as a statuette while I massaged baby shampoo into her coat. The kitten was soon wreathed in a cloak of bubbles.

I was proud of her nestled in the basin. Fortunately, Cleo couldn't see what a bath was doing for her looks. With her fur slicked down and whiskers pasted against her cheeks, she could've been mistaken for a rat. Nevertheless, Rosie had to be impressed with Cleo's understanding of hygiene requirements.

"Good girl," I crooned.

"See? Nothing to it," Rosie said. "Every cat needs a bath now and then."

Cleo suddenly let out a primeval yowl. It was a shocking noise that penetrated my maternal genes as instantly and powerfully as the cry of a child lost in a supermarket. Cleo's little head drooped sideways and, to my profound horror, she went limp as a dishcloth in my hands.

"Get her out! *Get her out!*" Rosie bellowed.

"I *am* getting her out!" I bellowed back. As I lifted the little creature from the water, her head and legs swung lifelessly. "Oh . . . !"

What was Rob going to say? His heart had already been shattered. He wouldn't be able to take another blow. I'd already proved myself a failure as mother. No way should I have been given command of something as small and helpless as a kitten. I was barely capable of putting my clothes on.

Snatching the towel from Rosie, I engulfed the lifeless form.

"Oh Cleo, I'm so sorry!" I cried, rubbing her with the towel and hurrying her through to the living room. I flicked the gas heater on, held Cleo as close as possible to the flames, and massaged her frantically.

"You were right, Rosie. I'm hopeless with cats. This is terrible!"

Rosie towered over us disapprovingly. "The water was too cold," she said.

"Why didn't you *say* something?"

"I thought it would probably be all right. Or it could've been the wrong shampoo . . ."

The tiny body lay lifeless in my hands.

"I've killed her, Rosie!" I sobbed. "She's the only thing that cheered things up around here. Now I've drowned her! I know you don't think I'm a cat person, but I was starting to love this kitten."

So this was going to be my life from now on. Everything I touched was destined to shrivel up and drop dead in my hands. For the sake of the world I'd have to climb a mountain at the bottom of the South Island, crawl into a cave and wait for things to end.

Then, to my astonishment, the rag on my lap emitted a single, demure sneeze. A shudder of life rippled through her body. She raised her head, climbed unsteadily onto her paws and shook herself indignantly, showering me with water.

"Oh, Cleo! You're back! I can't believe it!" She hardly needed the additional rinse of my happy tears.

The kitten fixed me with eyes the size of satellite dishes and bestowed a lick on my finger, as if she'd woken from a pleasant dream and was wondering what was for breakfast. Jubilant with relief, I rubbed her precious fur until it was nearly dry. Not since the boys were born had I felt so ecstatic to see a creature alive and functioning.

"Listen, she's purring!" I said to Rosie. "Do you think she forgives me?"

Rosie didn't look convinced. "Just as well she has nine lives," she said. "One down, eight to go. That poor kitten's going to need every one of them in this house."

After Rosie left, I kissed Cleo, thanked her for coming back to life, and held her close to my chest to keep her warm.

From that moment on, Cleo and I had an understanding. Baths, as far as she was concerned, were strictly for the birds.

Cleo was turning out to be quite a teacher. Like all good educationalists, she adopted her techniques according to the abilities of her students. Her near-drowning experience demonstrated I wasn't doomed to destroy everything in my path, after all. For the first time in my life I'd actually revived a living creature. And Cleo was giving me a second chance.

Compassion

Even though the cat is a solitary creature, it is capable of acts of great kindness.

"Sure you're going to be okay?" I asked, clicking Rob's school lunch box shut. His sandwiches were made of wholemeal bread, the healthiest available on supermarket shelves. Rob would've preferred white fluffy bread, naturally, but I was determined he'd sprout to a vigorous adulthood. If he couldn't learn to love broccoli and bean sprouts I was going to stuff them into him, anyway. No more bad things were allowed to happen to this boy.

The school had been understanding about us keeping Rob home for an extra couple of weeks. It was his second year of school, so he knew most of the kids in his grade. Nevertheless, his first day back without Sam loomed over us. Since Rob's education began, Sam had been woven into the fabric of every day. In playground warfare, the extrovert older brother provided a protective shield for the younger, quieter one. Nobody would pick a fight with Rob when they knew they'd also have to confront Sam (famed for his Superman kicks). Older and younger brother were Starsky and Hutch, Batman and Robin, each incomplete without the other.

"Will you drive me?"

"Of course," I said, fastening the buttons of his new shirt. Western style, it featured winged golden horses flying against a white background. Wings and feathers seemed to haunt every aspect of our lives. The shirt was on the lurid side, but Rob loved it, and I was encouraging him to express his individuality.

There were no arguments with Steve about the cost of children's clothes anymore. With Rob's help I'd managed to venture into an impressive range of shops over the past couple of weeks. Like most New Zealand primary schools, Rob's had a no-uniform policy. The intention was to create a laid-back atmosphere. The reality was, children's fashion trends absorbed more time and money than most parents would've liked.

On his first day back, everything about Rob was fresh from the packet, including the shoes with marshmallow-soft soles. ("They squeak," he said, as we wrangled with the spaghetti of his shoelaces. "People will laugh at me."—"They're just jealous," I assured him.) His clothes and professionally trimmed hair presented a mother's challenge to the world: this boy is precious; damage him at your peril. The only item on him that wasn't new was the Superman watch on his wrist.

"What if bullies get me?" he asked, clutching the stainless-steel band of his watch.

My insides melted. If only I could shadow his every step through the day ahead, monitor each breath that filled his six-year-old lungs, and roar at his adversaries.

"They won't," I said, fiercely hoping I was right. But what if I wasn't? His status as grieving brother had the potential to single him out for special attention from emotionally disturbed retards. "Tell the teacher to call me if you want to come home any time."

"Look after Cleo for me," he said, opening the fridge door and removing a jug of milk, too full for his child's grip. The jug wobbled as he poured the milk into a saucer, slopping a pond on the floor. Cleo arched with delight as the delicious liquid flowed. Her tail uncoiled and her tongue set about its work with crisp strokes.

Rob was sleeping more soundly since he'd moved back to his old room. His nightmares and dreams were less disturbing. No doubt the comfort of a centrally heated kitten had something to do with that.

A sharp tapping on the window jangled my nerves. The unmistakable cheekbones of Ginny Desilva, the most glamorous woman on the zigzag, pressed against the glass. Her perfectly shaped lips were arranged in a magazine smile. She raised three moisturized fingers, waved her glistening talons at us and called, "Hallooooo!"

Ginny was wearing a gold vinyl jacket, false eyelashes, earrings the size of chandeliers and a ponytail that was perched high on one side of her head. My regulation track pants and stained T-shirt didn't stand a chance.

A boy about Rob's size was holding Ginny's hand. He had spiky hair and a pixie face.

"That's Jason!" said Rob in awe.

"What's he like?" I hissed through my teeth, while nodding and smiling at Ginny.

"He's one of the Cool Gang."

Ah yes. The legendary Cool Gang. I'd heard Rob and Sam talk as if they'd rather paint their willies blue than join the Cool Gang. That was only because the Cool Gang hadn't asked for their membership.

The only thing cooler than the Cool Gang was the Cool Gang's parents. They were doctors, lawyers and architects who arranged tennis matches on a rotation basis so they all had a chance to show off the courts in their back gardens. Ginny and her husband, Rick, were Queen and King of the Cool Gang's parents because they transcended the run-of-the-mill professionals. Rick ran a record company. And Ginny, well, all she had to do was drape herself in fake fur and be Ginny.

Journalism had trained me to make snap judgments. Fashion model means way too beautiful *and* skinny plus shallow plus competitive about physical appearances and men plus dimwitted equals an excellent person for me to avoid. Ginny, in the single conversation I'd had with her when we'd bumped into each other on the zigzag, claimed to be a midwife, though this seemed too outlandish to be true. I'd assumed she was on something at the time.

"Hi," I said, almost blinded by the sheen of her mahogany hair as I opened the back door.

"Wow! A kitten!" her son yelled before any of us had time to exchange formalities. Weaving around my track pants, Jason burst into the kitchen.

"Rob, you didn't tell me you had a kitten!" said Jason. "It's so cute! Can I hold it?"

"She's Cleo," said Rob, proudly presenting his pet to Jason. "Her dad's a tomcat. He was wild. We're pretty sure he was a panther."

"Jason adores cats," Ginny laughed, as we watched Jason burying the kitten in his neck. I was waiting for her eyes to settle critically on my track pants and the lake of milk on the floor (which Rata was obligingly slurping), but she seemed oblivious to our chaos.

"I heard Rob's going to be in Jason's class this year," she said. "Jason was wondering if Rob would like to walk to school with him today, weren't you, darling?"

Jason nodded, though somewhat dutifully. Rob walk to school *with Jason?* But the morning was all planned. I'd played it over in my head so many times—mother and son make tragic appearance at school gates. Mother gives son invisible injection of power and protection before son steps boldly into new school life.

"Thanks, but we're driving," I said, immediately aware how clipped and ungrateful I sounded. What was *wrong* with me?

Not so long ago I'd been considered a warm, friendly person. When I was at primary school the other kids gave me the nickname "Happy." There was no danger of a name like that anymore. "Would Jason like us to give him a lift?"

Of course she was going to say no. She'd do it on the grounds of politeness and respect for the hermit shell of misery I'd retreated into. I'd escape with the appearance of having made the offer. She'd decline, and we'd get on with our appropriately separate lives.

"That would be lovely," Ginny replied, fixing me with brown eyes conveying unexpected warmth and something else. What was it—a fleeting spark of wisdom? "Byeee!"

Byeee? Must be retired fashion model speak. Watching Ginny sauntering away like an apparition from a punk rock magazine, I felt ambushed. With a tap of her fingernails on our kitchen window she'd gazumped our ceremonial drive to school.

Not only that, she and Jason had blustered into our kitchen as if it was the most natural thing to do. Her audacious swoop of neighborly intimacy was unnerving. She was crazy, obviously. Either that or unbelievably compassionate, with greater depths than I'd assumed she was capable of. Yes, Ginny had to be insane. Or incredibly wonderful. How else would she know that the best way to treat traumatized people is to behave normally (give or take a byeee or two)? I hadn't been prepared for a guerrilla attack of kindness, not so soon after breakfast.

I couldn't help admiring the woman. A gold vinyl jacket *and* leopard-skin tights? What was that perfume trailing behind her—tiger musk? And how come those chandeliers didn't pull her ears apart? I was too thickheaded to realize I'd just made a friend for life.

With his punk hairdo and purple schoolbag covered with rock band stickers, Jason was the personification of

Cool. Yet he was besotted with Cleo in an unself-consciously boyish way.

"This is the cutest kitten!" Jason said, rocking the black bundle in his arms. "You're so lucky!"

It was the first time in ages that anyone had put the words luck and our family in the same sentence.

"She likes friends," Rob replied.

A tingle fizzed down my spine. Rob was remembering Cleo's so-called promise to help him find new friends in the talking cat dream.

"Can I come over here and play with her after school?" Jason asked.

"Course you can!" we answered in unison.

Cleo settled herself in a pool of sunlight on Rob's bed and we headed out the door. Rata paddled behind us like a steamboat. Halfway up the zigzag, the old dog seemed to run out of puff and plonked herself down. I waited with her a moment. Even though she was panting, she slapped her tail reassuringly on the path as if to say, "Nothing to worry about."

Once Rata had recovered her breath we climbed the rest of the hill. The boys watched anxiously as she straggled to the car. Suddenly aware she was being observed, the dog rallied, lifted her tail and leapt youthfully into the back of the station wagon.

The school gates hadn't changed, which seemed strange considering so much else had. Those gates were at least seventy years old. The first children who ran through them were old men and women now. Their bodies were disintegrating around them in retirement homes, while the gates had merely gathered a layer of rust. The deal hardly seemed fair. Yet, given the choice, I'd still rather come back as human, with a limited quota of laughter and pain, than gates that lasted one hundred and fifty unfeeling years.

Kids were pouring through them, still buzzing with stories from the summer holidays. No doubt Sam's demise had been a hot topic around every kitchen table. Were they going to smother Rob with too much attention or, not knowing what to say, simply ignore him? I fought the urge to scramble out from behind the steering wheel and escort him through every nanosecond of the day.

Rob and Jason climbed out of the car.

"I'll pick you up here at three-thirty," I said.

"S'okay," Jason said. "We'll walk home together, won't we, Rob?"

Rob squinted through the sunlight at Jason and smiled. "Yeah, we'll walk."

Walk? Meaning *cross roads*? My insides swirled at the thought of Rob's feet going anywhere near roadside tarmac without my protective shadow. But Jason and Ginny were right. The sooner Rob adjusted to a new routine, maybe even created new friendships, the easier his life would become. Their advice had arrived in the most powerful package—generosity wrapped in action, not words.

At the risk of Jason thinking I was deranged, I took an old shopping list from my handbag and scribbled on the back the exact route they needed to take walking home. The pedestrian crossing outside the school was monitored by senior students who presumably had some respect for traffic. Following the footpath along the bend of the gulley, they'd have to cross one quiet street before reaching the busy road Sam had died on. They'd cross not at the bus stop farther down the hill but at the zebra crossing several hundred meters higher up, near Dennis's grocery store and the new deli. Pressing the shopping list into Rob's hand I made him promise not to cross until he was certain every car was safely distant. "And remember to ask the teacher to call me if you want to come home early," I called, the unmistakable whine of smother love in my voice.

But Rob was already halfway through the school gates, laughing at something Jason had said. Jason strolled alongside him, turned, waved at me and flung an arm across Rob's shoulder.

Huntress

Unlike most humans, a cat embraces the Wild Side.

Waiting on the zigzag that afternoon with Cleo in my arms, I listened for children's voices. Rob and Jason should have taken about twenty minutes to walk home if they'd followed my map. They were now seven minutes late.

My head filled with what-ifs. If Jason had persuaded Rob to take a longer, more dangerous route, if he'd forgotten Rob was going to walk home with him and gone off with a bunch of cool boys . . . A river rock sat in my chest. Then boyish laughter echoed up the valley. Some of those whoops, the like of which I'd never imagined hearing again, were unmistakably from our son. His first day back at school must have been more successful than I'd dared hope.

I watched as two heads rounded the corner of the leafy path—not two blonds but one fair-headed, one dark.

"How was it?" I called to Rob.

"Fine," he said. The sincerity in his voice sounded genuine.

Jason's face lit up when he saw Cleo.

"Let's teach her to hunt!" he said, sliding his schoolbag off his back.

"Isn't she a bit young?" I asked, nursing the black bundle I'd become so protective of since bringing her back to life. "She's hardly left her mother."

97

"No way!" said Jason, dumping his bag in our hallway as if it was already his second home. "Have you got a piece of old paper and some wool?"

Why hadn't I thought of it before? We'd been so engrossed in our misery I'd forgotten an essential piece of kitten development. Rob, Cleo and I watched as Jason scrunched a rectangle of newsprint and with a string of red wool tied it into a bow.

"Here, girl," Jason whispered, laying the newsprint bow like bait on the floor and twitching his end of the wool. "It's a mouse! *Catch it!*"

Cleo looked puzzled. Maybe she really was an Egyptian princess trapped in a feline body and unable to lower herself to playing with scraps of paper.

"C'mon!" he said, trailing the lure across the floor towards the rubber plant. "It's running away!"

Cleo's ears flicked forwards as she watched the thing skip across the carpet. A paw shot out, almost involuntary in its speed. Paw and paper collided briefly. Jason pulled the string. The kitten tuned into some ancient programming. Crouching on her hind legs, she shimmied her nether regions and tried to hypnotize her target.

Why cats sway like that before they pounce is a mystery. The closest to the cat shimmy I've seen in humans is when professional tennis players propel themselves from side to side as they wait to bash back a one-hundred-miles-per-hour serve. Maybe the shimmy, for cats and tennis players, is a subconscious way for them to prepare muscles on either side of the body for sudden action.

The boys laughed as Cleo pounced on the paper bow and juggled it between her front and back paws.

"Here, you try," said Jason, handing the string to Rob. Generosity was second nature to that child. "Hold it higher so she has to jump."

Cleo hid behind the rubber plant and waited like an assassin.

When the paper bow flew past above her head she grabbed it in midair, between her teeth and front paws. Sailing towards the carpet with her prey locked in a death grip, she looked up at us for the admiration she deserved before crashing in a bundle of legs, fur and paper.

The hapless bow was shredded in minutes.

Jason was even more impressed when Cleo demonstrated her prowess at sock-er. He became a daily visitor to our house after that, while I was gradually introduced to the glittering world of Ginny Desilva. The first time I ventured through the leafy shield up the white gravel path to her place, I felt like a naughty girl escaping from a correctional institution. A hedge of gardenias emitted sensual perfume. A fountain trickled and splashed. With every step I could sense Steve's disapproval. The racy Desilvas weren't our kind of people.

"Come in, darling!" cried Ginny, flinging her front door open. "You're just in time for bubbles."

Nobody on our side of the zigzag called anyone darling. Certainly not people they hardly knew. Ginny, with her false eyelashes and cheekbones to die for, was the first person I'd ever met who could make drinking champagne at four in the afternoon seem the most natural thing in the world. I was amazed at her capacity to never wear the same outfit twice. I was in awe of her white leather sofa and the stainless-steel sculpture that towered like an electric pylon over a corner of her living room. She couldn't remember the name of the artist, or at least she said she couldn't. With Ginny, it was hard to know if she was genuinely vague or just pretending to be in order to put you at ease.

After an hour or two at Ginny's, the world seemed a softer place. When streetlights sparked to life and windows of the office blocks glowed yellow in the city below, I knew it was time to leave. The gravel path undulated under my feet as I wandered home to cook dinner and deal with a hungry cat.

Like everyone else in our family Cleo had a highly developed interest in food. Being half-aristocrat, she made it clear she considered herself a cut above pet shop rubbish.

Once she'd figured out the fridge was the source of high-class menu items, such as salmon, she spent many hours worshipping its great white door. Occasionally she'd run an exploratory front paw along the plastic seal, but her attempts were fruitless.

When I opened the fridge door one morning, she accelerated like a furry cannonball across the kitchen floor and jumped right inside the crisper. When I yelled at her to come out she burrowed farther into the carrots. No way was she relinquishing the right to live inside her own five-star restaurant. When I tried to pry her out she batted me with a claw.

I closed the fridge the door to a crack and peeked inside. Eyeing the ice cliff of the door, with its built-in cartons of milk and juice, Cleo didn't look so confident. When I flung the door open again she pounced from her nest of carrots and shook herself on the kitchen floor, as if to say, "I was only doing it to keep the vegetables happy."

Abandoning the idea of fridge habitation, Cleo worked on other ways of adding gourmet flair to her diet. Emptying her litter box one day I discovered two rubber bands and a length of cotton thread had worked their way through her digestive tract.

With newly discovered power in her back legs, she'd spring onto the kitchen bench for a gastronomic preview of whatever we were having for dinner. Chicken breast and fish were favorites, but she developed a taste for mincemeat, cake, raw eggs and, of course, butter.

If I didn't stow the butter safely away in the fridge, suspicious-looking tracks would appear on its surface. It's hard to know if Cleo really liked butter or just pretended to enjoy it to taunt Rata, who was trapped unwillingly down at ground level. Our omnivorous golden retriever was genuinely obsessed with processed animal fats. At Sam's fifth birthday party she had wolfed down an entire slab of butter that had been left inadvertently on the coffee table. We waited for her to turn green around the whiskers, and prepared for an ambulance run to the vet, but Rata remained cheerful as ever. The dog's Teflon-lined stomach could handle anything from shoelaces to picnic lunch leftovers, including (if available) the paper napkins.

As the days shortened Cleo discovered the sort of food she liked best. Thanks to Jason's hunting lessons, she tuned into her wildcat side and learned the thrill of self-service. Prowling through the flowerbeds like a black panther she explored the victim potential of everything that moved, including blades of grass. Even the daisies were in danger. A crack in the path near the front gate revealed an exciting potential prey: ants. Her head would dart from side to side as these corporate workers of the garden went about their business. Cleo would tease them with her paw, only to be disappointed. Instead of playing a game, the ants would simply keep marching ahead, oblivious to fun or danger.

Her first triumph was a praying mantis she discovered on the window ledge in Rob's bedroom. I've always had a soft spot for praying mantises. Their revolving eyes and articulated limbs make them look like visitors from outer space. Geeks of the insect world, they live quietly and are endearingly harmless (except to the occasional fly or grasshopper). Unlike other insects they have no interest in sucking blood, stinging or spreading fatal illness.

Which is why I was upset to find one in Cleo's clutches one sunny afternoon. She was teasing the poor thing, letting it imagine it had escaped and then pouncing on it again. My first instinct was to rescue the insect. But it had already lost a leg. There was no hope.

For the first time I was mildly repelled by our kitten. Then again, if I tried to stop her hunting and occasionally killing other creatures I'd be denying her essential catness. Somewhere in the back of my head I could hear Mum saying *You can't interfere with Nature.* Not that her pioneering upbringing mirrored the sentiment. Our ancestors had no qualms reducing huge tracts of land to ash.

Guilty with praying mantis betrayal, I backed out of Rob's room and closed the door. Ten minutes later, I discovered Cleo dozing in the sun on Rob's pillow. She opened a self-satisfied eye at me and closed it. The headless torso of the praying mantis lay on the floor under the window ledge.

Cleo swiftly graduated to mice and birds, much to my horror. Headless corpses were deposited on the front doormat like little gifts. Digging graves for them beside the forget-me-nots was a reminder life has always been a struggle for living creatures. Somewhere along the line, we humans got hung up about death. We invented expressions like "passed away," and took pains to conceal the process of transforming a cow in a paddock into a hamburger. We hid away the sick, old and disabled, so that suffering was a mystery and death the ultimate abnormality.

People persuade themselves they deserve easy lives, that being human makes us somehow exempt from pain. The theory works fine until we face the inevitable challenges. Our conditioning of denial in no way equips us to deal with the difficult times that not one of us escapes.

Cleo's motto seemed to be: Life's tough and that's okay, because life is also fantastic. Love it, live it—but don't be fooled into thinking it's not harsh sometimes. Those who've survived periods of bleakness are often better at savoring good times and wise enough to understand that good times are actually *great.*

I wondered if I'd ever feel strong enough to follow her example.

Letting Go

A touch of a paw can work better than aspirin.

Autumn was upon us and the hills around the harbor were burnished gold with gorse flowers. The new season had crept in so gradually I'd hardly noticed the change as it was happening. One moment Cleo was making herself so hot sunbathing on the front path she had to retreat to the shadow of the house to cool off. Next she was jostling for prime position in front of the gas fire with the rest of us, and somehow always getting the best spot. Suddenly there was a bite in the wind and poplar trees were shimmering bronze. My powers of observation had been equally remiss with Cleo. I'd grown so accustomed to telling visitors we shared our house with a cat who looked like an alien I no longer regarded her through accurate lenses. I was taking it for granted that we lived with an ugly cat.

I was out in the garden raking leaves one morning when I noticed an extraordinary cat sitting on Mrs. Sommerville's roof. Sleek and elegant, its beauty sucked the breath out of my lungs for a moment. It was an awe-inspiring sight. My semirural background ensured I wasn't usually affected by animals like that. Mum had raised me to believe anything with four legs that wasn't a table was at best an economic unit, at worst a bloody nuisance. But this being was beyond in-built parental prejudice. Its profile was noble as any lion's. With its head tilted slightly to one side and its tail curved in mathematical perfection around its rump, it was a feline version of a top model posing for a *Vanity Fair* photo shoot. Except there was no self-consciousness in the cat's pose. It wasn't even interested in me. Ears forwards, nose slightly aloft, its attention was focused on a potential meal in a nearby tree.

I felt a stab of envy for the human who belonged to such a beast. I could see him sitting smug by his log fire, one hand encircling a decent red wine, the other massaging the handsome cat's fur. Although black from tip to tail like Cleo, it was obviously a pedigreed cat of impressive lineage. It probably had enough papers to set a house on fire. Going by the sheen on its coat, it dined on fresh sardines every night. Next to a cat like that, poor Cleo would resemble something that had just crawled out of the drains of Calcutta. Fortunately, Cleo was nowhere in sight. She was probably inside investigating the fruit bowl, which had recently proved an interesting source of insect life. I put my head down and continued raking. I have yet to discover the Zen approach to raking leaves. Autumn leaves are disobedient at the best of times. Trying to do anything with them on a windy day is physical and emotional torture. The moment I herded them into a satisfactory mound a playful breeze scattered them like kittens and shook another shoal down from the poplars. It was a frustrating job that would've been considerably more pleasant if Rata had been able to understand the intricacies of human plumbing services and why they'd been invented.

Muttering one of Sam's forbidden rude words, I scraped Rata's contribution to global soil fertility off the sole of my sneaker on a stone. The pleasures of autumn gardening, if there were any, were lost on me. I was about to give up and go inside in search of tea when I heard a familiar meow.

"Cleo!" I called, checking her favorite sunbathing place in the weeds under what once had been a rose bed. The only evidence of her there was a flattened oval of long grass. Scanning the window ledge outside Rob's bedroom, I called again. The black cat on Mrs. Somerville's roof stared down at me with steady curiosity.

"It's fine for you, you spoiled snooty thing!" I growled up at it. "We can't all be best in show."

The cat yawned and rose effortlessly to its feet. I watched it float along the roof guttering and sail into the branches of a tree. It then slid gracefully down the trunk and skipped toward me, meowing delightedly.

"Cleo?" I said bending to stroke the bridge of her back as she nudged her chin against my calf muscles. I lifted the manifestation of feline perfection into my arms and sank my nose into her fur to make sure it really was her. "Goodness, when did you become so gorgeous?"

I'd been so absorbed by grief over the summer I hadn't noticed Cleo had undergone a makeover beyond extreme. Over just a few weeks our skinny runt with unnerving eyes and hardly any fur had evolved into a drop-dead gorgeous cat. Her fur, jet black, grew thick and glossy in preparation for her first winter. She no longer looked like E.T.'s cousin. Her face had been sculpted into the aristocratic angles of her mother's.

It was time to make up for my shocking lack of observation, haul myself out of distraction and notice Cleo. The changes she had gone through while I wasn't looking were a reminder that life's relentless cycles were rolling on no matter what. Whether I was going to miss out on some magnificent episodes of change and rebirth was largely up to me.

Scooping her up, I carried her to the front porch and sat on the step with her on my knee. Cleo writhed ecstatically and rolled onto her back, her legs paddling the air. This un-catlike position was one of her favorites. She often fell asleep that way draped upside down across someone's knee in front of the television, her head drooping backwards so the underside of her neck and chin were exposed to whomever she was sitting on.

Stroking her was a tactile adventure, a journey of discovery through Cleo's landscape of fur. Her ears were cool and slick the way I'd imagined a seal's skin would be. Their design was vaguely aerodynamic, potentially giving her descendents the option of flight. The velour ridge of her nose was tipped with a patch of damp leather. On the slope descending between her ears and eyes, the fur was sparser, the closest thing Cleo had to a bald patch these days. But it was in no way unattractive. In fact it was intriguing and stylish in the way Yves Saint Laurent could make tartan a perfect match for polka dots. Taut skin around her eyes was helpful whenever I needed to roll specks of sleep from their corners, which was surprisingly often. Strange there were no eyelashes in this plethora of fur. Two pairs of antennae, a memory of eyebrows, sprouted from her forehead. No doubt they had some stealthy purpose such as measuring rat holes. Her whiskers were like dried grass, her chin a fuzzy beard.

The fur on her torso was fluffy, softer than a rabbit's. Her "underarms" sprouted longer fringes that seemed vaguely out of place, like human underarm hair, filing cabinets for ancestral memory. A raised ridge of fur ran like a mini Mohawk down the center of her chest. The growth on her lower abdomen was coarser and longer, but still soft. On the inner sides of her legs the fur was silky, the outer thighs slippery and smooth.

Her purr intensified as I rubbed her long back legs with their elongated kangaroo feet. The pads, smoother than vinyl, gleamed purple black in the sun. They were lined with closely cropped hair concealing the sheathed scimitars of her claws.

No decent petting was complete without attention to Cleo's pride and joy, her tail. Smooth and oily, it had sprouted into an elegant accessory. Serpent-like in appearance and flexibility, it had almost as much personality as Cleo herself. It lay in wait beside her when she woke in the mornings, and coiled stealthily around her last thing at night. Every time she looked over her shoulder there it was again, the stalker snake, shadowing her every move.

Most of the time, Cleo regarded her tail as a playmate. They could spend the best part of an afternoon chasing each other in circles around the floor until they collapsed from dizziness. On other occasions, the tail took on a more malevolent mood. When Cleo was dozing on the window ledge the tail would sometimes twitch, disturbing her sleep. She would open one eye to examine the mischievous appendage. Rippling under her gaze, that tail was asking to be taught a lesson. Cleo would attack, tumbling off the window ledge so she could grab the creature with all four sets of claws and sink her teeth into it. Twitching and writhing between her jaws, the snake put up a noble fight, inflicting mysteriously brutal pain on its attacker. Cleo and her tail were like a warring married couple, glued together for reasons they'd long forgotten and fighting several times a day over imagined insults. It took a long time for them to settle their differences and cohabit in peace.

I resisted the temptation to call Rosie and boast how our "ugly" kitten was transforming into a beauty. Cleo's newfound elegance aroused two hopes in me. One, that she wouldn't realize how gorgeous she was and become vain (few weaknesses are more tiresome to live with than vanity, especially in someone who has suffered the indignity of plain looks in their past). Two, that the theory about dog owners developing a physical likeness to their pets might also apply to cat owners. Neither of these aspirations seemed likely to happen. Cleo was too playful and fascinated with life to start behaving like a movie star. And I continued to resemble a food-addicted golden retriever.

Cleo awakened a depth of tenderness in Rob I hadn't seen before. He'd always been the baby of the household, the one everybody else looked out for. Now, for the first time, he was responsible for something smaller than himself, and a gentle, caring side of him began to emerge. Feeding, combing, cuddling his lovable kitten (often with enthusiastic advice from Jason) was helping him grow stronger and more self-assured. I watched in awe as he carved a fresh identity for himself at school, and a trickle of new friends made their way down the zigzag to our place.

Our affection for Cleo was fiercely returned. As her adopted slaves, we were duty-bound to include her in everything. If she heard a conversation going on in another room she scratched and called at the door until she was part of it. Occasionally she was content to witness goings-on from a vantage point in the sun on the back of the sofa. Mostly, though, she preferred to be wedged into a warm lap, her paws tucked neatly under her body, purring approval.

If someone was reading a book, particularly if the reader was lying comfortably on his back, Cleo knew she was being invited to position herself between him and the pages. Supremely confident that a cat was far more fascinating than any printed word, she'd be astonished when the reader lifted her, evicting her gently to the other side of the book. How could an inferior human be so rude? Once she'd regained her composure, she would examine the outside cover. She could only presume it had been placed there for grooming purposes. Cleo discovered cats don't need toothbrushes when they can run their teeth along the cardboard edge of a paperback cover.

She waited on Rob's window ledge with more than a hint of accusation in her eye whenever we went out. Was time going to limp by while we were away? As if. The moment she'd seen the back of the last raincoat disappear up the zigzag she'd get up to secret cat's business. A potted plant would tumble mysteriously on its side. Telltale paw prints appeared on the kitchen bench. Half-eaten blowflies sprinkled themselves over the carpet. The joint certainly jumped while we were out. When we arrived home Cleo would be waiting in the window again. She seemed to have an inbuilt radar that told her exactly when we'd be back. She would dance down the hall to greet us, her tail raised in an elegant curve of greeting. Anyone who picked her up in their arms would be rewarded with a kiss from her damp, licorice nose.

If dogs could talk, Rata would have been a reliable informant. Gazing mournfully at a tangle of pulled threads on the sofa she'd sigh as if to say, "What can you expect from a cat?" But when Cleo snuggled into the dog's belly to be slobbered with giant retriever kisses, all was forgiven. For all her uppity, occasionally murderous, habits, we adored her.

The more we let ourselves love our young cat, the more readily we seemed able to open our hearts and forgive the unfamiliar people we'd become since the loss of Sam. As we turned towards each other and started to rebuild a sense of family, a hopeful warmth resurfaced in our marriage. Steve dismantled the barricade of his newspaper one night, looked me straight in the eye and said: "You look so terribly sad and beautiful." His words stretched across the icy distance and enveloped us.

I'd forgotten how amusing his quirky sense of humor could be. That's what had drawn us together in the first place. Both outsiders, we'd been hopelessly uncoordinated at school sports and shared a talent for feeling awkward in groups. Together we'd created a separate universe and tried to persuade ourselves that life as a pair of misfits on the edge of the mainstream was a comfortable place to be.

Vulnerable as a pair of oysters without their shells, we put on our winter coats and went on our first movie "date" since our lives had changed so drastically. A divinely youthful and sexy Richard Gere in *An Officer and a Gentleman* diverted my attention long enough for me to feel surprised, then guilty, I'd gone for a few minutes not thinking about Sam. When the credits rolled, the lights went up and Joe Cocker and Jennifer Warnes launched into the theme song, "Up Where We Belong," reality crashed in again.

Soon after, Steve visited a specialist to investigate the prospect of a vasectomy reversal. Complicated microsurgery would be involved, and he was warned the chances of success were minimal, as low as ten percent. Nevertheless, taking our circumstances into account, the surgeon was willing to give it his best shot. Even though we knew our marriage was on a fault line and on the verge of crumbling, we both desperately wanted another child. A date for the surgery was set.

We weren't looking for a replacement for Sam. We both knew that would be impossible. But our house and hearts felt empty. I still set the table for four every night, until a cold gong in my heart reminded me I was living in the past. One set of knives and forks had to be put back in the drawer.

I longed for sorrow to shrivel and sail effortlessly into oblivion. If an autumn leaf could release the memory of summer and float into nothingness, fearless and with such grace, why was it impossible for me?

An inner lioness of motherhood refused to relinquish anything connected to Sam. Alone in the house, I'd carry his blue Boy Scouts jumper around with me like a comfort rug, over my shoulder. His name tag had been hand-sewn clumsily inside the collar. After he'd earned the red patches for Reading, Art, Chess and (laughably) Housework, I'd shared his pride by sewing them on the sleeves with small careful stitches. The garment had shrunk to the shape of his torso. It was redolent of him and now also of my tears.

Mothers are the ultimate power junkies. When we lift a newborn human from our bodies we experience an adrenaline high far headier than anything Bill Gates or Pablo Picasso ever knew. Multi-zillion-dollar businesses and the world's greatest art fade to trinkets alongside the miraculous creation of a human being. The reason so few women become great concert masters, politicians and inventors isn't so much because of prejudice (not that there's a shortage) or lack of opportunity (hardly a drought of that, either). Why would anyone bother writing a symphony when she can create a collection of cells that will one day ask to borrow her car?

Our passion for our children springs straight from the jungle. Would Bill Gates lay down his life for Microsoft? Picasso commit murder for one of his paintings?

Mothers have power beyond politics, art and money. We're the people who give life, nurture babies and make them grow. Without us humanity would wither like seaweed on a rock. Knowledge of our power is so deep we don't talk about it often, but we use it all the time.

Ancient mother's power is employed to make our kids eat green vegetables, aim straight at the toilet bowl and grow a few centimeters every year. When we yell *"Come back here!"* across a supermarket or a playing field, they freeze, turn around and obey—most of the time, anyway. It's magic. It works. Because we say so.

I'd brought Sam to life when he slid out of my body all those years ago. Surely I was strong enough to muster enough mother's power to will him to life again? *"Come back here!"* I yelled across the universe. The silence was darker than midnight. I longed to see even his ghostly form standing at the end of the bed. But Sam had flown farther away than the distance between stars, to the empty nothingness of space.

I dreaded bumping into Sam's old school friends. Their innocent faces still fired me with irrational resentment, then profound shame at my reaction. Rage flared whenever I saw a blue Ford Escort. It had yet to occur to me that the events of 21 January could have ruined the woman's life almost as drastically as ours. I often wondered how events had unfolded that day. After Sam had fallen, Rob had run up the zigzag to find Steve. Had she climbed out of her car to comfort the dying child?

But the sight of our young cat scampering down the hallway invariably lifted my mood. Not so long ago Lena's instruction to simply love our kitten had seemed an impossible ask. Yet Cleo overwhelmed us all with affection so freely, we couldn't help loving her back. The youngest, most joyous member of our family, she had woven herself into our life after Sam. I couldn't believe I'd ever contemplated giving her back to Lena.

◆

Leaves of a birch in our garden transformed themselves into a curtain of gold medallions that shimmered against pewter branches. Oblivious to its chances, a late summer rose unfurled on a bush.

A squall direct from Antarctica pummelled the harbor to stainless steel, scattering birds across the sky. No wonder birds greet a translucent dawn with consummate joy. They don't dwell on the previous night's storm. Their chorus betrays no concern for the winter ahead, either. They simply embrace the miracle of being alive in this instant on one perfect autumn morning. I had so much to learn from them.

If anything, the beauty of these sights was heightened now I understood how achingly brief the life span was of any living thing. Maybe the key to healing isn't found in books, tears or religion, but in affection for small things—a flower, the smell of damp grass. Love for a kitten was helping me embrace the world again.

Observer

A wise cat steps back from emotional response and observes without judgment.

Our first winter after losing Sam was particularly harsh. Snow draped itself over the hills across the harbor. Giant bruises of clouds rolled up from Antarctica and pushed against our windows. Rain pelted sideways at the glass. Wind tore our coats as we scurried down the zigzag, which had become a waterfall.

I gradually trained myself to drive under the footbridge. The first time I held my breath and focused on a triangle of harbor in the distance as the car hurtled down the hill. Next time, driving slowly up the slope, I allowed my eyes to drift to the bus stop and the curb Sam's foot had left.

A reluctant spring arrived with spikes of yellow bloom. Reliving Sam's last steps, I forced myself to walk down the zigzag and onto the tired wooden planks of the footbridge. Pausing in the center, I gazed down at the road. It was an unremarkable strip of tar seal. No stains, no hollows or irregularities. Nothing to indicate a boy had lost his life there. I hoped he hadn't died frightened and alone.

I gave up scouring the streets for mousey-haired, thirty-something largish women with or without spectacles in navy coats. A Ford Escort parked on the side of the street was no longer an invitation to inspect its headlights. The damage would've been fixed months ago, anyway. It was probably beetling up and down hills, pretending it had never killed.

With warmer weather a gut-wrenching series of firsts had to be endured: what would have been Sam's tenth birthday, closely followed by our first Christmas without him, then the anniversary of the accident. I've never been able to love summer wholeheartedly since.

Sometimes I'd been paralyzed with guilt if a few minutes went by without grief for Sam. A moment of laughter or happiness would shame me into thinking I was letting Sam down. But I gradually realized that being locked in a state of misery wasn't helping Rob or honoring the life we'd had with Sam or the fact I was still alive.

With courage worthy of Superman himself, Rob had settled back well into school. Teachers whined about learning difficulties but the main thing was he seemed to have plenty of friends. While Steve and I hadn't fallen in love again, we'd accepted some of our differences and were getting along better. Cleo was constantly springing out at us from behind doorways, reminding us life was too profound to be taken seriously.

I was beginning to relate to Cleo's attraction to high places. Even if it was just a hereditary Abyssinian thing, the notion of taking a step above daily life and gazing down at it from a distance had compelling logic. I'd been doing it myself at night recently, standing at the top of the zigzag, the chill wind slicing my cheeks, and staring down at the glittering city. When observed from a great height, pain sometimes shrinks and subsides into the wider pattern of life. With practice and time I was learning it's possible to disengage emotion occasionally and experience the serenity of a cat observing the world from a rooftop.

Gazing down at the grids of streetlights, I would wonder if a person's life is packaged in a predestined design. When

Sam was just two years old we'd walked through a picturesque old cemetery one morning. He ran ahead and stopped at a gravestone engraved with the name "Samuel." Pointing at the headstone, he howled uncontrollably. I'd had to lift him, red-faced and sobbing, in my arms and carry him away from the place. He couldn't even read at the time and had no way to understand the technicalities of death and cemeteries. How could a toddler comprehend so much, let alone experience a terrifying premonition? The memory of that day still makes me shudder.

The night sky that had once seemed so icy and indifferent would draw me into its magnificence. Maybe the cloak of space wasn't empty after all, but full of profound energies humans have yet to perceive. Instead of limitless nothing, that giant bowl of stars could be where we've come from and the place we return to. So far away and yet intimately close. Light that had left those stars years ago traveled across time to enter the retinas of my eyes and become part of my experience. They were as close to me now as darling Sam, distant as the stars and yet an integral part of every breath. The sky, stars, Sam and I were closer than I'd dared imagine. Maybe that's what Mum had been talking about when she'd said Sam was part of the sunset. Perhaps she wasn't insensitive after all, but incredibly wise. When it's my turn, maybe I'll discover death isn't a terrifying full stop but a return to the eternal mystery that is home.

◆

With help from Jason and Ginny we plowed through another winter into a second spring. As nights grew longer, evenings after school were a favorite time for the four of us to get together. Ginny and I would meet in the garden and soothe the day away with a glass of bubbles while we watched the boys burn off the last of their energy before bedtime.

I'd gone along with Ginny's dizzy act in the beginning. With her whacky earrings and fabulous hairdos, she gave the impression of being a blonde in brunette's clothing. Nothing could've been further from the truth. I was amazed when she confessed to not only being a midwife but studying for a science degree as well. More important, she introduced me to fake fur and lent me some of her earrings, including some orange dangling Perspex lightning bolts that were beyond electrifying. Ginny taught me how to put false eyelashes on straight and to not be scared of platform shoes. She was becoming the friend I'd always dreamt of—zany, wise, kind and equipped with an almost psychic ability to turn up when needed.

Rob and Jason were bonded by their devotion to Cleo. They thought it was about time she had kittens. They were disgusted when I explained she'd had an operation.

"That's *so-o* mean!" said Jason, shaking his head with bewilderment.

"Yeah," Rob added. "Why didn't you let Cleo have babies?"

Standing on the grass against an orange sunset, Ginny and I exchanged smiles. We'd become such close friends it felt as though we were living in an Antipodean version of an African longhouse. With one short zig of the zigzag between our homes, the boys ran freely from one house to the other. Even though Ginny and Jason lived in two-storied splendor, they seemed oblivious to our shabby kitsch.

"Well," I said, "a cat can have babies three or four times a year. And if she had five kittens in each litter that means Cleo would have twenty babies in one year. Imagine twenty kittens running through the house."

Rob thought that sounded fantastic. When I asked where they'd all sleep, Jason volunteered that at least one kitten could live at his house.

"They'd still have nineteen kittens left," said Ginny. "And it wouldn't be long before *they* were able to have kittens. They'd end up with hundreds and thousands of kittens."

"Wow!" said Rob, turning to me. "Why *were* you so mean?"

I tried to explain the operation's benefits. Without it Cleo would want to go out on dates. She'd get moody when we kept her inside. The vet had assured me having her spayed protected her from infections and some types of cancer.

"Nobody stopped *you* having babies," Rob grumbled.

This surgical reproductive talk was reassurance we'd done the right thing in not revealing to Rob details of Steve's vasectomy reversal, which had involved considerably more time under the knife and greater discomfort than Cleo had undergone. The patient hadn't once complained, though his eyes sometimes clouded with pain. The surgeon reported that the operation had gone well, though it would be some time before we knew for certain if it had worked. After a stoic recovery, Steve had packed his suitcase and hobbled off to the ferry for another stint at sea.

Cleo tuned into the boys' disapproval of me. Squirming in my arms, she demanded to be put on the grass. She stalked around the side of the house looking like Naomi Campbell. Watching her disappear I felt a momentary twinge of guilt. Perhaps a creature as graceful as Cleo deserved to populate the world.

"You should've let her have babies!" said Rob, harrumphing off down the path. "C'mon Jason. Let's dig."

The boys' shared love of Cleo had expanded to other interests, including a vast excavation they'd undertaken in a corner of our garden so wild and neglected I'd barely noticed it before. Shaded with ferns and an air of forbidden mystery, it was a perfect spot for male bonding over a major dig.

Day after day they dragged Steve's pickax and shovels out from under our house. The equipment looked huge and dangerous in their hands. Today's parent would probably be sued for letting them loose with such man-sized weaponry. But the hole-digging enterprise really mattered to the boys.

A fireball sun was sinking over the hills. A shawl of frost nestled in the valleys. The city hummed companionably below us. When I asked Ginny if we should call the boys back to get them inside and fed she shrugged. Digging was obviously an important rite in the passage to manhood.

Even though I was tempted to swathe Rob in Bubble Wrap and protect him from every potential dent, I knew it would be a mistake. I had to ease up and allow him the freedom a boy needs to develop into a confident young male. The hole-digging mission went on week after week, much to Rata's delight (the only expert digger among them). Perched on a branch, Cleo kept lookout for inadvertent birdlife while the boys swaggered like cowboys and exchanged grown-up cursewords below.

Nobody, including the boys, knew exactly why they were digging the hole. Its purpose changed all the time. They were tunneling through to the other side of the earth for a while, until they started feeling sweaty and wondered if they were getting too close to the core. Changing strategy a few days later, they decided to search for the chest of gold that Captain Cook had almost certainly buried there on his last voyage. A few days later they discovered an old wire mattress base under the house. They carried it outside and stretched it across the hole and made a lethal-looking trampoline.

I wondered if handling the moist weight of the soil was therapy for Rob. The sight of him spattered with dirt and flushed with satisfaction after a digging session reminded me of my grandmother. Mother of nine children, she'd spent most of her life on the same patch of farmland, and must have faced countless anxieties and disappointments. Whenever worry scratched at her innards she headed down her back steps, past the henhouse to her garden. The cure for every sorrow, she said, could be found on her knees on a patch of earth with a trowel in one hand. The ritualistic comfort of turning the earth was her psychotherapy. Deep engagement with her garden's volcanic loam kept her earthed and connected to the planet's ancient rhythms.

Though she'd long since moved on, I was beginning to understand her better now, especially since I'd spent more time outside while the boys were digging.

In a frivolous act of optimism I planted tulip bulbs for spring. To cover a seed with soil is to demonstrate faith in the future. Tearing out weeds, watering and nurturing the sleeping seed are acts of trust in Nature. When a green shoot appears the gardener experiences a similar rush to someone who has just created a work of art or given birth. Gardening is the closest some people get to feeling like a god. To watch a seedling sprout and unfurl into a flower or vegetable is to take part in a miracle. The gardener also learns acceptance of decay and death, to almost welcome a season of withdrawal as part of the cycle.

Cleo, on the other hand, had another way of dealing with life's hiccups. She headed for high places. As we wandered down the path to inspect the boys' earthworks, Ginny suddenly stopped and pointed a crimson fingernail at our roof. Perched on top of a chimney pot was a familiar silhouette.

"What's Cleo doing up there?" she asked.

"Probably sulking about the operation," I said. "She must be feeling pretty fit to get up there. *Cleo!*"

But our cat sat still as a statue against the orange sky, her back to us, her tail in a graceful loop over the chimney.

"Are you sure she's okay?" said Ginny doubtfully.

"It's her way of dealing with things."

"Do you think she's stuck?" asked Ginny.

"Maybe she's enjoying the view."

Cleo must've had fun climbing up there, but getting down looked impossible, even for an agile cat.

"Why do these things always happen when Steve's away at sea?" I complained. Trudging around the side of the house to find a ladder, I suddenly thought of a new motto: "Keep one eye on the stars and the other on the ground to watch out for dog shit."

Ginny, whose generosity knew no bounds, offered to climb up and get Cleo. But even a circus performer would think twice before scaling a ladder in fishnet stockings, platform shoes and earrings the size of post office clocks.

Thanking her, I leaned the ladder against the house and looked skywards.

Two tiny black ears stood out against the sunset. The ladder seemed suddenly frail and rickety—and far taller than I'd remembered.

As I climbed, a wave of nausea washed up from my knees to the top of my neck, threatening to burst out from the back of my throat. Vertigo had never had such a physical effect on me before.

"Shall I call the fire brigade?" Ginny called helpfully. I regretted glancing down. Ginny, her face turned up in concern, had shrunk to the size of a brightly colored beetle.

I reached the top of the ladder and edged onto the roof. Except it wasn't so much a roof as a collection of rusty holes holding hands, hardly ideal support for a not very petite woman.

"Here, kitty!" I called. The shape on top of the chimney remained motionless. The poor feline was frozen with terror. "Oh, Cleo! Don't worry. I'll get you down."

The roof squeaked and groaned in protest as I crawled toward the chimney, my stomach churning. The thought was just occurring to me that if Cleo, an agile animal equipped with four legs, was having trouble getting off the roof it might be close to impossible for a lumbering vertigo victim.

"Hold on! I'm nearly there," I called.

A pair of luminous eyes loomed above my head and narrowed to a bad-tempered glower. Cleo shook her head in a bored, dismissive manner. She rose gracefully to her feet on top of the chimney, arched her back and yawned. Without hesitation she sprang nimbly down to the roof, leapt across the rusty tin, jumped onto a nearby tree and slid groundwards, landing inches away from Ginny's platform shoes.

"I think I'm going to throw up!" I wailed down at Ginny.

"You'll be fine. Just take it slowly. Crawl back to the ladder, that's right. Turn around. Watch out for the gutter . . . there you go!"

When I finally reached terra firma I took three steps and threw up in a hydrangea bush.

"Why didn't you say you were scared of heights?" asked Ginny.

"It's not usually this bad. I haven't felt this sick since I was . . . pregnant."

Indulgence

Stress—a waste of nap time.

A cat's lips are arranged in a permanent smile. Even when it's miserable, the edges of its mouth point skywards. This is not the case with humans, whose mouths have a tendency to turn down at the corners, especially as they grow older. A human who wears the effortless smile of cat is in possession of a happy secret.

A smile appeared on Steve's lips when he heard the news. He carried it with him back to sea and was still wearing it a week later. I had a cat's smile too. We agreed not to make it official for a few weeks in case the pregnancy came to nothing.

When we decided it was safe to tell Rob, his smile was an explosion of sunlight.

He immediately put in an order for a baby brother. It had to be a boy, he said, because boys were what we had in our family. I agreed and promised to do my best. Then he ran across the zigzag to tell Jason, who of course told Ginny.

Arriving breathless on the doorstep, she enveloped me in the spicy embrace of her Opium perfume and did an excellent job feigning surprise. "Congratulations, darling! It's going to be wonderful." She offered to deliver the baby when the time came. I still had trouble believing my zany friend had another life in sterile gloves. Still, I liked the idea of our baby's first glimpse of humanity including a woman in false eyelashes and a zebra-skin jacket.

I sank into a pregnancy that combined squeamishness with ravenous hunger. It didn't seem so long ago that New Zealanders had survived on a diet of grey mince and mutton. During my teenage years, Mum introduced me to an exotic new food called pizza. We'd grown more sophisticated since then. We'd learned wine didn't necessarily come out of cardboard boxes, bread could be sold in sticks and there were more than two types of cheese in the world. When a smart new deli opened around the corner we knew we'd arrived.

Profiterole. ProfEETerole, if pronounced correctly, according to the deli man who baked them. Roll your tongue around the word and it sounds almost erotic.

The grumpy profiterole man was Michelangelo in a chef's apron. How he could produce the lightest, puffiest, most delectable pastries on earth was beyond me. But who would guess a beige moth could produce a gorgeous green gum emperor caterpillar?

He laid them out every morning like naked sunbathers in his shop window. Lightly tanned, each oblong encased a glob of cream. Mudslides of chocolate sauce trickled over the cases. The shop window steamed around the edges, inviting—no, *insisting*—I venture inside.

"One profiterole, please," I asked.

"ProFEETerole!" he snapped.

"Make that two."

After all, I was eating for two now (three, in fact, counting Cleo).

Profiterole man grunted. Anyone would think I was trying to buy his children.

Waddling back up the zigzag I could feel the pastry crumbling and the cream oozing through the paper bag.

It was tempting to lower my globular body onto the seat halfway up the zigzag and scoff them there. But there was a danger I'd encounter Mrs. Sommerville. She'd shoot me that Look of hers. Disapproving as ice cliffs, the Sommerville Look was designed to make boys confess to throwing snails at postmen and grown women suddenly feel as if they'd forgotten to put their underwear on.

I decided to slog on. Besides, I wasn't the only one holding out for profiteroles. Cleo had developed an obsession with profiterole cream. The day she stole a splodge off my finger was like a heroin addict's first hit. Ever since, she'd taken to licking empty paper bags, the edges of my plate, my sleeve, anywhere trace elements could be found.

Every morning she waited, outlined against a stained-glass panel in the porch and looking like an Art Nouveau poster, for my return. The moment I arrived puffing at our front gate she galloped towards me, tail high, head slightly tilted. Together we'd trudge inside and sink into the recliner rocker, footrest up, headrest down, and rip open the paper bag.

Cleo was changing my attitude to indulgence. Guilt isn't in cat vocabulary. They never suffer remorse for eating too much, sleeping too long or hogging the warmest cushion in the house. They welcome every pleasurable moment as it unravels, and savor it to the full until a butterfly or falling leaf diverts their attention. They don't waste energy counting the number of calories they've consumed or the hours they've frittered away sunbathing.

Cats don't beat themselves up about not working hard enough. They don't get up and go, they sit down and stay. For them, lethargy is an art form. From their vantage points on top of fences and window ledges, they see the treadmills of human obligations for what they are—a meaningless waste of nap time.

I loved lazing around the half-renovated bungalow taking chill-out lessons from a cat. I slowed down, zoned out and tried listening to my body. It was screaming for rest, not just to cope with the demands of pregnancy, but to harvest energy for deeper levels of recovery. We became shameless sleepers, indulging in afternoon naps and morning ones, too. Eventually, after I'd waddled home from an after-school visit to Ginny's, Cleo and I discovered the delights of the early evening snooze.

I was her hot-water bottle. Either Cleo sensed the presence of new life inside me and wanted to be part of it, or she simply enjoyed the extra warmth and curves of the expanding mound. Almost horizontal in our recliner rocker, we had an ideal padded nest in which to laze away the weeks.

During the middle months of my pregnancy Cleo arranged herself around the top of the bulge, her head perfectly positioned for an idle tickle. Cleo adored small circular massages in the dent behind her ears, interspersed with full-length body strokes from her forehead to the tip of her tail. The experience was equally pleasurable for the masseuse, and at night my hands tingled with the memory of her fur.

As weeks progressed and my mound grew, Cleo reverted to snuggling wherever she could, stretching up my side or sometimes around the lower regions of my expanding abdomen. Claws were politely sheathed, until she could bear it no longer. Overcome with pleasure, she would knead them rhythmically into her protesting human heater.

A cat's fur has many textures, from the dense velvety covering on her nose to the silky pads of her paws; the sleek fur on her back to the fluffy undergrowth on her belly. Strange that such softness contrasts with claws and teeth sharp as pins. But every feline is a puzzle of contradictions—adoring one moment, aloof the next; a nurturing parent but also a murderer so cold-blooded it toys with wounded prey.

Sprawled in the armchair with Cleo I had an urge to feel wool nudging through my fingers again. To knit the spiderweb delicacy of baby clothes was beyond my capability, so I bought three balls of blue wool (thick) and some chunky needles, and embarked on a plain-stitch scarf for Rob.

The rhythm of needles clicking is soothing, like a heartbeat. How a single thread of wool can be knotted together to create a three-dimensional item of clothing is almost as much a mystery as how a conglomeration of cells multiplies to make a baby.

Every stitch is complete in itself, though attached to stitches past and future. As I wound the wool around the needles to form each stitch, I thought of Sam, and I gently cast off. Cross needles, wind wool, *release* . . . cross needles, wind wool, *release* . . . If I practiced this ten thousand times, or a million, perhaps my soul could do the same. *Release, release* . . .

Cleo was mesmerized; her eyes revolved in unison with the needles. With precision timing, she swatted them as they swept past her face and caught them between her teeth. The enemy of the knitting needles made such a nuisance of herself sometimes I'd scrape her off my lap and put her on the floor. Yet that was no punishment—the snake of blue wool unfurling from its ball was a thrilling foe.

Apart from occasional squabbles over wool and needles, our days drifted away companionably eating, dreaming and following patches of sun around the house. Every moment was a stitch in a larger fabric that was gradually becoming a life connected to the one we had before with Sam, yet entirely different. Household rhythms unfurled effortlessly as a ball of wool. Spoons clattered into kitchen drawers only to be taken out, used, washed, dried and put back again. Each morning Rob and Jason trudged through long shadows down the path to school to return at that time in the afternoon when the day is getting tired. Piles of laundry waited to be sorted, washed and pegged on the clothesline overlooking the shipping terminal below. Then taken down, folded, ironed, put in cupboards, worn and dumped in familiar-smelling piles again. Complete in themselves, each with a beginning, middle and end, these comforting cycles interwove into the semblance of a normal life.

Watching sun ripple against the wallpaper I wondered why we'd been in such a rush to fix up the house. What was so offensive about the wallpaper? If it stayed attached to the walls long enough the frenzy of black floral arrangements against a white background might become fashionable again. Even the shaggy carpet didn't get on my nerves much anymore. Pregnant euphoria ensured everything could wait.

Steve's reaction was the opposite. Every room reeked of fresh paint. Ladders leaned at drunken angles all over the house. Plunging into feverish activity, he finished renovating the bathroom. He hauled out the peeling blue bath with its tasteless gold taps and dumped it on the lawn in front of the house. I was so hormoned-out I wasn't bothered when grass grew tall around its edges.

When I wondered aloud to Ginny if she thought he'd ever take the bath away she suggested we turn it into a lily pond with goldfish. God, I loved that woman.

Cleo and I developed a taste for Mozart, not just because of the theory that babies could hear through the walls of the womb and classical music helped their brain cells grow. Cleo seemed to genuinely appreciate the composer's soothing music, particularly the second movement of the Clarinet Concerto in A. As the clarinet pulled notes of liquid gold from the air, Cleo's eyes narrowed to silver slits. Rainbows of sunlight danced across her fur. Nestling snugly around my belly, she purred accompaniment while Mozart resolved life's heartache in one exquisite movement. Listening to that piece I was assured even the most profound sadness can be transformed into beauty.

Replacement

A cat listens carefully to every story, whether she has heard it before or not.

"It's a boy!" every cell in my body shouted. There was an unmistakable masculinity in the way his feet ricocheted off my ribs. The tiny fists that pummeled my bladder in the middle of the night had the force of a miniature boxing champion. My feet marched "boy, boy" down the darkened hall to the bathroom for the third time in as many hours.

I sewed a tiny baby's gown and embroidered the neck with blue daisies. We talked about names. Joshua, maybe. Certainly not Samuel, though perhaps as a middle name.

Not a replacement for Sam, I explained to anyone who was interested. The new baby would have his own personality, with just a touch of Sam's roguish sense of humor, the same shaped eyes, maybe, perhaps even a similar grassy smell to his skin. He wouldn't *be* Sam, of course. I'd respect the baby's individuality. However much he did or didn't resemble Sam, the baby would make us a family of four again. I'd tell Joshua Samuel everything about the brother he never knew. A thread of continuity would be woven into our lives.

Steve allowed himself to smile more often. To think all this hope was blossoming against the odds because of a surgeon with a microscope and clever fingers! For the last two babies

Steve had scrounged a secondhand bassinet from the For Sale columns of the local newspaper. Certain there'd be no more babies, he'd quickly disposed of it after we'd moved Rob to a larger cot.

This time he went out and bought a brand-new bassinet trimmed with yellow satin ribbon, a tactfully asexual color. Peeling away its shiny wrapping, he assembled it in our bedroom. With a net canopy draped over its sides, the cradle was fit for a prince. I smoothed sheets the size of tea towels over the mattress.

Running my hand over the yellow ribbon, I wondered how people handled raising girls. All that tulle and Barbie doll stuff would be complicated. I knew how boys worked. Looking after them involves a lot of physical energy—chasing, mostly, and yelling. Boys are emotionally straightforward. They have special bonds with their mothers. Sam and I had a Kissing Game, a sort of tag, we used to play. The winner was whoever planted the last kiss on the other's face, and it always ended with both of us purple with laughter.

Yes, I thought, examining the latest styles in blue booties and cuddly rugs, I'd teach the new baby the secret Kissing Game, even though it had belonged exclusively to Sam and me. I wondered if Joshua would like Sam's old wooden train set, and if there was anything else of Sam's he'd like. Not that I was in any way planning to replicate what we had. Was I?

◆

Rata was overjoyed when Mum's Japanese hatchback slowed to a halt at the top of the zigzag. It was a car the retriever associated with jaunts to the beach, farms and other happy places. Mum had come to "help out" before the baby arrived. The length of her stay was unspecified, but if it was like any other it probably wouldn't be more than a couple of nights. Mum and I loved each other dearly, but we both had strong personalities and were prone to amateur dramatics. We usually rubbed each other the wrong way after a few nights.

As Mum emerged from the driver's door Rata sprang on her hind legs, plonked a paw on each of the old woman's shoulders and swiped her cheek with a sloppy lick. Staggering slightly under Rata's weight, Mum smiled broadly. She'd always been a dog person, and Rata was her favorite dog on earth.

After being showered with saliva, Mum patiently lowered each of Rata's paws. Rob ran forward and wrapped his arms around her waist. Tail waving a welcome banner, Rata led us in procession down the zigzag. Second to Rob, there was no one now who Rata adored more than Mum.

Unpacking her bag in the spare room she presented me with her pièce de résistance—a shawl she'd knitted in wool so fine and needles so tiny the entire thing could be passed through her wedding ring. Dazzling white, with scalloped edges and a web of intricate stitches, it was the Ultimate Baby Shawl.

Since Dad's death, Mum passed her nights in front of a flickering screen with only knitting needles for company. Most of the time she created blankets and big bulky rugs made from carpet wool she bought direct from the factory. This baby shawl was in a different league, knitted with such love and attention to detail it glowed with some sort of energy. It was a shawl that might be filled with protective spells to become a magic cloak.

"It's beautiful!" I said, admiring her handiwork. "He'll love it."

"How do you know it's a boy?" she asked.

"I just feel it." But Mum was already onto another topic.

"Well, back in the twenties cousin Eve, that's *my* first cousin, which would make her your second cousin or something along those lines . . . She's the one who went to the Sorbonne and had the fling with the married hairdresser until the family found out and stopped her allowance. She arrived back in New

Zealand wearing a fur coat and lipstick. Everyone thought she'd had her lips tattooed . . ."

Poor Mum. What she missed most these days, she often said, was having someone to talk to. Sadly, this inflicted her with the lonely person's disease—she talked too much. As a result, some of her oldest friends had withdrawn to become occupied with bridge, charity work or grandchildren. I couldn't blame them. Some of her stories were amusing, like this one about cousin Eve (which interested me the first time she told it. I was intrigued a family not known for glamorous and wicked women could have produced someone as wonderful as Eve). But Mum was a heavy-duty talker. It demanded great loyalty and affection to endure a barrage of words with a noticeable absence of polite questions about health and weather offered in return. As Mum launched into yet another monologue, smiles would set like raspberry jam, faces went flat as piecrusts. When the listener retreated into a private world of shopping lists and which underwear really should be thrown out, Mum would suddenly startle them with a loud "You're not *listening*, are you?"

Even though we lived four hundred kilometers apart, Mum and I had always been emotionally close. Listening to her on the phone several times a week, I longed to ease her loneliness. She invariably mentioned the other widows in her community of concrete block townhouses and how lucky they were to have regular visits from their families. The guilt missile hit bulls-eye every time. If we'd lived closer I could have been one of those responsible daughters who, every Sunday, arrived on their aging mother's doorstep nursing a warm casserole dish.

"Let's see how it looks on the bassinet," I said, leading her and Rob into our bedroom, where the baby's bed waited, a semitranslucent cocoon.

Flourishing the shawl, I prepared to spread it over the miniscule mattress.

"Wait!" Mum yelled.

I froze mid-swoosh. Curled up inside the bassinet was the unmistakable silhouette of a sleeping cat princess. Cleo flicked an ear, and opened a lazy eye to examine us in a bored way.

Our cat had obviously recognized the bassinet for what it was. Her subjects had finally got around to understanding her regal status and provided the level of comfort she was entitled to.

Mum ran forwards, bent over the bassinet and boomed "*Shooooo!*" Cleo flattened her ears and hissed back. I watched helpless while two of the most powerful females in my life declared war on each other.

"It's okay, Nana," Rob said. "Cleo's just trying out the baby's bed. She wants to make sure it's comfortable."

"There's only one place cats belong," Mum proclaimed, grabbing Cleo around the belly and marching her to the front door. "Outside!"

After her abrupt landing on the veranda Cleo shook herself in disbelief. Why on earth had the giant grandmother woman tossed her out of *her* bed?

Back in the kitchen, Mum filled the electric kettle while Rata sat devotedly at her feet.

"That cat will smother the baby," she said.

Through the window I saw Cleo licking herself all over with long comforting strokes. No doubt she was hatching a plan.

"Cats and babies don't go together," Mum continued. "They drop fur everywhere. Have you seen? It's all over Rob's pillowcase. The whole house is covered in cat fur. It gives babies asthma. And the claws. Cats have no patience. They lash out and scratch babies on the face. Cats aren't like dogs, are they, Rata? They get jealous . . ."

"Cleo's not jealous," Rob said.

"Just wait till the baby's here," said Mum.

"Cleo's looking forward to the baby," said Rob. "She says it's a blessing."

Mum's hand froze on the kettle's handle. She shot me a worried look.

"What do you mean *says?*" she asked Rob. "You think the cat's *talking* to you?"

"No," I said quickly. "He just had a couple of dreams about Cleo. I don't think it's anything to worry about. You know what kids are like."

"He's been through an awful lot," she said to me under her breath. "You don't think he's going a bit *strange*, do you?"

"He's fine," I said firmly, arranging mugs on a tray.

"Frankly, I don't know why you've bothered with a cat when most people would give anything to have a dog like Rata," she continued. "Rata's practically . . . a human being. She's like having another person around."

I'd forgotten what a dyed-in-the-wool dog person Mum was. Rata thumped her tail amiably on the floor. Mum was right: Rata was the most lovable dog in the world.

"Whenever Rata stays with me she keeps me company at night. I never feel scared because she always barks at strangers. She's a wonderful guard dog. Her fur's so silky. Don't you love the way it feels? And the best thing about her is the way she *listens*. Haven't you noticed the way Rata *listens to everything I say?*"

My heart stopped. How had a woman who'd once been so strong and forceful suddenly grown into an old lady with wavy grey hair and bifocals? The once regulation stiletto heels and pointy toes had surrendered to sensible shoes made of soft leather and with toes rounded enough not to trouble her bunions.

But she was giving decrepitude a run for its money. With her fashion flair (vibrant jackets with shoulder pads highlighted with chunky jewelry) and a lifelong commitment to coral lipstick, she was at the stylish end of the late seventies age group. Nevertheless, she looked more fragile than before. And for the first time she was actually *asking* me for something. She wanted company, protection, someone to give and receive love, and most importantly a pair of attentive ears.

As I poured the tea Mum wandered down the hall towards our bedroom with Rata at her heels. Compared to hers, my life was brimming with adults, children and animals. And now there was the baby to look forward to. Mum wanted more than television and knitting needles. She needed healing as much, if not more, than we did. A grandparent's grief is a double dose—grief for the lost grandchild and empathy for the unhappy adult child whose dream of family has unraveled.

"*I don't believe it!*" Mum yelled.

I followed her voice into our bedroom. Cleo had ensconced herself in the bassinet again. She and Mum were locked in a mutual glower.

"How did *you* get back inside?" she growled at the cat.

Cleo raised herself on all fours, curved her tail down to look like an old-fashioned pump handle and growled back.

"Through a window, probably," I answered.

"That cat's a liability!" Mum snapped, scooping Cleo up and putting her firmly outside again. "You're going to *have* to keep your bedroom door shut."

The Battle of the Bassinet went on day after day. Even though I tried to keep our bedroom door shut, it constantly seemed to glide open. Cleo never missed an opportunity to reinstate herself in her new bed, and Mum was constantly at the ready to toss her out.

My attempts to call a truce between two determined females were pointless. Tensions between cat and grandmother were driving me crazy. Unable to sleep one night, I climbed out of bed around midnight, went under the house and fumbled in the dark for the hand mower. Mowing the lawn by moonlight calmed me down for a bit (and probably provided Mrs. Sommerville with entertainment).

"Getting restless, are you?" said Mum the next morning. "It's a sign the baby can't be far away. You'd better get rid of that cat."

I gave up trying to fix things. Mum announced her departure, early as usual. Good-byes were always clumsy. Our family wasn't big on displays of affection. As she stowed her bag into her hatchback, she looked suddenly frail again, a lonely old woman in a brown coat. We hugged briefly while Rata looked on, her tail at half-mast.

"Take care," I whispered.

"You too," Mum said, her vein-roped hand on the driver's door.

The drive ahead would take her five solitary hours, after which there'd be toast and scrambled eggs in front of the television and more knitting. Around eleven p.m. she'd have a mug of tea and a biscuit or two before heading off to bed— all of which added up to twelve hours of not talking to anyone. For someone who needed to talk, the prospect must've been torture. But Mum never complained.

"Would you like Rata to stay with you for a while?" I asked. "I've talked with Rob and Steve, and they're okay with it."

Mum suddenly straightened her back and shed ten years.

"I think we'd get on very well together, wouldn't we, girl?" she said without hesitation.

Rata looked adoringly up at her with an expression of absolute devotion and barked happily. It'd been a long time since Mum had been the focus of such adulation.

"Just a minute," she said, looking young and pretty again. She reached into the backseat and produced one of her green knitted rugs, which she smoothed over the front seat. Tail flying, Rata leapt gleefully onto the seat and waited for the engine to start.

If animals are healers, Mum needed one as much as anyone else. The silver-haired woman and the golden-haired dog looked a perfect match as they drove off up the street.

Raising my arm to wave good-bye, I felt a pang—strange, yet familiar. Exciting and frightening at the same time. A new person was about to arrive on planet Earth.

Rebirth

Love, for cats and people, can be painful.

A mother cat is rightfully called a Queen. Personally, I think it would be great if pregnant women were also called Queens. If the gay community protested too much we might possibly accept Baroness, Duchess or Fairy Princess. Anything instead of those glamour-sapping medical terms Gravida, Multigravida and the dreaded Geriatric Multigravida.

Cats arrange to have four or five babies in one hit. If humans did the same the number of months a woman spends gazing into a toilet bowl would be dramatically reduced. She'd have to buy only one set of hideous maternity clothes in her entire life. Children's clothes would be bought in bulk. Deals could be made with baby gear manufacturers and schools. (Five educations for the price of four?)

Restlessness is a surefire sign that a female cat is going into labor. It's the same with humans. I'd been wrong to assume the Battle of the Bassinet was responsible for my moonlight escapade with the hand mower. I should have realized it was primal instinct telling my body to rev up for a big one.

"Hello? Is that the hospital? Look, I think I might be going into labor. Contractions? Well, they're not all that strong—maybe five minutes apart . . . What do you *mean* try and get some sleep? How can I go to sleep when I'm having a baby? . . . You want me to calm down and take a pill? Are you joking? So what if your beds are all full? I'll give birth in the broom closet."

"Who does that stupid nurse think she is, turning me away from the hospital like that?"

"Here's the pill," Steve said. "Try and get a good night's sleep."

"I think we should call Ginny. She'll know what to do."

"I did. The babysitter answered. They're at some rock music awards."

"Rock music awards?"

"It's okay. They'll finish around midnight. Ginny will meet us at the hospital, if we end up going there. Try and get some sleep."

◆

"What time is it?"

"Haven't you gone to sleep yet? It's ten-thirty."

"These contractions started seven hours ago. I think we should go to the hospital."

"They don't want you."

"They're hardly going to turn us away if we arrive on their doorstep, are they?"

As we pulled into the hospital parking lot I immediately wanted to go home again. Hospitals creep me out, especially when you're not entirely welcome. Even this one, with its "homely" new birthing unit, could've doubled as a set for a Frankenstein movie. As if I didn't notice the gleam of the machinery, the holes in the wall expecting tubes and wires to be plugged into them, the nasty implements lurking under green surgical cloth. Frankly, I'd have preferred a cardboard box.

My birthing machinery was proving inefficient. I took a bath, breathed and paced. I crouched like an animal, knelt like a peasant woman from the Amazon and would've willingly hung upside down from one of the bad-taste paintings on the wall if it might've got things going. None of it worked. Even though the contractions were increasingly uncomfortable they refused to get businesslike.

The doctor arrived around midnight and went to sleep in the next room. I was boring everyone, including me. I wanted to burst through the hospital doors and run away into the night.

Even though I was planning a natural birth with no pain-killers, I developed an attachment to a mask that exuded sickly smelling nitrous oxide. Why it's called laughing gas I'll never know. Nothing remotely funny happened, except everyone started talking in Donald Duck voices. They were only doing that to annoy me. Whenever they tried to pry the mask away from me, I clamped it over my face and refused to let go.

The doctor appeared and said she was going to rupture the membranes around the baby's head. Baby? Was there a *baby* involved in all this pain? Suddenly a shimmering white cat glided into the room and stood over me, gazing at me with beautiful glittering eyes. Except it wasn't a cat, it was Ginny!

"You're making great progress," she purred in my ear. "We can see the head. The baby has a fine crop of black hair. You can give a push with the next contraction."

"That's it," said Ginny. "One more push . . ."

Just as well there was a spectacular waterfall to look at. A comet of diamonds, it arced toward the ceiling and landed somewhere beyond my right knee.

A loud cry filled the air. Miniature crimson legs and dainty feet were intertwined with red and purple rope thick enough to tie Steve's ferry to the wharf. Umbilical cord. Tiny hands curled like pink camellias. A face wise as a guru, fresh as dawn, peered curiously around the room from under a cap of dark hair. Never had I seen anyone look so confident they were in the right place. The baby. *Our* baby! A tidal wave of love surged out of me and enveloped the child.

"She's absolutely perfect," Ginny said, lowering her into my arms. "What are you going to call her?"

A girl was the last thing I'd planned for. My longing for a daughter had been so deep I'd been too scared to admit it to anyone, especially to myself. This child's femaleness was a statement she had no intention of being a replica of Sam. Staring up into my face with shortsighted intensity she exuded such strong individuality I wasn't tempted to mention Samantha, even as a middle name.

"Lydia," I said. "After my father's mother. I never met her, but everyone says she was a strong woman."

"Lydia, little one," said Ginny tenderly. "May you journey lightly through life's rain showers." As she delivered her impromptu blessing I noticed for the first time how Ginny's eyes gleamed with unspoken wisdom, like Cleo's.

Risk

A cat's movements are fluid as milk and
she always lands on all fours.

Rob was right. Cleo wasn't the slightest bit jealous of the baby.
Surrendering the bassinet without complaint, our cat seemed
to understand Lydia was a precious addition to our household.
Fascinated by the new human, Cleo welcomed Lydia's interest in
staying awake most of the night. In fact, Cleo seemed to think
Lydia had invented a three-hour feeding schedule specifically
to relieve the boredom of long, uneventful darkness. Whatever
time the baby stirred, two a.m., three-thirty, or four-fifteen, a
four-legged silhouette meowed as if she'd been merely napping
in anticipation of this fun event. Cleo would spring onto the
rocking chair to snuggle into the warm, damp intimacy of mother
and newborn. Sometimes she perched on the chair's headrest
and, purring loudly, gazed down at us through huge translucent
eyes. Standing sentinel over us, Cleo seemed to gather mystical
power from the night and envelop us with love and protection.
The spirit of Bastet traversed the centuries and beamed from
our small black cat.

I'd never met a baby more comfortable in her own skin.
Clasping my finger with her delicate hand, Lydia seemed to
know she was where she needed to be. It was incredible to think

she would never have existed if Sam hadn't left us two and a half years earlier. I still wept for Sam and searched for him in the shape of her head, her eyes. But Lydia was determined to be accepted on her own terms. Great joy doesn't obliterate grief. Both can be encompassed at the same time.

Winter was under way again. Lashings of rain iced southerly gales as they roared through Cook Strait to harass the city. Umbrellas exploded on street corners. Old women clung to lampposts. As citizens struggled up hills to their homes, not a single one could be accused of having a good hair day. When the wind finally exhausted itself, the hills wrapped themselves in petticoats of cloud and sulked. The city closed in on itself. And still it rained.

Wellingtonians seldom mentioned these minor irritations. Their reward for living on a series of climactically challenged cliffs staring straight into the jaws of the frozen continent was the knowledge that they inhabited the nation's capital, and were therefore (there was no way to put it tactfully) important. They certainly were a cut above those rough Aucklanders, dreary Christchurch people and (heaven forbid) country bumpkins from the provinces. If the weather made day-to-day survival tough, the capital's inner life was furnished with book clubs, night classes and more theaters per head of population than any other city. A cultured lot, they were.

"You must've brought the weather with you," they'd say in accusatory tones to drenched and shivering visitors from out of town. "If only you'd arrived yesterday. We've just had two weeks of glorious sunshine."

But after the tenth consecutive day of rain and wind, Wellington could do something extraordinary. Shaking off its grey cloak, the city would suddenly emerge in crisp primary colors. A smiling yellow sun would turn the harbor blue. Scarlet roofs would glow against green hills. Wellington looked fresh out of a children's picture book. Once again, locals could congratulate each other for living in what they called a tropical paradise (well, practically).

Six weeks after Lydia's arrival Rob was due to turn nine years old. The prospect of another ninth birthday cast an irrational shadow. Would it be an unlucky number for all our children?

"How do you want to celebrate?" I asked Rob one morning, nervous he might ask for a repeat of Sam's eerie ninth birthday "party."

"What I'd really like," he said while I held my breath over the kitchen sink, "is a pajama sleepover party."

"With Jason?"

"And Simon and Tom and Andrew and Nathan . . ."

"A big party?" I asked, imagining happy noises resounding off the wallpaper. "Let's do it!"

"Can I ask Daniel and Hugo and Mike, too?"

"Of course! Do you want girls?"

Rob looked at me as if I'd suggested he have broccoli and onions on toast for breakfast.

The morning of Rob's birthday we woke him early and presented him with a small packet wrapped in red tissue with a blue bow. Superman colors.

"Do I open the card first?" he asked breathlessly.

He was delighted to find Cleo had added her signature to his birthday card in the form of a paw print made in blue finger paint. Always a careful child, he coaxed the cellophane tape off with his fingernails instead of tearing at the paper the way other boys would have done. Watching his face, so sweet and expectant, I wasn't sure he was ready for the gift, but Steve and I had talked it over countless times and chosen it with care.

"Wow!" he cried, his face blazing with joy. "A real Casio digital watch!" It was out of its box and on his wrist before anyone could say "Multiple Functions."

"I *love* it!" he said. "It's even got a light, see? If you push this button you can tell the time in the dark."

There was no doubt Rob's ease with technology hadn't come from my side of the family. He pored over the sheet of instructions and told us the watch could do just about anything except fly into space. Flushed with satisfaction, he peeled off the protective seal over its face, folded the instructions and placed them respectfully inside the box the watch had arrived in.

"It's the best present I've ever had," he sighed, lifting his Superman watch from his bedside table. "But I can't wear two watches."

His thumb circled the face of the Superman watch. Something jarred in my throat. How could we have been so insensitive?

"I really love this Superman watch . . ." Of course. It was too soon for him to give up the comfort and connection with Sam it provided.

"Don't worry, Rob," I said. "We'll take the Casio back to the shop and change it for something else."

"No! That's not what I meant!" he said, shaking his head earnestly. "I mean . . . do you think Sam would mind if I put his watch away in my drawer?"

The sharp lump in my throat dissolved as I drew Rob into my neck and stroked his hair.

"Sam wouldn't mind at all," I said, swallowing back tears of pride. "In fact, I think he'd say you're ready for a big boy's watch."

♦

Later that night, boys trooped down the zigzag wearing their pajamas and smiles bright enough to blind the possum who was busy demolishing the tree by the gate. Rob welcomed them inside, decked out in a bright-red dressing gown and his brand-new watch, with more digital functions than the space shuttle.

The house filled with loud, raucous, running boys. Walls shook. The rubber plant trembled. Potato chips were ground into the shag pile. Sausages were thrown across the kitchen. It was the sort of party that would've set my teeth on edge in the old days. Not anymore. Tie sheets and dangle them out the window? Why not! Cricket in the hall? What's a broken lamp or two? I slid into my blue dressing gown to match the party theme and prepared for boys to run wild.

I hadn't realized how many friends Rob had made in the two and a half years since Sam's death. They weren't dutiful friends who'd taken him on purely out of sympathy, either. They teased, laughed and treated Rob with genuine affection. He'd journeyed such a long way since 1983. The shy younger brother had transformed into an outgoing friend magnet. I almost wept with gratitude and respect for him.

Cats, babies and parties tend not to mix. I'd arranged for Lydia and Cleo to be tucked away in a room at the quiet end of the house. But they were intrigued rather than spooked by the visitors. I let them out to circulate—Cleo on her own and Lydia in my arms. Cleo swiftly adopted Simon, a red-haired cat lover, and spent most of the night on his lap sampling slivers of ham. Lydia, wearing one of her blue baby suits (bought when she was going to be a boy) greeted our guests with the gracious smile of the Queen Mother on a walkabout.

The boys played Pass the Parcel or, in their case, Throw the Parcel (thankfully neither Cleo nor Lydia played the role of Parcel). Rain flung itself at the windows. A drumroll of thunder rumbled above the roof. A flash of lightning coincided with the front door knocker slamming on its hinges.

An elderly magician stood on the doorstep wearing a false nose and glasses. Holding a large suitcase in one hand, he was oblivious to the storm, as if it was just another theatrical prop that followed him around. He must have been close to eighty years old. Apologizing for being late, he removed his raincoat and slapped a fez on his bald head. I feared for him. No audience is harsher than a collection of rowdy boys. The boys sneered when he stepped boldly into the living room. He wasn't going to last thirty seconds in there.

His hands were square, with fingers the size and shape of cigarette stubs. Bricklayer's hands, yet they proved deceptively nimble. The magician made ropes change their lengths inside a plastic bag, and ink-spattered scarves wash themselves clean in the privacy of a cardboard box. Though the boys had no intention of being impressed, they couldn't help themselves.

Towards the end of his act the old man produced a top hat. He asked the birthday boy to tap it three times with a magic wand. To everyone's amazement a pure-white living, breathing dove emerged from the hat.

Cleo, who had been watching the show with detached amusement from Simon's knee, suddenly shot across the floor like a licorice bullet and sprang at the bird. The old man tumbled backwards. Alarmed, the dove squawked and slipped out of his grasp. The boys watched in awe as the bird flapped across the room to perch clumsily in the rubber plant. Steve grabbed Cleo and carried her out of the room while I helped the magician to his feet.

"Wow! This is the best party I've ever been to!" yelled one of the boys, as the magician retrieved his bird and carried it out to the kitchen. The others whooped agreement and sent the old man off with enthusiastic applause.

Later, the magician soothed his dove along with his nerves over a mug of tea. Spacey strains of David Bowie reverberated through the walls.

"They call *that* music?" he sighed, sliding his plastic nose and glasses into his pocket. "I'm a Bing Crosby man myself."

The old man drained his tea, packed up his suitcase and headed back to the safety of the thunderstorm. I waved him good-bye and ventured into the party room. The sight of fifteen boys in pajamas jumping off furniture and leapfrogging over the shag pile would have reduced me to a screaming shrew not so long ago. But I'd wasted too many years trying to yell boys into shape: surrendering to the noise, the untidiness and the celebration of it all was much more fun.

I searched the sea of heads for Rob. He was easy to spot in his red dressing gown with Cleo in his arms.

"You're going to love this one, guys!" he yelled, turning up the stereo even louder. As Bowie boomed out Rob's favorite song, "Let's Dance," I had only one choice. Surrender. With Lydia perched on my hip I swayed, twirled and waltzed till my legs ached. The room shimmered with joy. I hadn't partied like this since Sam was alive—no, since *ever*. Along with all the tears, I'd shed ideas about what mattered. I didn't have to be in control all the time anymore. The boys weren't disasters waiting to happen to our furniture. A few extra scratches would improve the coffee table. We laughed. We danced. We were alive.

◆

A few weeks after Rob's birthday, there was a phone call from newspaper editor Jim Tucker. Jim was starting up a national broadsheet, the *Sunday Star*, and wondered if I'd like to join his team as a feature writer. Listening to Jim's energy-charged enthusiasm, I had to concentrate on his voice to convince myself I wasn't dreaming. A fresh start in an exciting work environment was something I'd longed for. Up till now, I'd been confident that would never happen. After all, my weekly pieces about family life in the Wellington newspaper were hardly Pulitzer Prize material.

Jim was offering every mother's dream—flexible working hours. But there was one thing he wasn't prepared to negotiate. If I wanted the job we'd have to pack up the family, cat and all, and move six hundred kilometers north to Auckland. Heart throbbing in the back of my throat, I thanked Jim and asked if he could give me some time to think.

Cleo glided into the kitchen and stared up at me through crescent-moon eyes. I lifted her up and ran my fingers through her silky fur. We'd made good friends in Wellington. How could we leave Ginny and Jason? Rob was happy at school. The success of his birthday party proved the great progress he'd made. Lydia was young enough not to notice, but even then I'd have to find quality care for her while I was working. And what about Cleo? Cats are famous for being more attached to places than people.

Then there was the job. Jim was obviously confident that I could write about subjects other than babies, carpet fluff and supermarket trolleys, but what if he was wrong? After a decade languishing in the 'burbs, I'd forgotten most of my journalism training. Parts of my brain had almost certainly shriveled. Why else would I scribble shopping lists in code I couldn't decipher by the time I reached the supermarket? Failure would be embarrassingly public.

I loved Wellington and had learned to appreciate the character-building aspects of its weather, hills and earthquakes. On the other hand, the allure of a larger, warmer city was appealing. I sometimes wondered if the zigzag bungalow was built on an unlucky fault line and doomed to bring sorrow to whoever lived within its walls. Even though Steve and I had sailed a cloud of elation around Lydia's conception and birth, we were starting to drift back into old patterns of withdrawal and resentment. Love was on ice again. Maybe the romance of hibiscus flowers and long summer nights would muster our strength for one last try.

Always supportive of my writing "career." Steve was prepared to put up with the inconvenience of selling the house and commuting to his ship every few weeks. Accepting Jim's job offer was risking a lot. Turning him down, however, would be taking other, possibly more dangerous, risks.

I'd seen Cleo in a similar dilemma, with her back legs wedged in the fork of a tree and her front paws stretched down and perched perilously on the top of a fence. She knew she had to get down from the tree, and the fence was the only viable option. Her confidence wavered every so often, and she'd try to twist herself back up into the tree. But it was too late—she'd made the move, stretched her body across the space between the tree and fence and there was only one way to go. She had to use every ounce of concentration to land her back legs accurately on the fence. If not, a humiliating tumble into the garden would be involved. Cleo was a risk expert. She took them every day and they nearly always paid off.

We'd survived two Christmases without Sam, and two of his birthdays. The days when grief was still raw were interspersed with a slowly increasing number of "good" days. Optimism was fragile, though. Like a shoot forcing itself through the earth after a long winter, I was easily crushed.

Bolstered by Jim's offer, I was walking through the city center one morning feeling unusually buoyant. Valerie, an acquaintance from Sam's preschool, approached, arranging her face in that funeral-parlor expression that had become so familiar. "How *are* you?" she asked in the old terminal-diagnosis voice. "I was thinking of you the other day when my great-aunt Lucy died . . ."

After listening to Valerie's story (great-aunt Lucy dropped dead digging potatoes, aged ninety-seven) I hurried home and picked up the phone. "Jim? I'll take the job."

Resilience

There are no changes in a cat's life.
Only adventures.

The saddest thing about leaving Wellington was saying good-bye to Ginny. She stood at the top of the zigzag, wind blowing her earrings horizontal. But with the house sold and the car packed to the roof, it was too late to change my mind. I sensed we'd always be part of each other's lives.

"You'll be fabulous, darling," she said, blowing a kiss through the passenger window. "Byeee!"

Rosie predicted our cat would be traumatized by the move north. Cleo didn't do predictable. The more we treated Cleo as an honorary human, the more she behaved like one—though she was always angling for goddess status. (Why sit on someone's lap at the dinner table when you can climb onto the table and graze free range?)

An eight-hour car journey cooped inside a basket was hardly luxury travel for a feline deity, but she didn't complain. She dozed contentedly with a sock for company most of the way.

We'd bought an old tram conductor's cottage in Ponsonby, a scruffy inner suburb. I adored the laid-back atmosphere on Ponsonby Road, where Polynesian women glided alongside street kids and drunks pretending to be artists. Even the graffiti was worth reading. I didn't realize it then, but it was just a matter of time before the espresso machines and earnest young couples moved in.

I had fallen in love with the cottage the moment I saw it. Sunny, outward-looking and easy to reach, it was everything our Wellington house wasn't. With big sash windows and woodwork furled like lace around the veranda it smiled out onto the street. Wisteria coiled through the latticework. Flower baskets swung in the breeze. A white picket fence flashed its teeth at a bottlebrush tree.

The inside layout was pleasantly predictable, with three double bedrooms off a central hallway that led to an open-plan living area. Sometime during the seventies a morose hippie had renovated the place. He must have been depressed. Why else would he have laid dark brown carpet in every room and lined the kitchen with treacle-colored wood? While character features such as paneled ceilings and brick fireplaces had been kept, there were occasional lapses of taste. I was willing to forgive the penchant for redwood fence stain, but had to seriously avoid dwelling on the Spanish archway between the living room and kitchen.

The backyard was perfect for kids. From a sunroom off the kitchen, French doors opened onto a redwood deck, with built-in benches around the edges. Under a pergola groaning with grapes was, joy of joys, a hot tub. Beyond the deck, a luscious patch of grass, miraculously flat, had enough room for a jungle gym and trampoline. A banana tree waved its glistening fronds from over the back fence. Everything about the place screamed happily ever after. Steve wasn't so sure, but was willing to go along with my enthusiasm.

The basket on the backseat emitted a regal meow. Obeying Rosie's pre-trip instructions, Rob carried Cleo, basket and all, through the gate. He went inside and lowered the basket onto the floor. (I'd known the house was meant to be ours the moment I slapped eyes on the carpet. We were destined to live with offensive floor coverings.) Carefully, slowly, he opened the lid. Rosie had warned us Cleo could be so disoriented from the trip she might cower in her carrying case for hours.

A pair of black ears rose from the wicker rim, followed by two eyes, black whiskers and a nose. The eyes rolled sideways to inspect the shabby hallway, then upwards to check all people slaves were present. Cleo then sprang daintily from her bower and, like a sniper sussing out an enemy village, padded through the house, sniffing the carpet and investigating corners in every room.

In the bathroom her search for spiders under the decrepit claw-foot bath was rewarded with a satisfyingly crunchy snack. The kitchen revealed another treasure—a colony of hyperactive ants under the sink. With this much live-in livestock, the house was custom-made for her.

Cleo particularly approved of the French doors' ability to intensify solar rays. Yawning, she stretched across the doorway, her fur shimmering blue-black in the heat. Her eyes shrank to translucent slits while the human slaves heaved boxes and suitcases over the threshold, all the time trying not to trip over our Egyptian princess. No doubt her ancestors had dozed through similar scenes while the pyramids were being built.

Rosie had instructed us to keep Cleo inside for two days in case she panicked and attempted to escape back to Wellington. Basking happily in her personal tanning clinic, our cat showed no interest in cutting loose. The genes that had adapted to cope with the heat of ancient Egypt reveled in Auckland's subtropical climate.

✦

I hoped the rest of us would be able to follow Cleo's example and adjust to all the changes, but the fresh start had no hope in the marriage department. Steve's commute to Wellington was going to mean more time apart. We'd given up trying to reach across the valley of our differences and started having separate social lives. The friends I made he found offensively loud, while I found his friends unnervingly introspective. He set up camp on a sofa bed in the sunroom. We tried to kid ourselves that for the sake of the children we could still be friends, but not in *that* way.

Although Rob had been popular at his old school, its formal approach to learning had proved an uncomfortable match for him. I'd begun to dread perching on dwarf-sized chairs during parent interviews listening to twelve-year-old teachers drone on about Rob being bright but needing to work harder. Having spent most of my school career gazing out classroom windows admiring the quality of sunlight on distant trees (and once a pair of dogs demonstrating something I'd only ever seen in line drawings in a book about teenage health Mum had left on my bed), I sympathized entirely with Rob. The only difference between Rob and me was he *was* working hard at school. He was frustrated that his Herculean efforts at reading and arithmetic were acknowledged with Cs and Ds. Even though his teachers were barely old enough to chew solids they had power and (like most dictators and children) knew they were right. I was tired of hearing them imply Rob had "problems," not the least of which was a dead brother and unhappily married parents. They were unable to appreciate his unconventional methods of absorbing information and were too lazy or unimaginative to go out of their way to help him.

The Auckland move gave him a chance to try a more laid-back school, though I hadn't expected it to be quite so relaxed. Every surface, inside and out, was smothered with children's artwork in violent primary colors. The playground equipment (concrete pipes, giant wooden cable spools) resembled leftovers from major roadworks. His new teacher, Mrs. Roberts, had a fuzz of red hair and aquamarine eyes with an otherworldly sparkle. With a tie-dye silk scarf looped over her shoulders she casually mentioned Rob's lovely aura.

"She's Alternative," I explained to Rob as we scrambled through a giant pipe to get back to the car. "Everything around here is, a bit."

"What do you mean?"

"They don't expect you to work too hard. If you don't like pottery classes, you get an alternative, like dance or theater. Nobody here knew Sam. You don't have to be the boy whose brother died anymore. Just be you."

It had yet to occur to me that dance, theater and pottery might not be a perfect match for a boy who'd built so many model airplanes his bedroom was a miniature version of the Battle of Britain. At the beach while other kids jumped mindlessly in the surf he spent hours constructing cities complete with drainage systems and overhead bridges. I should have realized such a child is unlikely to squeeze himself into tights and beg to play the prince in *Swan Lake*. Nevertheless, he was willing to give the new school a try.

The next challenge was finding someone trustworthy, lovable and entirely faultless to look after Lydia. Even though Jim had promised flexible hours I knew I'd have to show up at the office most days. My heart ached at the thought of leaving one-year-old Lydia with a stranger.

What I was looking for, I explained to the nanny agency, was a cross between Mary Poppins and the Virgin Mary. The nanny agent laughed, but it wasn't the cynical snort of someone who was about to offer a child molester in nanny's clothing. It was a crystalline laugh of recognition. "I have that exact person on my books," she said. "Her name is Anne Marie, and I can hardly believe this, but she's actually available. She has people lining up asking her to work for them, though. You'll have to find out if she likes you first."

The *nanny* interviews *us*?

Anne Marie's credentials couldn't have been better. Not only had she trained at the prestigious Norland nanny school in London, she'd raised four children of her own.

I was awestruck when she appeared on our doorstep wearing a combination of pastel pink and white devoid of a single stain. Her shoes glowed like a pair of snowballs. Her brown eyes were warm, though, especially when she saw Lydia (who adored Anne Marie on the spot). When the baby beamed a welcome, raised her chubby arms and wrapped them around Anne Marie's neck I experienced the primitive stab of jealousy every working mother feels when she hands her child over to a caregiver.

After a day of anxious waiting the phone rang. Anne Marie said she was willing to take us on.

I could hardly believe my luck to be working on a newspaper again. I'd forgotten how much I'd missed the sad/funny/clever misfits who inhabit newsrooms. Like a lost wanderer returned to her tribe, I finally belonged again—alongside all the other outsiders who'd chosen journalism because no other employer would tolerate their quirky antisocial ways.

I loved Mary, the glamorous, self-doubting Irish fashion writer, and Colin, the rock reporter whose sexy melancholy had women sticking to him like plasters. Tina, the features editor, was highly strung, and could erupt into platinum rages. Yet every now and then her ice-queen mask melted to reveal a heart that was passionately pure.

Nicole, the television writer, was beautiful and blond, with legs she'd stolen from Marlene Dietrich. I assumed Nicole wouldn't waste her time with mere humans. But she'd been a teenage bride like me, and was wading through a divorce and custody swamp. Nicole was offbeat and wounded like the rest of us, and tough as a terrier when she sunk her teeth into a story. I adored them all.

I also reveled in wearing proper clothes again. For the past decade my wardrobe had consisted of track pants, maternity clothes and dressing gowns (in tones of mostly grey, black and brown). It was exhilarating to slip into a fuchsia-colored suit with a cobalt blue bow tie (in retrospect a crime against fashion). Applying makeup every morning and learning to walk in shoes with heels again was thrilling. I felt like Cinderella, who'd just found out the ball wasn't over after all. The music was louder, the guests were zanier and I was invited back to collect my size 10C glass slipper and get back on the floor.

As a general features writer, I didn't care what stories they were going to assign me. I'd have been grateful if they'd asked me to write about bedbugs. To my astonishment, Jim and Tina trusted my abilities beyond logic. They assigned me interviews with international performers like James Taylor and Michael Crawford and writers such as Margaret Atwood and Terry Pratchett. Crazier still, they sent me to meet our nation's porcine prime minister and even (for heaven's sake) the president of Ireland, Mary Robinson. I soon learned that the more elevated on the global stage people are the more humble and approachable they tend to be, despite the bewildering jet lag involved in getting to our agricultural outpost. Mary Robinson was more animated when she talked about helping her kids do homework around their kitchen table than anything else we discussed. (Which was just as well. International politics was hardly my beat.)

Jim also had me writing editorials, where I'd switch into pipe-and-slippers mode and hammer out the paper's views on everything from atomic energy to zoos. Producing one of those within the required forty minutes was the equivalent of being spun inside a microwave oven on high.

Distraught with panic one morning, I wrote an entire leader raging against the perils of "alcahol." Either my fingers fumbled on the typewriter keys or all those years gazing out of classroom windows had finally come home to roost. My bizarre spelling slipped through the subeditors (spellcheck was yet to be invented), no doubt lowering the newspaper's status to litter-box liner for several weeks. To my disbelief and eternal gratitude Jim and Tina refrained from throwing me back on the streets. They kept on nodding, smiling and tossing plum stories my way. Maybe all the real journalists had caught some form of plague through drinking too much and sleeping with each other and died off.

But much as I loved the office the best part of the day was when I slid the key in the front door of the old cottage to see Cleo prancing down the hall to greet me with a welcome meow.

I'd started to notice Cleo was developing her language skills. Apart from the charming *hello* meow she gave whenever any of us arrived home, and the polite mew when someone picked her up, there was the assertive *let me come in, you heartless morons!* wail when she was shut out. She had better manners than the four of us put together. Whenever anyone opened a door to let her in she always responded with a clipped and demure *thank you* as she sailed past.

Mealtimes, especially if they were delayed, reduced her to a stream of alley cat language. Standing in front of the fridge she'd yowl, *If you don't feed me right now I'm going to jump on your head and tattoo your eyeballs.*

Cleo moved houses and cities without so much as a twitch of a whisker. I worried that living on a street for the first time she might get run over—especially with her penchant for after-dark expeditions. Who'd see a black cat against a darkened street? Once again I was underestimating her. She had a traffic-smart gene, no doubt inherited from her father.

After a raucous fight with a larger cat under the house one night she appeared at the front door with a torn ear. I tried to keep her inside after that, but every night she wailed until I let her out. Even though the fight had been serious, she must have established her territory with it. We never heard another scrap.

Her bird-hunting skills shifted to new levels. The shoes in my wardrobe were stuffed with tiny corpses and clusters of feathers. After persistent begging from the kids, I dug a hole in the corner of the back garden and fitted it with a fishpond and water plants. The resident goldfish became a voyeuristic fixation for Cleo. I doubted they'd survive past Christmas. Fortunately, they were wily enough to spend most of their waking hours up to no good under the lily pads. They made so many babies I wondered if there was such a thing as goldfish contraception.

Cleo demonstrated how good manners and charm can coexist under one skin, along with backstreet resilience. Following her example, I tried to shrug off embarrassing moments at work (for example, when I took too long to realize the man panting on the other end of the phone line hadn't been for a run but was indulging in a less wholesome activity. Or the time I had to field dozens of calls after getting the names of two fashion models confused and captioning a classy one with a slutty one's name.) Like Cleo on the rare occasions she slipped off a fence to tumble into the hydrangeas, I endured the humiliation, shook it off, hoped I wouldn't be stupid enough to repeat the mistake—and prayed lawyers wouldn't be involved.

Over the following year, Steve and I settled into a pattern of avoiding each other when he was at home. According to statistics, women are far more likely to end a relationship than men. I've never been a fan of statistics. Another theory is that men who want to end relationships make themselves impossible to live with, so the woman is forced into ending it.

Our marriage was like a bowl of egg whites. We'd both sweated over it, whipping air through, occasionally working it into peaks. At times it looked like we might make a decent meringue out of it, but as any cook knows, if you whip egg whites too long, if you try too hard, they simply go flat.

Things came to a head one afternoon when I arrived home from work. He was standing in the driveway. I can't remember exactly what the conversation was about, probably something trivial, like who'd left the butter on the bench so Cleo could get it. It escalated into an argument—and we *never* argued. Suddenly we were talking about divorce.

We both knew he couldn't go on sleeping in the sunroom the rest of his days. Nevertheless, it was shocking to finally have the D word out in the open.

Steve looked sideways at a red bottlebrush flower and said he wanted to keep lawyers out of it as much as possible. The flower nodded agreement. A car backfired farther down the street. The front garden seemed an unlikely place to be having such a conversation. But where *do* people talk about divorce? Certainly not candlelit restaurants or incense-scented bedrooms, as far as I knew.

He said he'd move out next week. He wanted to take the painting of yachts that was in the hallway if I didn't mind, and some other things as well. I was shocked at how carefully he'd thought it through, though realistically he'd had years to mull it over. He wanted the kids fifty-fifty and suggested we'd sort the money out later.

Oh, and I could keep the cat.

Openness

*The only people less enlightened than those who claim not to be
cat people are those who swear they're strictly dog people.*

The house was hollow as a cave at night without children sighing
and turning in their beds. I worried if Rob needed help with his
English homework, if Steve was watching Lydia closely enough.
At two and a half years of age, she was all confidence and no
sense. Cleo wasn't happy about it, either. She carried their socks
around and slept on their beds.

I made excuses to see them during Steve's allocated week,
collecting Lydia from daycare, driving Rob to Sea Scouts. I tried
to make the most of the empty hours, rearranging the bathroom cupboards, reworking feature articles, but my imagination
refused to rest. It hovered like a giant telescope in the sky,
trained on their every move—was Rob watching for cars before
he climbed on the school bus? Was Lydia catching a virus?
I wondered if they sensed my presence.

Sam's photo beamed at me from the mantelpiece. A cheeky
smirk. I thought about the Ford Escort woman. Her memory
of Sam would be different. I accepted now she wasn't at fault.
I wondered what I'd have done in her shoes. Moved to another
country, tried to bury myself in a new identity. Out late one night
with Rob, collecting him from a Sea Scout meeting, I'd run over

a cat. It'd happened so suddenly. A flash of white fur, a thump and a grinding thud as the wheel crunched into bone. There was no way I could've stopped in time. The woman would've felt the same. Shocked, sick with remorse, I stopped the car. The animal was crushed, lifeless. I felt wretched enough running over a cat. Killing a child would be infinitely worse.

Sometimes it seemed I was destined to lose children one way or another. I'd never liked self-pity. Undignified, tiresome. I'd begun to discover ways out of it. One was to accept invitations to meet grieving parents and to interview people experiencing loss. Their trauma was often recent and more raw than my own. On the few occasions I was able to offer reassurance, my pain was replaced with a sense of doing something vaguely worthwhile. The past five years had informed me about human sorrow. While no two griefs are the same, nobody understands suffering like those who've been there.

◆

The shrink had a box of tissues on her table. Tears were her trade. Not wanting to give the impression I was one of her run-of-the-mill weepy clients I was determined to keep my eyes dry.

"What you need," she said, crossing her legs and gazing through her salmon-pink lenses, "is a fresh start, something to boost your self-esteem."

Even though I wasn't crying, my body badly needed to ooze. My nose started streaming uncontrollably. I glanced longingly at the tissues, but reaching for them would be an admission of defeat. The only alternative was to emit loud regular sniffs.

"Do you know what would do you the world of good?" she asked, sinking into a chair carefully positioned under a Rothko print in pastel pinks and yellows. Presumably the painting was intended to soothe anguished clients with its gentle shades. It probably worked for those who didn't realize poor Rothko succumbed to depression and killed himself. "A one-night stand."

Her words sailed across the room and exploded in my ears like missiles. Mum (due to a range of sexual hang-ups of her own not worth delving into here) had raised me from the cradle to treat my body as a temple, preferably open to only one dreary but dependable worshipper for my entire life.

"You mean finding a man I have nothing in common with but am mildly attracted to and just sleeping with him for the sake of it?"

She nodded. The shrink was obviously mad. She wanted me to die of guilt.

"It would be a healthy way to start a new phase of life," she said.

"What about the kids?" I asked.

"They needn't find out," she said. "It's nothing to do with them. Arrange it for one of the weekends when your ex-husband has custody."

Arrange it? People *arrange* one-night stands? She asked me to make up a list of potential victims. The only blokes I met were at work. Male journalists are unbelievably indiscreet. I had no desire to be added to the list of women in the office who "do it with anyone." A couple of friends' husbands had dismayed me by turning up at the house and thoughtfully offering their services, but I was in no way willing to betray my women friends. My list was blank.

"Good luck," said the shrink, smiling as I scribbled a shaky signature on the check. "And remember, be *open*."

◆

An opportunity to put her advice into practice turned up a few weeks later when Mary the fashion writer set me up on a date to accompany her friend to a fund-raising dinner. Mary assured me I'd love Nigel, who was recently divorced from his second wife, though not for the usual reasons of being disgusting to live with and a total reject. I'd read about Nigel's activities in our business pages. He was the corporate equivalent of a giant with an eating disorder, a compulsive devourer of small companies. He was an unfamiliar type, potentially dull, if all he could talk about was money. But I was used to interviewing people. I assured myself I could draw out the interesting side of a house spider if necessary. Mary said Nigel had ticks in all the right boxes. I wasn't sure what she meant. It was years since I'd been on a date. The rules must've changed. In fact, there was only one rule back in the old days—don't let him go all the way unless he's at least hinted he might want to marry you. During the years I'd spent buried in suburbia, dating seemed to have turned into a clinical cross between supermarket shopping and animal husbandry.

The night of the date arrived. I was so nervous my hands were trembling. Cleo always liked to supervise my clumsy attempts to apply makeup. She sprang up on to the bathroom vanity as I opened the makeup drawer—one of Cleo's favorite places in the entire house. Her passion for makeup must've been a throwback to her Egyptian heritage. Given half a chance, she'd steal a sable brush, run away and de-hair it bristle by bristle under my bed. Cleo jumped into the drawer and patted the shiny pots of eye shadow. She seemed to favor purple tonight. With no other beauty consultant available, it was logical to take her advice. She mewed encouragement as I applied two brooding streaks of shadow to my eyelids. The effect was more post–encounter with Muhammad Ali than cocktails with Mark Antony, but I was running out of time. Cleo toyed idly with my lipstick, a lurid crimson, which I snatched from her paws.

"What do you think?" I asked, applying a final circle of lipstick.

Sitting on her hind legs with her front paws arranged as neatly as a ballet dancer's, Cleo put her head on one side and winked. She approved. I doubted my legs would be able to hold me up long enough for the evening to ever qualify as a one-night stand, if that's what it was going to be.

Sensing my nerves, Cleo took over the meet-and-greet role, her tail curled graciously as she trotted towards Nigel. He was unusually tall and regal, with a sandy moustache. I wasn't confident facial hair was part of my one-night-stand scenario, but inside my head the shrink's voice echoed. "Be *open!*"

"A cat!" Nigel's eyebrows ricocheted like lines on a stock market chart. "I'm allergic."

"Oh," I said, lowering her to the floor, "sorry."

Unfazed by Nigel's reaction, Cleo stood on her toes and arched her back prettily. She arranged her tail in a gracious curl as she escorted him to the living room. Trotting ahead of us, Cleo really was the perfect hostess. The back of Nigel's suit, I noticed, was frighteningly free of creases.

I guided him toward the most pristine cushion on the sofa and asked if he'd like a drink.

"Chardonnay would be excellent," he said, perching on the sofa arm. I couldn't blame the poor man for protecting his Armani threads from our crumbs and cola stains.

While the fridge contained an assortment of drinks ranging from milk to cordial, Chardonnay wasn't among them. The closest on offer was a half empty cardboard box of Riesling. Depressing the plastic plunger, I hoped Nigel wouldn't notice.

He seemed agitated, crossing and uncrossing his long scissor legs. Cleo settled a few inches from his feet and fixed her eyes on him like interrogation lights.

"The problem with cats," he announced as I handed him a wineglass smudged with fingerprints, "is they always like me."

Cleo shuffled closer to him as he spoke and intensified her gaze, then hoisted her back leg aloft and proceeded to lick her most private parts.

"Shoooo, Cleo!" I growled. But Cleo resented being spoken to as if she was a mere animal. She rolled on her back and writhed seductively at Nigel.

"There's a compliment," I said. "She wants you to rub her tummy."

"Oh, I couldn't do that," he said, drawing a green paisley handkerchief from his pocket and dabbing his moustache. "The allergy, you see. In fact, you know, I think I'm going to . . ."

The curtains trembled in the aftershocks of Nigel's sneeze. Startled, Cleo leapt to her paws, dug her claws into the carpet, and bushed out her tail.

"Don't worry, I'll shut her in the back," I said.

When I bent over to collect the cat she slithered out of my grasp and scrambled up the bookshelves. Confident I couldn't reach her and Nigel wouldn't try, she strutted along the top shelf, tapping a precious Victorian vase with her tail. Cleo was extremely pleased with herself.

"You're not getting away with this!" I muttered, dragging a dining chair toward the shelves. The instant I stood on the chair and reached for her, Cleo bounded down from the shelves on to Nigel's lap. He emitted a boyish yelp and I lunged and got my hands around Cleo's belly. But she wasn't surrendering without a fight. As she sank her claws into the Nigel's thighs for leverage, man and cat emitted a simultaneous yowl.

"I'm so sorry," I said, unhooking each claw while Nigel focused valiantly on the ceiling.

I returned from shutting Cleo away to find Nigel sneezing discreetly into his handkerchief.

"The thing is," he said, pocketing the handkerchief and absentmindedly brushing real and imaginary cat hair off the sofa's arm, "I'm really a dog person."

"So am I," I said, trying to improve the atmosphere. "At least, technically speaking. We have a beautiful golden retriever, but she's gone to live with my mother. She's pretty old now. The dog, I mean."

"Dogs are less aggressive," he added. "When I was a kid I was attacked by a cat."

"Really?" I said.

"Yes, I was on my bike on my paper round, and this wildcat threw itself at me."

I tried not to smile at the image of a mini version of Excellent Nigel pedaling the streets of Whakatane, being felled by a murderous tabby. Nevertheless, it was clear Nigel's phobia sprang from deep, Freudian waters. It wasn't a mere quirk Cleo and I would be able to iron out in one night.

"Do you think the experience might've given you the drive and determination to become a successful businessman?" I asked, hating myself for employing pop psychology to make a sarcastic joke, but Nigel seemed to consider the question seriously.

"You know I've never thought of it that way, but you're probably right," he said, reassembling some of his dignity. "I wouldn't be where I am today if it hadn't been for that cat attack."

He was reminding himself aloud to tell the hack ghost currently writing his autobiography *Nigel's Nine Notches to Excellence* to include the cat attack when I noticed the bedroom door glide ajar. A four-legged shadow wafted into view. Cleo could open just about any door that wasn't locked and bolted.

As Nigel warmed to recounting his triumph over childhood trauma, Cleo slithered like a commando along the edge of the skirting board. Invisible to him, she crouched in the shade of the bookshelves and listened to details of a cat nightmare he'd suffered over two decades ago. She was still as a stone with a Cheshire cat grin settled on her lips.

Suddenly, Cleo darted out of her hiding place and ran at Nigel. In a single movement she sprang on to his lap, sending his wineglass flying through the air. Nigel emitted a roar straight from his primeval core. Horrified, I leapt to try and catch the glass, but everything was happening in slow motion. As my hand swiped at the glass it tumbled toward the carpet, drenching us both in a wine fountain.

Nigel stood up and brushed his trousers with agitated strokes. I grabbed paper towels from the kitchen and dabbed the blotches on his knees, while he attended to the more intimate areas.

"I'm so sorry!" I cried.

"Excellent," he muttered, sinking back into the sofa and crossing his legs. Before there was time to stop her Cleo climbed on his shoulder and wove herself in a knot around his neck.

"She seems to like you," I said. "Sorry—your allergy. Here, let me take her."

"No, seriously," Nigel sputtered, disentangling Cleo and arranging her uncomfortably on his knees. "I'm quite comfortable. She can probably smell Rex on me. He's my Doberman. A very athletic, straightforward dog."

"Yes," I said, wondering if we'd ever progress towards anything that could be classified as conversation. "Dogs are . . . straightforward."

"Dogs are more like men in that respect," said Nigel. "Whereas cats are more like women, don't you think? You could write a book about that."

Nigel's face suddenly turned the color of Australian Shiraz. As Cleo dived on the floor and disappeared down the hall Nigel's eyes rolled towards the ceiling. For a dreadful moment he appeared to be having one of those allergic reactions that seize people's throats up.

"Are you okay?" I asked.

He raised his hands and his mouth curled down in disgust. "Your cat," he whispered. "Just. Peed. On. Me."

Nigel insisted on returning to his apartment to change his suit. While he was gone I searched Cleo's favorite hiding places under the bed and in the wardrobe to punish her, but she'd successfully dematerialized. Satisfied the evening was drained of potential romance, Cleo had melted into the walls.

Later I spotted the silhouette of a cat on the roof. Its eyes shone down at me like lighthouse beams. Even from that distance, I could see a glow of satisfaction in them.

◆

If nothing else, the one-night stand that wasn't made a good story to share with Mum when she phoned. She sounded distracted. Her outings with Rata were getting challenging. When they'd walked down a hill to a beach at the weekend, Rata hadn't been able to get back up the slope. Mum said she'd had to carry Rata up the hill. Rata was no small animal. How Mum had managed to lift her was beyond me. The vet had diagnosed emphysema.

At work on Monday morning Nicole asked if I'd do her a favor. Her flatmate was getting married in a couple of weeks. He and his bride were from the States and didn't know enough people to make up a decent wedding celebration.

"*Please* come along?" she begged. "You won't have to stay more than an hour. Just long enough to make the room look fuller."

Her confidence that my presence could overflow an empty room was hardly flattering. I wasn't keen on being a one-woman rent-a-crowd. But we both knew I had nothing else to do on Friday nights, except maybe shovel Lego bricks back in their boxes while the children were at their father's.

"*Pleeeeease?*"

The couple had arranged to get married at sunset on the steps of the city museum. As the sun hovered like a commitment-phobe on the horizon I locked the car and climbed the hill to the museum. Glancing up, I saw the bridal party. She looked like Barbie. He looked like Ken. But it was the best man who caught my eye. He was stunningly good-looking. Not just handsome in an ordinary aftershave advertisement way, but glowingly breathtaking in the manner of a Greek god. Or gay man.

Gay, of course, I thought, admiring the sweep of well-groomed hair over the wide, tanned forehead, and the broad shoulders accentuated by a well-cut suit. Or married. If not, most definitely girlfriended.

To say it was love at first sight would be exaggerating. Lust at first sight would be more accurate. As the sunset glinted on his aviator glasses and I saw his flashing blue eyes I was overcome by another sensation that was less carnal and even more powerful—a sense of recognition. If we hadn't met before in this life, we'd almost certainly known each other in earlier lifetimes. Even though he was a stranger, I felt I knew him at a deep level.

The wedding reception was held at the home of Sir Edmund Hillary. Apparently the groom worked with someone who was related to the famous mountaineer. Sir Ed, who was away doing something bold and heroic on the other side of the world, had graciously opened his home to the wedding party. It was a modest, understated home, not unlike the man himself. The walls were a soft yellow and the decor extremely tasteful. Every painting, every handwoven rug, seemed to hold a story of great meaning to its owner.

By the time the gay/married/girlfriended best man walked over and introduced himself as "Philip with one l" I was over him. He was too good-looking to be real. When I discovered the reason for his athletic profile (freshly honed from eight years in the army) and that he'd just entered the professional arena of banking, it was obvious we had no future. To thrash the final nail on its head, he confessed his age. Twenty-six. Practically a baby, he was eight years younger than me. Unmarried, undivorced and childless, he seemed to spring from a completely different (still possibly gay) world. I was practically his mother. Nevertheless, he seemed a nice young man, devoid of the creepy complexities so many males were burdened with. And I hadn't forgotten the shrink's advice. If I drank a lot of wine and didn't tell a soul, and he was crazy (or desperate) enough to consider it, he had definite one-night-stand potential.

I told him I didn't go out much at night, but I did do lunch. I scribbled my work number on a paper napkin. He seemed startled by my offer. Not that he had any reason to. I was more than happy to take on the role of Mother Confessor and counsel the poor boy on his love life. Or just be friends. I was O-pen.

Next morning at work I studied the phone. No one called,

except for a disgruntled reader and the same old Heavy Breather in his phone box. It didn't ring significantly the next day, or the next week, either. By the time the third week came around I'd forgotten all about "Philip with one l." Which is why, when he eventually *did* call, he had to remind me who he was and how we'd met at the wedding.

"Oh, God, it's that army-banking kid," I sighed after we'd hung up.

"Maybe he wants instructions on how to find the nearest kindergarten," Nicole said.

"He's invited me to a play," I said.

"A *playground?*"

"No, a proper play. A theater dinner, or a dinner theater or something."

"I have to warn you . . ." Nicole said, pointing her pen at me. "Apart from the age difference . . ."

"You don't have to warn me. He just wants someone to talk to."

"He's way too conservative for you."

Red flags have been waved in my face at several important crossroads, resulting in profoundly unimaginable consequences. One was at primary school, when a bossy art teacher instructed the class that if *any*body dared put their fingers in her wet pottery clay they would be in bigger trouble than anyone in this god-fearing world could imagine. Another was at journalism school, when a tutor said in unequivocal words I had no future whatsoever as a columnist. As I listened to Nicole, a familiar, thistly sensation prickled the base of my spine. Its message was the same as the last two times: *You think so, do you? Well, let's see about that.*

After work that day I flitted through the part of town famed for strip clubs and thrift shops, and picked up the perfect outfit to impress a conservative young banker—a black satin Chinese pantsuit with flamboyantly embroidered trimmings. It was gorgeous.

The Kiss

Nothing is more damply magical than a kitten's kiss.

Cats kiss. Cleo did it all the time. It starts with a gentle head butt, a raising of the chin, a narrowing of the eyes, followed by a fleeting union of lips. Hormones are presumably exchanged. Nothing beyond that is asked, except perhaps a soothing stroke. A cat kiss is complete in itself.

Philip with one l was late. Too late to be even considered half-fashionable. He'd obviously forgotten that he'd asked me out to see some trashy play, or that I'd gone out of my way to arrange it for a weekend the kids were at Steve's. I was *that* forgettable. Hot rashes of emotion prickled up and down the back of my Chinese jacket. My skin stuck to the unbreathable fabric, which was proving itself not even a distant cousin of any upmarket natural fiber. Insult flared to anger. I didn't want to see him, anyway. What on earth would we have to talk about? To think I'd gone to the trouble of buying a new outfit.

If Philip with one l had the nerve to show up now I'd demonstrate Helen could be spelt with two ll's. Nicole and Mary would have words to say about this at work on Monday. He's not worth it. You're too good for him. What a dick.

Darker thoughts nudged to mind as I sat on the bed and shook off one of the dressy sandals that matched the Chinese outfit perfectly. Maybe he had a genuine excuse for not turning up, like catching a glimpse of his own reflection in a shop window and smashing into a lamppost.

Truth was, I had no reason to like him enough to care. I was content orbiting kids and work every day. They were the center of my universe. Every week that we survived without sore throats, crises at school or disturbing mail in spidery backhanded writing from a deranged reader was a miracle. It didn't matter if ninety percent of my remaining world consisted of black holes. The shrink was nuts suggesting all that one-night-stand rubbish. Boy, that woman had issues. I should've been shrinking her, not the other way around.

Cleo sprang onto the bed, made one of her squeaking noises and snuggled into my lap. *I'm here, I'm here*, she purred. Calm washed over me like baby shampoo. Hurt and outrage shrank until they weren't much bigger than a pair of bubbles resting in the bathroom plughole. Kicking off the other sandal, I smiled (partly from relief—they were giving me blisters, anyway). The only damage was to my ego. There was nothing wrong with a night at home in front of the fire with Cleo after a long working week. In fact, it was downright welcome.

I carried Cleo down the hall. She watched expectantly while I crouched at the fireplace and arranged the kindling in an uncertain teepee. We were both startled by urgent hammering on the front door.

"I've been driving around the neighborhood for ages," Philip said as soon as I opened the door. "I knocked on the door of 33 *Albany* Road. It's the street parallel to this one. The woman there was confused. In fact so was I. It took me a while to work out you're *Ardmore* Road . . ."

So. Not only was he too young and conservative—he wasn't in danger of becoming the world's next Mastermind, either. Just as I was starting to feel irritated, I noticed his face. His eyes were trailing up and down my Chinese suit with the look of someone witnessing the aftermath of mass terrorism.

"You don't like it?" I said, suddenly. "I can change into something . . . more conventional, if you like."

Philip didn't object. I was profoundly, unspeakably insulted. Thrusting Cleo into his arms, I hurried back into the bedroom. On the other hand, I thought, changing into a brown skirt and cream blouse, maybe I should be relieved he was honest enough to imply he'd rather reenact a scenario from the Vietnam War than appear in public with me wearing the Asian rhapsody.

"Nice cat," he said, as we headed out the door.

We were late for the play. Sitting in the shadows watching an appallingly amateurish version of *Cat on a Hot Tin Roof* I quietly assembled a list of why this was a ridiculous choice, even for a one-night stand: he was hardly out of high school; he couldn't have made more screwed-up career choices if he'd tried (the army *and* banking?!); he had bad taste in plays; he was unable to appreciate my approach to fashion.

I wasn't that shook on *his* clothes, come to think of it. His shoes were so shiny you could pluck your eyebrows in them. The striped shirt, the corduroy trousers, the carefully chosen leather belt. It was all straight out of some old fogey's catalog.

Yet there was no doubt he looked good in that stuff. He smelled fresh as an alpine forest, compared to male journalists, who invariably reeked of booze, cigarettes and substances I preferred not to know about. His eyes flared like blue gas flames when he laughed at my jokes (possibly too loudly). One of my jokes was about the inadequate snobs who drive European cars. I'd been too traumatized by our dash to the theater to notice what sort of car he drove. The satirical twinkle when, after the show, he opened the passenger door of his elderly Audi, was nothing short of admirable.

He was obviously a very pleasant young man who probably wanted to download his love-life woes on a pair of understanding ears. There was no harm offering him friendship. I invited him inside for coffee.

"I'd like to," he said. "But I don't generally drink caffeine this late at night. Do you have any herb teas?"

While I knew a few people at work who drank herbal teas, I doubted they were the type he was talking about.

"Sorry, I only have black tea."

The house was unusually quiet without the children. Even when they were asleep I was aware of their shifting blankets and dream-laden sighs. I kicked my shoes off and clattered through the kitchen cupboards, searching for a pair of cups that matched.

"Interesting cat," I heard from the other room. "She's almost like a person."

Carrying the tray with two tea bags cunningly concealed in a teapot and the cracked cup on my side I was surprised at the vignette in the living room. A purring Cleo wound herself through Philip's legs, leapt onto his knees, climbed his shirt and applied neat licks over his chin. Never before had Cleo warmed so affectionately to a stranger.

"Sorry, I'll put her away," I said.

"No, she's fine," he said, tenderly running his hand over the mound of her spine. "You're a good cat, aren't you? So tell me about the kids."

I stiffened. He had just blundered into No Go Territory. Of course I'd made no secret of the fact I had kids. They were as much part of me as my hands and feet. I couldn't have hidden their existence even if I'd wanted to. Everything about the house screamed "Kids!" The living room was ankle deep in Lego bricks. Lydia's fauvist playgroup artwork was taped to the kitchen cupboards. Rob's school bag lay like a drunk on the floor outside his room.

The kids were the core of my life, so precious I'd tear my heart out for them. He had no right to ask about them. They had nothing to do with a potential one-night stand who was rapidly losing any chance of becoming one.

"So tell me about your life," I replied. "Ever been married?"

He went blank, as if I was asking if he'd ever dressed up in fishnet stockings and lip-synched to Judy Garland.

"No."

Helen Brown

"Kids?"

He shook his head, his smile vaguely bewildered.

"So you're having girlfriend trouble?"

Cleo, having finished with his chin, moved on to his ears.

"No, apart from the fact I don't have one. How about some music?"

Music? He wanted to be interrogated to *music*? Without waiting for an answer he sifted through my record collection and put on my latest purchase and current favorite, Ella Fitzgerald and Louis Armstrong singing "Can't We Be Friends?"

Philip obviously had some kind of problem. Why else would he be here? I was going to have to muster all my journalistic skills to get him to unravel his woes, so he could pack up, go home and let us both get some sleep.

"Would you like to dance?" he asked.

"What?! Here?"

"Why not?"

Now it was getting silly. Still, if I danced with him he might be satisfied and go home. Standing up, I put my damp, flustered hand in his cool, dry one and lurched painfully over the Lego bricks. If I'd known the room would be transformed into a ballroom I'd have put the kids' toys away and kept my shoes on.

As Ella's liquid voice wrapped the room in a haze of sensuality I noticed his excellent sense of rhythm (years of marching on parade grounds probably had something to do with it). And his body, as it brushed offhandedly against mine, seemed to be encased in some kind of metal suit. Until I realized the curves were too well formed to be metal. They were made of a material totally unfamiliar to me—lean muscle.

"So how old are the kids?" he asked.

Oh no. What was it with him and the kids?

"Nearly three and twelve."

Painfully, patiently, he dragged their names out of me, what they liked to do at weekends and how they handled having parents who were separated. I changed the subject, and we danced in silence for a while. He did have an exceptional body— but either he was clumsy, or he was deliberately moving closer. With the shrink's words ringing in my ears, I didn't flinch when he lowered his godlike head and pressed his lips onto mine.

The room whirled in a kaleidoscope of toys, cups and saucers against apricot-colored walls. Cleo looked on approvingly as I savored the magical kiss. Soft, damp and luscious. It was perfect, beyond perfect. *Too* perfect!

I stopped swaying to the music and straightened my spine. No, dammit! This wasn't how things were meant to happen. The whole point of the night was that I was supposed to be running the show. This man-boy had no right to schmooze with Cleo and then ask me to dance. As for all that probing about the kids . . .

He froze, too. At least he was sensitive enough to notice my mood had changed.

"Shall we go to the bedroom?" he said softly.

For several moments, possibly six months or twelve hundred years, I couldn't summon up a response. She the unshockable was—there was no other word for it—shocked.

"It's not that I don't *like* you . . ." I said, stepping backwards.

He tensed like a cardboard cutout doll.

"In fact, I'd probably sleep with you if I *didn't* like you. At least that's what my shrink says I should be doing . . ."

He was starting to look almost as horrified as he'd been at the sight of the Chinese pantsuit.

"The thing is, I like you too much to sleep with you . . ."

He stood stunned, like he'd wandered into a friendly camp and was suddenly under enemy fire. It was beginning to dawn on me that probably no woman in the multidimensional universe had ever turned down the opportunity to exchange bodily fluids with such a suntanned Adonis.

"It's getting incredibly . . . late . . . and I don't know about you, but I'm bushed by the end of the week."

"Can I call you sometime?" he asked icily, as he gathered up his jacket and I escorted him to the door with Cleo in our wake.

"No. I mean, yes. Yes. Definitely. Um. Good night."

I closed the door softly but firmly. Cleo flicked her tail at me and stalked down the hall.

Exposure

In the face of real danger a cat freezes.

"He made you change your outfit?!" Nicole was trying to control the volume of her laughter, so only half the newsroom could hear.

"He didn't *make* me," I said, giggling, yet already regretting the capacity women have to be mercilessly indiscreet about their intimate encounters with men. Especially when somebody makes a fool of himself. Except this time the personal humiliation involved was mine.

If only I'd been wise enough to have said "fine" when she'd asked how the date went and left it at that. But then she would have suspected serious emotional entanglement, and nothing could be further from the truth. "He just looked mortified, so I offered to change."

"*Seriously?* I wouldn't have bothered."

The annoying thing was, Nicole would never *have* to bother. She could walk down the street in her grandmother's dressing gown and hair rollers and still turn every male head within a square mile.

"And it was a *terrible* play! There were so many ham actors you could've made a pork roast. Honestly, he has no idea . . ."

"Probably trying to impress you. Did you . . . did he try to . . . take things further?"

"Course not!" I said, my face suddenly feeling like it was in a sauna. The kiss was nothing. An aberration best deleted from conversation and memory. "I think he's just lonely. I won't be seeing him again, anyway. Too young and boring."

"Told you so," said Nicole, her fingers galloping over her keyboard. "Got to get this story in by eleven o'clock, and I haven't done a word."

"What would a guy like that want with an old solo mum with two kids, anyway?" I muttered, trying to decipher a notepad of shorthand that had made perfect sense when I'd scribbled down the words of a fading international author the previous week. The jottings now resembled ancient Arabic. "He must have a screw loose."

"Who?" said Nicole, her attention focused on finding the home number of an elusive television director she needed to interrogate.

"The boy."

"Oh, the toy boy. Forget him."

Yes. That's what he was. Toy boy, an excellent, freshly invented expression with a cleansing ring to it, like mouthwash. With a label like that he could be sealed in cellophane, put in a box and shut away as one of life's more regrettable experiments.

Tina slid a list of story ideas onto my desk. At the bottom of the list she'd scrawled "Halloween feature. Find some way to make this interesting. We did pumpkins last year. Awful!"

Work. Where would I be without it? There was no better anesthetic.

"Phone call for you, Helen," Mike, one of the nosier political reporters, shouted across the room. "Some snooty-sounding bloke. It's come through on my line for some reason. I'll transfer it to you."

There's an art to how a woman journalist answers her phone. She must sound fresh and approachable, in case the caller has a story that has potential to wind up on the cover of *Newsweek*, which is about as likely as dinosaurs stirring themselves out of their graves and plodding through suburban neighborhoods. And there must also be a Teflon edge to her tone, in case it is a nutter or the Heavy Breather.

"Thank you for last night," the voice was measured and formal.

"Oh!" I said, stupidly.

Nicole's fingers froze mid-air over her keyboard. She put her head to one side and whispered, "*Who is it?*" Her instinct for a story was always spot-on.

I nestled the phone under my chin and mimed "one l" with my fingers.

"I had a great time," he continued.

Oh God. He was lying. He would've had more fun giving blood.

"So did I."

Nicole rolled her eyes and shook her head at me slowly.

"Sorry the play wasn't up to scratch," he said.

"It was fine, honestly . . ."

Nicole took a pen from her desktop and ran it like an imitation scalpel across her neck.

"I was wondering if you'd like to go out for dinner next weekend?" he asked.

Shock rippled through me and settled on my feet like a pair of leaden shoes.

"I've got the kids next weekend," I said, cool and sensible. Nicole nodded approval and resumed her keyboard tattoo. That was it. Finito. No joy, toy boy.

"What about the following weekend?" he asked.

"Oh!" my lead shoes turned molten hot. "Well, no. I don't think I'm doing anything."

Nicole towered over me, the steam from her nostrils almost visible.

"Good. How about seven-thirty Saturday?"

"Sounds good."

"See you then."

"*Damn!*" I muttered, clattering the receiver down.

"Why didn't you say no?" asked Nicole, my frustrated life coach.

"I don't know. Couldn't think of an excuse."

"Don't you know 'no' is the new 'yes'? If you say no to something you don't want to do now it saves you having to go through all sorts of demoralising situations in the future. Do you seriously want to go out with someone who made you change your clothes?"

"What can I do?"

"Call him back a couple of days before the date and say your aunt died and you have to go home to the funeral."

"Good idea. I'll do it."

I didn't. For several reasons. It never feels good to lie; saying my aunt had died might tempt fate—I was very fond of Aunt Lila; Cleo approved of him and . . . there wasn't really a fourth reason, apart from the memory of that extraordinary kiss.

Considering how many awkward and embarrassing things had happened on that first so-called date he was fool enough to sign up for more. He had to be mad. Or special. Or mad in a special way, or the other way around.

I often told the kids that anything's worth trying if your chances are better than winning Lotto. Yet the possibility of there being more to the toy boy beyond his perfectly groomed surface was almost zero. On the other hand, he'd called my bluff a couple of times. Maybe I'd underestimated him.

Despite Nicole's assurances there was no future in it, the dinner became the first of many. And I was facing a dilemma. I was beginning to enjoy the company of multifaceted Philip. If our relationship went any further, it could no longer be classified as a one-night stand, even in the loosest terms. After all, the whole point of a one-night stand is it's impersonal, possibly unsatisfactory, and therefore not worth repeating. Sleeping with him now would be tantamount to disobeying the shrink's instructions.

Besides which, there were other more uncomfortable matters to consider. A woman who has given birth three times is unwilling if not insane to expose her body, especially if she has avoided the rigors of the gym. "Drop a dress size in one week" diets invariably ended in "gain two sizes a week later." After the birth of a child the female form arranges itself in mounds and folds that can charitably be described as "interesting" to artists such as Renoir and Rubens. After the birth of three, her body is more or less a Henry Moore sculpture carved in sponge rubber. A young man whose greatest physical imperfection was a subtly crooked nose (due to a rugby injury) had every reason to be warned against the dangers of unraveling acres of unruly womanly flesh. Yet, like Livingstone in search of the source of the Nile, he refused to give up.

I gradually began to understand why queen-size sheets were invented. They're the Western woman's equivalent of the Muslim female's chador. With careful planning, a queen-size sheet can be arranged to cover the entire body and head with just a slit from which the eyes can peer out. "Gosh," she says, trying to sound offhand as she peers through the slit at the impossibly toned male body, "these sheets have a mind of their own." The other merciful invention is the light switch. Due to a condition that has afflicted her since childhood, known as Extreme Sensitivity of the Eyes to Artificial Light, it must be switched off. My body was no longer a temple. It was a garden for the blind.

It was during a lull in one of these nonvisual encounters that he invited me to spend a weekend at his family's holiday cottage on the shores of Lake Taupo. This was starting to sound scarily on the edge of being beyond a several-night stand to something complicated.

"But I'll have the . . ."

"Make it one of the weekends you don't have the kids."

He'd finally accepted the kids were sacred turf, part of a separate life he was banned from.

"But . . . there's no one to look after the cat."

"Cleo can come along with us, if she doesn't get carsick."

I told him Cleo adored riding in cars. So a couple of weeks later on a Friday night after work she jumped eagerly into the old Audi. Perched on my knee, she watched the countryside spinning past. As we headed towards the lake the hills turned gold, then crimson, before drenching themselves in deepest violet.

We arrived at the cottage after dark. The Taupo night wrapped around us like black velvet, making us blind but heightening our other senses. The air was heavy with piney smells. There was a spike of distant snow on the breeze. I could hear the intimate lap of waves licking the shore. The outline of the wooden house was plain and modest. Even though I couldn't see it properly, the place had unmistakable soul. Like a child on a mystery adventure I followed the thread of Philip's torchlight to a flyscreen door.

"Just a minute," he said. "There's a special hiding place for the key."

He disappeared around the side of the house and emerged with the key soon after. "Here we go," he said, sliding it in the lock. "Damn!"

"What's happened?"

"It's okay," he said. "I've just broken the key."

"Oh. *Is* that okay?"

"It's stuck in the lock."

"Can't we break a window?"

"That would set the alarm off."

"Let's do it, then."

"I can't remember the code."

We stood for what seemed several minutes in the dark together, Cleo tucked under my arm. Our courtship, if that's what it was, seemed destined to be laced with complications.

"We'll just have to stay in a motel," he sighed. "I'll call a locksmith in the morning."

♦

The sign outside the motel said "No Pets." Cleo was smuggled through the lobby inside my handbag, without so much as a mew. Next morning, we met the wry, smiling locksmith at the cottage.

Nestled on the lake's edge, the old house had been in Philip's family for three generations. With French doors opening onto a stretch of grass running down to a pumice-laden beach, the setting was more spectacular than anything I'd imagined the previous night. The lake sparkled blue as a Sri Lankan sapphire. A sage-green island rose like an afterthought in the distance.

Cleo stretched gleefully in front of a driftwood fire while Philip and I walked along the river track. We paused at a bend where the river widened and spilled over rocks. Ferns bent over the water's edge to admire their reflections. A group of midges hung expectantly in the air. If Philip wanted to understand who I was, sooner or later he'd have to know about Sam. There was a possibility the information would destroy our burgeoning romance. To take on an older woman is one thing. Add a couple of readymade kids and the scenario becomes more complicated. If Philip was willing to wade in any deeper, he'd need to try to understand the emotional picture of what it might be like to lose a child. Even if we spent the rest of our lives together and had our own children, there would always be

Helen Brown

part of me that would remain fenced off from him. The part that loved and grieved for Sam.

"There's something I need to tell you," I said, concentrating on a powder puff of cloud in the distance. "Rob and Lydia had an older brother . . ."

The edges of the cloud started peeling away as if it was about to dissolve into the sky. A breeze spiked off the mountains. I shivered inside my city rain jacket. If I'd had more outdoor experience I would've thought to bring gloves to a place like this in the depths of winter.

"I know about Sam," he replied quietly.

"How?" I asked, surprised.

"I read the articles you wrote around the time it happened."

"Really? What was an army boy doing reading that sort of thing?"

"Your stories were very moving," he said, staring up at the same cloud for what seemed a long time. "Tell me about Sam." He took my hand and rubbed it warm.

"Are you sure you want to know?"

He kissed my fingers, cocooned them in his and tucked them protectively in the pocket of his Gore-Tex jacket. "Absolutely."

As we trudged the rest of the river track with my hand nestled in his pocket he listened to Sam's story, the funny bits, the sad. I told him how losing a child was like having an arm or leg lopped off, except probably worse. That I wasn't sure how profoundly the experience had affected me, that in fact it still did. No matter how logical I tried to be, how squarely I faced the facts Sam no longer existed, I often continued to set an extra place at the table, and would probably do so for the rest of my life. No doubt there were mothers all over the world officially "recovered" from their grief who did the same thing.

I would have forgiven him if he'd said one of the old clichés like "I can't imagine what it must've been like" or one of the newer ones like "you must be so strong." But he simply listened. For that I was grateful.

Cleo was waiting in the glow of the fire when we returned.

"And this cat, she's part of it all," Philip said, scooping her into his arms. "She's your connection to Sam, isn't she?"

Purring loudly, Cleo stretched a lazy paw and patted his neck. She yawned and snuggled into his chest. There was nowhere else she, or I, wanted to be.

Later in the day we went fishing in a dinghy, against a backdrop of mountains tinged candy-floss pink in the sunset. A plump rainbow trout provided dinner for all three of us. We drank red wine and laughed. From a "ticks in boxes" perspective we had little in common, yet we shared something Philip had recognized from the start. We were both strong individuals, unwilling or unable to belong to an in-crowd. In my case, even the out-crowd wouldn't have me. It seemed incredible that Philip hadn't turned away from Sam's story or the scar of my grief. He'd intuited Cleo's part in it, too.

I began to realize I was falling in love.

Respect

A cat demands to be treated as an equal. She expects nothing less. Patronize a feline at your peril.

Carrying out a secret affair in a newsroom is like working in a chocolate factory and trying to stay skinny.

"There's someone called Dustin on the phone for you," said Nicole, cool and quizzical.

To make ourselves feel more relaxed about our age difference I'd summoned up famous historical love affairs in which the woman was considerably older—Cleopatra and Antony, Yoko and John, and of course, Mrs. Robinson and Dustin Hoffman in *The Graduate.*

Philip used the code name Dustin when he called me at the office. At his work I left messages that Mrs. Robinson had called.

"Who's *Dustin?*" Nicole probed.

"Distant cousin."

"Oh well, I suppose it's good you've moved on from that toy boy."

The times Philip and I spent together were growing more precious. I looked forward to them the way a child counts the days till Christmas. After two months of clandestine meetings, I wondered how much longer I'd be able to keep my life so neatly compartmentalized. Whenever he stayed the night while the kids were in residence, I woke him before dawn and made sure he creaked safely out the front door before an impressionable eye flicked open. The last thing I wanted was for them to have to deal with a transient adult male. Yet on our weekends alone together I'd see him looking so comfortable with Cleo draped over his knee it felt like he'd always been part of my emotional framework. Always—a risky word in anyone's language.

"So when do I get to meet the kids?" he asked. "You've told me so much about them it's like I know them already."

"Soon." Cleo looked up at me from his lap and winked.

"In twenty years' time?"

"Not here at the house. I don't want them thinking you're invading their territory."

"Okay. Let's get together on neutral ground. There's a new pizza parlor in town."

He'd obviously thought it through. How could I possibly object to a casual meeting in a pizza parlor? I was in love with Philip, but had ongoing proof that romantic love is like a swimming pool. People fall into it and scramble out of it wet and disheveled, usually in one piece but damaged, all the time.

The love for my children was a different beast altogether. It was fierce and unfathomable. I'd willingly fight to the death for them. Besides, he had no hope of comprehending the grief I carried for Sam. Not that I wanted him to shoulder my sadness in any way, but if he wanted to be part of our lives he needed to acknowledge its existence.

He had every reason to turn around and run. But if he burst into my children's lives and abandoned them brokenhearted I'd tear his limbs off, preferably one at a time, slowly and with no pain relief whatsoever.

✦

Rob slipped into his favorite sweatshirt, several sizes too big for him, with USA emblazoned on the front. I buckled Lydia's red shoes, licked a tissue and wiped mysterious goo off her cheek.

"Try and be well behaved," I instructed them. "He's not used to children."

"What sort of person isn't used to children?" asked Rob. "Anyway, I'm not a kid anymore."

The pizza parlor was carved out of the ground under a shopping arcade. Descending a fake marble staircase, complete with wrought-iron railings, the kids seemed impressed. Quiet at least. I was grateful the place hadn't been open long enough to reek of tired fat. Fake ivy clambered over polystyrene columns. Red and white checked tablecloths screamed at the glistening cash register. It felt like a movie set, with us as an unlikely set of actors auditioning for the role of Family Group.

I was relieved when the waiter escorted us to a discreet table under the stairs. Anyone from work could turn up at a joint like this. It would be through the office like chickenpox by Monday morning—"Brown and Toyboy Test Drive Family Outing. Has She Lost Plot?!"

We ordered pizza and Coke. Rob was no longer a bubbly kid; he'd elongated into a thirteen-year-old with a tank full of testosterone. He was sullen, silent and determined to show no interest in someone who wasn't used to children. I'd warned Philip it was a difficult age. Lydia, who had insisted on wearing three strands of beads around her neck, vacuumed her glass until it was almost empty. Philip seemed slightly unnerved when her slurping noises echoed against the plastic wall panels.

"Don't do that!" I hissed at the child.

"Why not? It's fun."

"It's not polite."

"But this is," she said, lifting the straw from her glass and tipping the remains of her Coke onto her tartan skirt.

"No, it's *not!*" I said, dabbing her skirt with a paper napkin. I glanced at Philip, who was studying the menu as if it was a legal document. Now he surely understood why I never wanted this collision of realities to take place.

"Haven't you got a mother?" Lydia asked, kicking the table leg and making the cutlery hiccup.

"Yes, I do," he said, lowering the menu to welcome the first unsolicited contact from the children.

"Why don't you go home and be with her?"

Silence. I waited for Philip to scrape his chair back and run.

"She's busy tonight."

"Tell her not to be. We've got our mother. You've got yours. You don't need our mother, too."

"Strangers in the Night" dribbled out of a nearby speaker. To the untrained ear the recording had been made inside a shipping container, with musicians scraping instruments made of tin cans. Their Muzak was a welcome silence filler.

Philip's attention moved to the paper place mats with games printed on them. He asked Rob if he'd like to play snakes and ladders. (*Not snakes and ladders!* I wanted to tell Philip. *Rob grew out of that years ago. He thinks it's a game for babies!*) But it wasn't Philip's fault he hadn't kept pace with child development. I held my breath waiting for the inevitable combination of rejection and scorn to catapult across the table.

"I'd rather play this," Rob said, indicating a mass of dots arranged in rectangles. I hadn't seen the game before, but it looked brutally competitive. Each player was allowed one pencil stroke to join two dots at a time, gradually amassing territories of fully formed rectangles. Whoever gained the largest number of completed rectangles won the game. This was the restaurant place mat version of war.

The game started casually enough for me to munch through a triangle of Hawaiian pizza while concentrating on keeping

Lydia's mouth full so no more conversational frogs could leap out of it.

To keep the atmosphere cheerful I read from a section of the menu about the history of pizza, since its humble beginnings when the Greeks first came up with the idea of decorating flat bread.

"The real turning point was in the early nineteenth century, when a Neapolitan baker called Raffaele Esposito decided to make a bread that would stand out from everyone else's. He started by just adding cheese . . ."

I was, of course, reading all this while surreptitiously monitoring the battle taking place between the two men in my life. Rob claimed a cluster of rectangles in the right-hand corner. Philip filled in a strip on the other side. The game was evenly matched.

"After a while he started putting sauce under the cheese. He let the dough fluff out to the shape of a pie . . ."

Rob's territory was spreading across the square. Philip, on the other hand, appeared to be making listless progress on his side. My lips wanted to smile, but I tried to keep them in a straight line. Philip was demonstrating unexpected maturity by letting Rob win. Maybe he was stepfather material after all. He certainly looked the part in his corduroy trousers and fisherman's knit jumper.

"Everyone loved Esposito's pizza so much he was asked to create a special one for the King and Queen of Italy. He made one in the colors of the Italian flag—red sauce, white cheese, green basil . . ."

The two blocks of rectangles moved closer together. Their pencils flashed like swords. It was starting to look like a draw. That would be okay, I thought, as long as Rob's dignity was kept intact. There was hardly any free space left now.

"He named his pizza Margherita, after the queen . . ."

The tension was unbearable.

"The new Margherita pizza was a huge hit."

I didn't dare watch the last few strokes. I knew it was over when I heard two pencils clatter onto the tabletop.

"You won," said Rob, with a brave smile.

"You *what*?!" I said, turning to Philip.

"It was a tough game," he said, shrugging with an unmistakable glint of satisfaction.

A tough game? Didn't he understand there's no such thing as a tough game when children were involved, especially *my* children? My kids' lives were tough enough without some jerk in pseudo stepdad corduroys turning up and knocking their self-esteem around.

I should never have let Philip near them. He was behaving like a child. Worse than a child. And the last thing I needed was another child. The relationship was doomed. Rob would be devastated for days after losing that game.

We drove home in silence and exchanged chaste farewells at the gate.

"It's good he's going home," said Lydia, echoing my thoughts. "His mother will be missing him."

"What did you think?" I asked Rob after I'd fed Cleo and put Lydia to bed.

"He's cool."

"I don't suppose he comes across as a very warm person."

"No, I like him."

"You *like* him? But he beat you at that stupid game."

"I'm sick of the way grown-ups always go out of their way to let me win," said Rob. "They think I don't notice. He treated me as an adult. He's cool. You should see more of him."

People and Places

*Cats have a reputation for being more attached to places
than people. But some remarkable individuals have
proved the generalization quite wrong.*

Mum's voice was jagged over the phone. She told me not to be
upset. I prepared for bad news. She'd had to take Rata to the
vet again. The old dog hadn't been coping. She couldn't walk.
The vet was wonderful, such a lovely young woman. She'd been
a friend of Rata's. She went red in the face when she and Mum
made the decision. Mum stroked Rata while it was happening.
She went out wagging her tail.

Video footage of Rata rolled through my mind. Sam and
Rata charging through the surf, Rata helping the boys dig holes
in the sand and scuffing it over disgruntled sunbathers, Sam
throwing driftwood for her to rescue. Rata shaking her coat and
showering us all in seawater. Rata galloping down the zigzag.
Cleo curled between Rata's giant paws. Tender, loyal Rata.

Rob didn't say much when I told him. We put our arms
around each other. He was so tall now. With the old dog's
departure another connection with Sam was broken. Mum
was going to feel it, too. I invited her to spend a few days with
us, though she never stayed long in our "busy household."

Frantic was a better word for it. In the weeks the children
were home it was a kaleidoscope of school runs and homework;

194

rushing home from work to make spaghetti bolognese; bedtime stories on the run. Once they were in bed I often worked on a feature that was due the next day. I was too exhausted to watch television.

It wouldn't have been possible to hold together without Anne Marie calmly folding laundry, vacuuming, making sandwiches, tidying toys and countless other things she said nannies never do. She'd sometimes stay on for a coffee after I arrived back from work. We learned to appreciate each other's strengths and tolerate the differences. Sometimes I'd arrive home so tired I'd collapse on the floor and doze in a patch of sun—something she said none of her employers had done before. She once commented she'd never seen anyone so tired. Yet I always managed to dredge energy up to sew fairy wings for Lydia or teach Rob how to make sushi. Nothing was perfect, but somehow things got done. I began to think there was a goddess of solo mothers who gave strength when it was needed and arranged for the right people to turn up at the right time. If there was such a goddess I reckoned she looked like a cat.

Steve was carving a new life for himself in a cottage five minutes' drive away. I was pleased when the kids mentioned he had some women friends. He deserved another roll of the happiness dice.

Even though Philip had won Rob's approval on the pizza night, I wasn't sure the kids and I had met whatever expectations were floating around inside his head. He'd seen us as a set, and was no doubt beginning to absorb the enormity of entering the lives of all three of us (plus cat). The phone stayed quiet for several days. Then, to my surprise, it rang. He obviously hadn't had enough punishment. He invited all of us, including Cleo, for a weekend at the lake.

The drive seemed longer by daylight with two extra passengers, one silent, one whining. The road buckled and bent like a cobra in its death throes.

"I've got a sore tummy," moaned Lydia as the car meandered up a hill.

"No, you haven't." Unlike more conscientious mothers, I treated children's health complaints as imaginary until proven otherwise.

"I'm going to frow up."

"Take some deep breaths," I said, turning to examine the backseat patient. Her usually jellybean-pink face had turned the color of a blueberry.

"I think we'd better stop," I said to Philip. While I was immune to the potpourri of stale vomit and various other bodily fluids in my own car, I was certain Philip wasn't psychologically equipped to have the ambience of his Audi permanently altered by Eau de Family.

He pulled into a siding near the top of the hill. I concentrated on the spectacular spine of ranges spread out below us while Lydia vomited copiously into a ditch.

•

Misty haze enveloped the cottage as the car pulled up under a silver birch. Rain was something I hadn't counted on. Philip said it wouldn't matter—there was always something to do at the lake. The leafy smell was intensified in the damp. Cleo recognized the place straightaway and sprang gleefully from the car into a thicket of ferns that was suspect mouse guerrilla territory.

The children were slower to be impressed. Rob gathered his sleeping bag and trudged inside, the screen door slamming behind him. Philip didn't seem the least fazed. No doubt he'd seen the full spectrum of male behavior in the army. Alternatively, having endured his own adolescence only a few years earlier, he probably remembered what it was like. Either way, Philip seemed immune to the ogreish male teenage stuff I was at a loss to deal with.

I helped Lydia slide from the backseat onto the moist earth.

"It's a forest," she said, gazing up at a tree.

We carried our bags inside, where the familiar combination of sea grass and burnt driftwood tweaked my nostrils. I paused at a noticeboard covered with family photos. Wholesome, smiling faces celebrating Christmas at the lake. Every one of Philip's family was handsome and tanned, with teeth so white they surely glowed in the dark. Apparently, there were no fat, scruffy, gay, dark-skinned or emotionally challenged people in their circle. Going by the photos, they were also all Olympic champions. Waterskiing, tennis, snow skiing, fishing were activities I'd never had the time or money, let alone the muscular coordination, to learn as a teenage mum.

Young women featured in the photos, too. Sleek, pretty bikini-clad girls, who were probably studying law or dentistry. So these must be the ticks-in-the-right-boxes girls, I thought. The type Philip and his two brothers were expected to marry. And why not? Every one of the smiling young women was prime breeding stock. But when I asked about them, Philip dismissed them as boring.

"Please use only a <u>small</u> piece of toilet paper," instructed a notice in the loo. I wasn't sure the kids and I could qualify as small toilet paper people.

"How about a swim?" Philip called to Rob.

"It's raining."

"I could help you get out the kayak if you like." The man was nothing if not persistent.

"Too cold."

"Bunks! It's got bunks!" Lydia called. I went into the bunk room, where Rob was roosting inside his sleeping bag on an upper bunk. Lydia bounced up and down on the lower bunk's mattress, circling her chubby arms in the air.

The lake stretched out like a wrinkled sheet of tinfoil. Drops of condensation raced down the inside of windows. Philip crouched over the fireplace and crunched newspapers into balls. After a few false starts the kindling flared and the room crackled to life. Cleo pounced on a spider in the woodpile and munched on its legs with the thoughtful appreciation of a connoisseur, before taking up her usual position in front of the flames. Gazing up at me through half-closed eyes she yawned and seemed to say, *This is how it's meant to be. Don't worry. Everything will be fine.*

"Back in a minute," Philip said.

Gathering Lydia onto my lap to read her favorite story about the elephant and the bad baby, I surreptitiously wiped her fingers. Even though the cottage exuded rustic simplicity it obviously hadn't been tainted by preschool fingers for decades. I'd hate us to be accused of leaving sticky fingerprints on the furniture.

Philip tapped on the window and beckoned us outside. The rain had eased. I slid Lydia into her gumboots. She scooped Cleo up and carried her upside down (a position Cleo had become nonchalant about since Lydia learned to walk). We opened the flyscreen to a gift more magnificent than a room full of diamonds: Philip had latched a rope around one of the higher branches of the silver birch and threaded an old tire through it.

"Wow! A tree swing!" cried Lydia.

She spent the rest of the day begging to be pushed on the swing—lying on her tummy with her legs flying out the back; sitting with her legs forward through the center of the tire; standing inside the rim and clinging to the rope. I'd never seen a man demonstrate so much patience with a child who wasn't his own. Still, something held me back. Even if this wonderful man was everything he seemed, with a soul deeper than the lake itself, the prospect of encompassing all three of us and a cat was surely too much for him.

As night enveloped the cottage, the rain eased enough for Philip to grill sausages on a brick barbecue nestled into a hedge. It was too wet for us to eat outside, so I set the Formica table. We shared the meal under the inquisitive glare of a light-bulb.

"How would you like to go for a bike ride tomorrow?" Philip asked Rob. "There are some great tracks up in the hills."

"No."

"We could hit a tennis ball around . . ."

Rob studied the tomato sauce on his plate. An experienced parent, worn by countless battles of will, would stop at this intersection, turn back and opt for a change of subject. I was hoping for all our sakes that Philip would do so now.

"How about taking the kayak out in the morning? I'll put the life jacket out for you."

"It's all very well for you!" Rob exploded at Philip. "You didn't see your brother killed on the road!"

The teenager scraped back his chair and stomped off to the bunk room, leaving us in a bubble of stunned silence at the table.

"He does this sometimes," I said quietly. Yet it was more than a teenage eruption this time. The lake cottage, with its garage choked with skis, boats and canoes, made the contrast between our two families all too evident. Philip appeared to have coasted through endless summers of pretty girls and sailboats. Our life, by comparison, was an endless struggle, overshadowed by death and divorce. How could anyone from Philip's background have the slightest understanding of the grief Rob and I shared—and, more to the point, why should he?

"I'll talk to him," Philip said, standing up to follow him.

"No, don't," I said. "He'll get over it."

In truth I was frightened by Rob's adolescent outbursts and had no way of handling them, apart from letting them blow over—which sometimes could take days.

Deaf to my instructions, Philip departed swiftly into the bunk room. Through the walls, I could hear him speaking gently to Rob. While it was impossible to hear exact words, the tone was unmistakable. Philip was meeting Rob's pain head-on, accepting their differences and talking him down.

"He's okay," Philip said when he emerged some time afterwards. "He says he wants to sleep now."

♦

We woke next morning with rain thrumming on the roof. Lydia, plodding around in her pajamas, was delighted when she found a box of old building blocks in one of the cupboards.

"There's been kids here!" she called.

Cleo was chomping on the remains of a moth while Lydia set about building an elephant castle with a swing for the baby elephants.

"Where's Rob?" I asked.

"Dunno," said Lydia.

Philip had no idea, either. A lump of fear settled in my stomach. If Rob had taken off during the night he could be anywhere by now. He could have hitched a ride back to Auckland on one of the logging trucks that roared along the main highway. Or maybe just wandered into the bush. Either way, it could be dangerous, especially in this rainstorm. His father would have to be called, possibly the police as well. It was a disaster. Why did I always land in the box labeled "disaster"?

"Look," said Philip, putting a hand on my shoulder and turning me slowly towards the French doors. Through the rain-spattered glass I could see waves, big as ocean surf, smashing on the beach. Purple clouds smothered the island. In the distance I could just make out a figure in a kayak.

The waves pushed the figure sideways and seemed to engulf him completely. He reemerged, plowing the oar into the water and turning the kayak around to surf another wave. The canoeist was fearless, intense in his determination to stay afloat.

"You're all crazy around here," I said. "Who'd go out in this weather?"

"Rob," said Philip, smiling enigmatically. "And I have to say he's making an impressive job of it."

Freedom

Human beings strive to claim ownership of everything they love. Yet a cat belongs to nobody, except perhaps the moon.

Around the time I became a single mother Cleo stepped up her hunting skills. Maybe she sensed we were down to one provider and thought I was doing a lousy job bringing home the bacon. Not only was I a pathetic, two-legged creature with (from her point of view, anyway) a hideously bald body, I couldn't hunt a mouse if world peace depended on it. Cleo more than compensated for my inadequacies with a stream of furry or feathered corpses scattered from the front doormat, through the bedrooms and down the hall to the kitchen. Our house resembled the workroom of an amateur taxidermist. To stem the tide of destruction I bought Cleo a hot-pink collar with fake diamond studs and a bell to warn potential victims to scurry back to their nests.

"Cats don't wear collars," Mum said in a tone implying she'd just delivered the Eleventh Commandment.

While the kids and I always looked forward to Mum's visits, she invariably found something not quite right with our setup. This time it was the cat collar.

"She's killing too many animals," I said, tightening the buckle around Cleo's reluctant neck. "Besides, it looks quite Audrey Hepburn, don't you think?"

"It's hideous," Mum replied. "And it's a cat's *job* to kill things."

For once Cleo agreed with Mum. The cat shook her head vigorously, making herself jingle like a Christmas accessory.

"See? It doesn't like that thing!"

"She's not an 'it.' She's a *she*," I said. "And she'll get used to it."

Cleo and I embarked on a serious battle of wills. She detested that collar with more focus than she'd ever hated anything, including non–cat people. Every waking hour was devoted to scratching and gnawing at it. Three fake diamonds fell out. The sumptuous pink strap faded and was reduced to a stringy neck brace. Cleo fixed me with a hooded look that said it all: *How dare you try and brand me with this degrading object! What makes you assume you have the right? Do you think you own me?*

"Is *that* your new boyfriend?" Mum stage-whispered in the kitchen. "I thought he was a policeman when I opened the door. His hair's so short and he's so clean-cut. Hardly your type, is he?"

I never enjoyed her reviewing my personal affairs. Her observation skills were astringent enough to qualify as an ingredient for aftershave. Philip's appearance in our lives provided her with a wealth of new material.

"Just out of the army, is he? Oh well, you were married to a sailor. I suppose it'll be the air force next."

Life at work was no easier. When the cat got out of the bag that I was still seeing Philip with one l there were enough arched eyebrows to form a Gothic cathedral. Toy-boy jokes echoed from one end of the newsroom to the other. Journalists pride themselves on being broad-minded, but I was learning they're broad-minded only in certain ways. If I'd taken to booze and boogied till dawn with an elderly drug addict they'd hardly have noticed. Movies were (and still are) full of old men as ugly as bulldogs slurping over models twenty-five years their junior. It hardly seemed fair that a woman going out with a short-haired, younger bloke in a suit was regarded as an act of indecency. I tried to retaliate with quips to assure them it was merely a fling. Except the fling was lasting a month or two longer than expected.

Things weren't straightforward for Philip, either. His circle of bright young things couldn't believe he was in such a whacky relationship. He continued to be inundated with invitations to lunches and parties by ticks-in-the-right-boxes girls. The town was packed with highly qualified wrinkle-free beauties all desperate for a man, and Philip in particular.

Falling in love with my one-night stand was the most pleasant surprise that ever happened to me. Getting to know him was like exploring an underground cave, dark and deceptively shallow at first. Yet dig a little deeper, turn a few corners, and there was a cavern full of rare and magnificent crystals. Not only was he handsome, great company and wonderful to the kids, he had a strong spiritual curiosity. He was the first man I'd ever met who seemed genuinely interested in my weird dreams and occasional off-the-planet psychic experiences. We were destined to be together, I thought, encircling him with an invisible version of Cleo's pink collar (camouflage pattern, perhaps; definitely no bell).

"It doesn't matter what wrapping people are in," I said to anyone who questioned our unlikely union. "It's what's inside that counts."

I even loved the aspects of him that had stopped me taking him seriously at the beginning. The age difference between us was fun and interesting (apart from the time he asked, "Who's Shirley Bassey?"). His conservative manner wasn't so deep-set that I couldn't joke him out of it sometimes. And I had a lot to learn about military life and banks. Our relationship was astoundingly close to perfect.

One of the many aspects of Philip I adored was the way he kept a perfectly ironed handkerchief in his pocket. The handkerchief was flourished whenever required to wipe a woman's tears or, occasionally by *very* special request, less glamorous outpourings from her nostrils. Even more impressive, he insisted on being on the outside whenever we were walking along a footpath. The only other man I knew who performed this ancient act of chivalry designed to protect a woman from oncoming horses as well as mud flying from carriage wheels was my father. The first time Philip gently took my arm, moved slowly behind me and slid my hand into the crook of his other elbow so I was closest to the shop windows and he was nearest the gutter I knew this was a man I'd willingly spend the rest of my life with.

But then . . . why does there always have to be a "but then"? Why can't the sad solo mother queen just meet her prince, fall in love, stroll down the aisle in a tactfully off-white suit and live happily ever after? Because life isn't written by Rodgers and Hammerstein. Real people have histories, hang-ups, phobias, anxieties, egos, ambitions, not to mention opinionated friends and family just waiting to pass judgment.

We no longer went to huge lengths not to be seen in public with the children. At least, I didn't think so. So when the four of us drove to town one Saturday morning on a T-shirt shopping mission, we parked on the main street and bundled out of the car. Walking down the footpath, Philip completed one of his elegant mud-protecting moves. The kids galloped ahead into the store. I felt like someone in a movie whose life has turned out wonderfully, when people have finished their popcorn and the credits are about to roll.

"I like this one," Lydia said, holding up a T-shirt featuring teddy bears dressed as fairies. The color was predictable.

"She's going through a three-year-old pink phase," I said to Philip. "I'm not fighting it. If I do she'll probably end up on a shrink's couch someday, blaming me for denying her an essential part of her development."

He didn't laugh. In fact, he'd frozen like a cat that has spotted a rottweiler.

"Sarah!" he said, smiling broadly over my shoulder.

I turned. Standing outside a changing room in a bikini so miniscule it could have doubled as dental floss was a blonde with legs longer than Barbie's. I recognized her from the photo board at the lake, one of the famous "boring" girls. Ticks in every single box.

"Philip!" she beamed. "Where *have* you been? We haven't seen you at tennis for ages. I've been missing you."

I waited for Philip to introduce me, but he snapped himself inside a Perspex bubble that denied any connection with me. I was just another shopper he happened to be standing next to, and the kids were invisible.

"Work's been full-on," he said, moving towards her. "You know what it's like this time of year."

"Same at the surgery," she said, rolling her eyes and flicking her golden mane. "There's heaps of cosmetic work these days. Everyone wants perfect teeth. You're looking so well!"

"So are you!" His voice ricocheted off the walls into my ears, collided inside my brain, spun down my spinal column and ruptured something in my chest.

"And your parents? How are they?"

As their conversation grew warmer and more intimate I stood like a Charles Dickens character shivering out in the snow and peering through a window at a flickering hearth surrounded by happy faces.

"Let's go!" I said quietly to Rob.

"But I want this pink one," said Lydia.

"Not now!" I said, thrusting it back on a neatly folded pile.

Grabbing her hand, I swept out of the shop with Rob jogging to catch up with me.

"Shouldn't we wait for him?" Rob asked, as we charged through a sea of faces.

"I don't think he even knows we've gone."

What a fool I'd been. A consummate moron. Why on earth hadn't I listened to Nicole and Mum and everyone else who'd warned me? They'd been right all along. The boy-man and I had no place in each other's worlds. He was no more capable of fitting in with my journalist crowd than I was of suddenly becoming a twenty-four-year-old Barbie dentist. Let alone the kids. It would take an incredibly special man to encompass my kids in his future.

How wrong of me to expose them to someone so shallow and immature. And yes, conservative. So damned conservative and dull he might as well take up smoking a pipe and marry a dentist.

"Wait!" Philip, panting from running to catch up with us, touched me on the shoulder. "What's the matter?"

I sent Rob into a McDonald's to buy himself chips and Lydia an ineptly named Happy Meal.

"Ashamed of us, are you?" I yowled.

"What do you mean?" he asked, feigning innocence.

"Why didn't you introduce us?"

"I didn't think you'd be interested."

"You mean you didn't think *she'd* be interested!"

"Look, I . . ." An inquisitive shopper paused to absorb as much of our argument as was politely possible.

"I thought you said Sarah was boring." I hated the vindictive quaver in my voice. It was hideously unattractive and about as un-ticks-in-boxes as anyone could get. "You did a pretty good impression of not being bored."

"She's . . . just a friend."

"If that's the case why did you act as if we weren't there?"

Philip stared up at a neon sign above our head. In a merciless act of cruelty it flashed the words "Engagement Rings."

"Do you think this is easy for me?" he erupted. "It's not that I don't like the kids. I think they're wonderful. It's just . . ."

I waited as a thousand shoppers changed color under the flashing sign.

"I'm not sure I want to be an instant father."

When he dropped us home and drove off I discovered Cleo's collar was missing. She'd finally chewed it off and claimed her freedom.

Witch's Cat

Sometimes it's easier to love the moon.

There aren't many options for a brokenhearted woman with attitude, except perhaps to become a witch. Witches fight off curses. They create their own luck. Witchery had potential. Cleo, with her ability to appear on a rooftop and in front of a fireplace almost simultaneously, was the perfect witch's cat, not to mention the ideal color.

A room is more beautiful when furnished with a cat. Her silken presence transforms a collection of chairs, discarded toys and crumb-sprinkled plates into a temple to soothe the soul. Poised like a goddess on a window ledge she observes the countless frailties of the humans she has blessed with her presence. The poor creatures make countless mistakes with their neurotic attempts to cling to the past and control the future. They need a cat to remind themselves just to be.

A cat's ears absorb the thump of a school bag hitting the floor or a mother's curse when she finds ants in the sugar bowl yet again. Humans and their tragic overreactions amuse her. Nothing they can do disturbs her composure, except for the young, when they go through that horrifying stage of wanting to dress her in baby clothes and imprison her in a pram.

Her paws absorb the earth's slightest tremor. Ever watchful, her eyes perceive more than human eyes can. When she sleeps, a cat draws a third eyelid, a translucent screen, over her eyes so no movement escapes her. A cat is always watching, but wise enough to refrain from offering an opinion.

A black cat is lucky, or not, depending on which side of the Atlantic you are born. If a black cat crosses your path in Britain expect good fortune. In North America, a black cat spells danger.

With their shimmering fur and mirror eyes, black cats were once regarded as malevolent spirits. They blended into darkness, which to some ill-informed minds made them the personification of evil—the devil himself stalking the rooftops of innocent peasants. Even in Britain, where black cats are considered lucky, the superstition isn't in the felines' favor. It's only because a person suffers no harm when a black cat crosses his path, and has therefore escaped evil, that he can congratulate himself on his luck.

✦

There was no point seeing the shrink again. She'd only tell me to have another one-night stand. We all knew how that ended up. Anyway, I'd learned from my mistakes. I withdrew from the dating world and tried to be wise. A scary replica of my mother, I developed the lonely person's syndrome of telling people the same stories over and over again. As their eyes glazed I'd stop and say, "Have I told you this before?" The polite ones said no.

When they asked, I said I'd never been happier. So what? A cat never loses its smile. I did everything possible to become a self-sufficient witch who didn't need a man. Compromise was no longer part of my vocabulary. The Chinese pantsuit enjoyed regular airings. I nailed kitsch pottery ducks to the wall, drank wine and farted when I felt like it. At night, sometimes, when the kids were at their father's, I turned the stereo up loud enough for the neighbors to notice and danced half-naked to Marvin

Gaye. (*Never* Ella and Louis!) Women friends approved. They said I was empowered.

Empowerment sounds wonderful, but frankly, it's not everything it's cracked up to be. Although a witch may seem in control of her life, she has a diligent stalker: loneliness. After the kids had gone to bed I'd pour a glass of wine. Cleo would pad across the floor towards me. The shadow of her tail, an eerie serpent six feet tall, would flicker against the wall. A charge of electricity would shudder up my arm as I ran my hand over her coat. I'd scoop her up and carry her out to the back deck. We'd sit under the stars together, licking our wounds and studying the moon's acne.

"Nobody touches a witch's heart," I murmured, burying my nose in her velvet fur.

Nevertheless, I leapt at the phone every time it rang. It was never him. Why should it be? He'd made it clear enough when we split up. He said he wasn't "ready," whatever that meant. If people waited till everything was ready, nothing would ever happen. Life isn't a menu; you can't order courses when you're "ready" for them. I hadn't been ready to lose Sam. And I didn't feel ready to say good-bye to Philip. His words were surgical, but his eyes brimmed with sadness and love. Even though I tried to accept what he said I still believed his eyes. Why had he walked away?

I missed his calm presence, his voice warm as a driftwood fire, his ridiculously conservative clothes, the crooked nose, the hairy groves inside his ears. One of the things I missed most was his smell. Even though he seldom wore aftershave, he always smelled like a grove of cypress trees. How come so few sonnets are written to a lover's smell? Rob was missing him, too. Philip had been a desperately needed role model that had turned out fake, heartless as a shop mannequin. What a fool I'd been. I vowed no man would ever hurt Rob that way again.

I wondered what Philip was up to. Had he shed us like one of his Italian jackets? No doubt he was being devoured by bimbo dentists and lawyers. If our worlds had been closer, a few discreet phone calls would have answered my questions. But we had no friends in common. He might as well have taken off to Pluto. Weeks dissolved into months.

If I was to be a witch, then Cleo needed to look the part. I taught her to perch on my shoulder. Our first attempts were dismal and painful to us both. But Cleo was a willing student with a sense of balance worthy of Cirque du Soleil. She was soon able to dig her claws into my clothes deeply enough to secure a platform without piercing my skin. I enjoyed the alarm that flickered across visitors' faces when I opened the door with a black cat glaring down at them from my shoulder. For all their technology and sophistication, people are wired like primitive beings. They still believe in witches. Not so long ago, neighbors would have gathered outside my white picket fence at dusk and dragged me and my cat to the nearest bonfire.

"A woman needs a man like a butterfly needs deep-sea diving gear," I said to Emma, who'd become a regular visitor. I'd met her at a book launch, where we'd both been hovering by the loo doors. Emma worked in a feminist bookstore. She helped me nurture a herb garden and introduced me to her circle of women friends, who had strong views on the male species. Listening to their wine-fueled discussions, I nodded fiercely. Men were a lesser species, slaves to the bulge in their pants and overdue for extinction.

Even if I couldn't contemplate cutting my hair short and bleaching it silver the way Emma had, I admired her flair. Turquoise was her color. Only a woman with no children would have time to sift through what must've amounted to hundreds of shops and market stalls to find so much turquoise junk— bangles, scarves, even a pair of turquoise sunglasses. One of her favorite accessories was a feather-trimmed pendant inlaid with turquoise, a gift from a Hopi Indian chief who had cleansed her aura, smudged evil spirits out of her house with sage smoke and identified her totem animal as a cougar.

Emma often brought over books from her shop—*Why Women Bleed*, *The Disposable Male*. Free from maternal exhaustion, she was honorary aunt to the kids. I envied the excess energy she had to bounce on the trampoline with Lydia or kick a ball around with Rob. I was grateful for Emma's company.

I was also thankful for the restless, throwaway atmosphere of the newsroom. A combination of deadlines and worldly quips from workmates helped stop up the holes in a shattered heart. I was grateful that nobody, not even Nicole, said, "I told you so." The toy-boy jokes dried up and gradually stopped. They accepted me back into the fold. I loved them for it.

While I didn't know Tina well, she was showing signs of being an empowerment witch herself. Not so long ago she'd asked me into her office and suggested I apply for a Press Fellowship to Cambridge University in Britain. My chances of being accepted were less than zero, but I filled out the form to practice applying for things. The form invited applicants to nominate an area of interest. Confident I wouldn't get in, I invented a zany topic—Environmental Studies from a Spiritual Perspective.

Another weekend without the children stretched ahead like a desert. I was pleased when Emma offered a Saturday night oasis, asking me over to her place for pasta and salad. Thank God, whoever She may be, for women friends, I thought, pulling up outside Emma's cutesy house nestled in the hills outside town.

"How are you?" she said, opening the door.

Emma was one of the few people I could be honest with.

"Good. Bad . . . Dunno . . . Tired."

She poured a glass of wine, a soulful Australian red. We dined outside under the hypnotic toll of a wind chime.

"You're a wonderful friend," I said, scraping the remains of home-baked lemon pudding off my bowl. "It's such a treat to have a beautiful meal just appear like this. It's magic. I can't get over it. I didn't have to peel a potato."

"My pleasure," Emma said, flashing her incisors. The Hopi Indian chief was right. There was something cougarish about her, especially in the evening light.

As I stood to help clear the table, Emma took my hand. "No. Sit down," she said. "Tonight's *your* night. I know how hard you work and how demanding it is raising the kids on your own. Tonight I'm taking care of you."

Her words made me want to crumble with gratitude. At last someone understood.

"What's that sound?" I asked. "Do you have an ornamental fountain?"

"I'm running a bath for you," Emma said.

A bath?! Did I smell that bad? I'd showered before leaving home.

"You said a good bath relaxes you more than anything," she added, sensing my alarm.

"Yes, but that's when I'm at home on my own," I muttered.

"This is going to be better than anything you've ever had at home," said Emma. "I've been saving some special French bubble bath for you."

"That's . . . very . . . kind," I said, wishing she could've just handed over the bottle of bubble bath and let me go home.

"I've put a robe out for you," she said, looking more cougarish by the second. "In the bathroom."

I felt suddenly hot and confused. Over the years I'd known lots of women, strong wonderful people like Ginny, who I'd trust with my life. We'd laughed and cried together, moaned about men and shared intimate details about our bodily functions. Those women had helped me grieve and give birth, let go of my marriage and laugh off life's indignities. So far not one of them had invited me to have a bath. A bubble bath at that.

"Don't worry," soothed Emma. "It's your special night."

Oh, well. What was wrong with taking a bath? She might think me unsophisticated if I said no. I liked Emma a lot. She was obviously trying to help. I didn't want to hurt her feelings or seem unappreciative.

The French obviously knew a thing or two about bubble bath. Giant rainbow domes rose from the water. A row of colored candles blazed on the window ledge. Surely a fire hazard. A robe was folded thoughtfully on the vanity. I instinctively raised a hand to lock the bathroom door. There was no lock.

Sinking into the bubbles, I examined the Women Can Do Anything poster on the wall. Had I sent unusual signals to Emma? I hoped not. She knew my tastes were straightforward. Perhaps I'd been naive to assume hers were, too. She certainly hadn't gone out of her way to talk about previous love affairs. I'd respected Emma's need for privacy. Maybe I should have been more curious. She'd mentioned a man once, and women friends. But I'd assumed "friends" was the operative word. Maybe I'd been loose in my use of language. When I'd told her I loved women I hadn't felt it necessary to add "but not in that way." Strange sounds warbled from under the door that I had closed firmly as possible.

"Whale song!" called Emma. "With subliminal messages."

"Oh," I replied nonchalantly. "What do you mean?"

"They recorded messages you can't quite hear under the whale song," she said. "To change your way of thinking."

Suddenly on edge, I craned my neck out of the water to listen for whatever hidden message there was behind the yodeling whales. Some sort of mumbling was definitely going on. Maybe Emma was trying to brainwash me to join some religious sect.

"What does it say?" I asked, trying to conceal my anxiety.

"Oh, relax, let go, that sort of thing."

If any whale, white, blue or sperm, tried to audition for a choir I was running I'd turn it down. Those things are tone deaf. I sank back into the bubbles and concentrated on relaxing.

"Is it warm enough for you?" asked Emma, bursting into the room and pressing her face so close to mine I could smell garlic on her breath.

"Yes, thanks," I said, sinking into the bubbles as deep as possible without drowning. "It's perfect. I think . . ."

"Yes?" said Emma, whose face rose like the sun over the edge of the bath.

"I'd like to get out now."

"Oh, but you'll miss the massage!" cried Emma, digging her large, practical fingers into my neck.

The massage?! Crouched unwillingly, I endured her attentions with the stoicism of a dog being forced to have its fur washed. Emma's breaths were hot and increasingly loud in my ear. The masculine tang of her perfume (aftershave?) made me vaguely nauseous.

Images arose of a future sharing a rose-covered cottage with a well-built woman and her turquoise collection. There'd been two women teachers like that when I was at high school. They used to drive to school in separate cars to keep the gossip down, but everyone knew. People said they'd arranged to be buried together.

Technically, I supposed it was an option. A life with Emma would avoid some of the cruelties inflicted by men. Testosterone wouldn't pose much of a problem, competition from blond dentists would be minimal and there'd be plenty of the affection women enjoy. Cuddles and hugs, not unlike the sort of stuff you get from a cat. I liked Emma. There was only one difficulty. I didn't love her. Not in *that* way.

As Emma turned my face in her hands and planted her damp lips on mine I knew straightaway. I wasn't that kind of girl.

✦

Six months had passed since I'd seen Philip. I was over him, at least I pretended to be. I hardly needed a man when I was flat-out with the kids and work, where I was becoming a minor authority on "wimmin's issues." Emma had put me on to a local witch, who'd agreed to visit the office for an interview on women's spirituality. Apparently witches needed publicity as much as anyone else. Apart from a few crystals dangling around her neck and sticking plasters wrapped around several gnarled toes protruding from her Birkenstocks, she resembled any mature woman I might clash supermarket trolleys with. I escorted her into the interview room. We exchanged smiles. I quietly wondered if she recognized my witch potential. She surprised me by asking if I had any pets. When I mentioned Cleo she hunched forwards, causing her crystals to clatter.

"A black cat is a perfect familiar for a witch," she said. "A spirit will often manifest in a black cat's body and attach itself to a witch to help her on psychic levels."

"You mean Cleo could help my dreams come true?" I asked.

The witch laughed, an ordinary old lady's laugh, not a cackle.

"On a simplistic level, I guess you could say so," she said.

We were interrupted by a tap on the door. It was Tina, casting her quick journalist's eye over the witch. From that one glance I could tell she was soaking up enough raw material to produce a thousand words.

"Sorry to trouble you," she said. "But there's someone downstairs wanting to see you. Says his name is Dustin."

Absence

A cat seizes opportunities whenever they arise.

Cleo was on edge, as if a low-grade electric current was running through her fur. Whiskers twitching, she paced the carpet. Up, down, under the table and back again. When a car hummed down the street, she froze and flattened her ears. Once the car had gone she'd regained her composure and resumed her carpet patrol. Our next-door neighbor's son shouted to a friend. She arched her back and sank her claws in the rug.

She kept returning to the desk under my bedroom window, which had the best view of the street. Its gravitational force pulled her back, and back again to survey our front garden and the houses across the road. At the sound of a bird's call she sprang up on the desk and wove through the curtains to peer out. She then dropped back to the floor with a disappointed thud. The clatter of a distant rubbish tin and she was back on the desk again, scanning the neighborhood before jumping down again to resume her restless stride.

Then the sound she'd been waiting for—the click of the front gate. Bounding on the desk and through the curtains, she stared intensely at the figure approaching the house. Her tail unfurled and quivered with delight. She sprang to the floor and sped down the hallway toward the front door squeaking mews of delight.

When I opened the door to Philip, Cleo lunged at him and stretched her front paws up his thighs.

"She's been waiting for you," I said, as he gathered her in his arms. Cleo clambered up his fisherman's jumper, licked his neck and burrowed under his chin. Not since Cleopatra made up with Mark Antony had a reunion been so loving.

The children's welcome was more cautious. Lydia glanced up from a wooden jigsaw puzzle she was working on with an expression that implied a certain amount of groveling would be required if she was ever to take Philip seriously again. Rob emerged from his bedroom door and nodded politely.

As weeks melted into months, warmth and trust gradually returned. The bond we'd had before grew even stronger. Even though I tried to keep part of my heart cordoned off in case it was shattered again there was no doubt I loved—we all loved—Philip.

Late one Sunday afternoon he bundled us all—including Cleo—into his car.

"Where are we going?" I had a longtime aversion to secrets and surprises.

"You'll see."

With Cleo perched on Rob's knee and Lydia beside them, the atmosphere in the backseat was surprisingly genial.

"Are you taking us to a circus?" Lydia asked. Her latest ambition was to become what she called an "upside down lady" in a pink sequin bodysuit and matching feathers hanging from the roof of a circus tent.

"Not this time," Philip replied. I was impressed how quickly he'd learned parents' language—using the word "no" sparingly.

"What are we going to the museum for?" Rob asked as we turned into the botanic gardens that lead up to the museum.

"You'll find out."

Philip drew to a halt in the same parking lot I'd used that evening we'd first met. He asked us to wait in the car for a minute and disappeared up the steps.

"Are we going to see dinosaurs?" Lydia asked.

"We can't," Rob replied, "it's too late. The museum's closed."

"That's right," I added. "It's nearly sunset."

A gold medallion sun sank in cotton-candy clouds. Long shadows stretched from the columns in front of the museum. It was a perfect night, an almost exact replica of how it had been when we first set eyes on each other. It didn't take much to envisage the bridal party standing on the steps and that powerful surge of recognition at the sight of my handsome army boy. I still wasn't certain if my physical reaction had been the result of a cosmic explosion of soul mates colliding—or simply undiluted lust.

Philip reappeared and beckoned us to follow him up the steps. We clambered out of the car. Normally, Rob would have left Cleo in the backseat, but he seemed to sense something momentous was about to happen. He carried her up the steps, while I took Lydia's hand.

To my surprise, Philip was standing where I'd first seen him, in a shaft of evening sun slightly to the right of the museum doors.

"There's something I want you to see," he said, standing aside and holding out his hand. He seemed to be pointing toward a concrete window frame so recessed and steeped in shadow it was difficult to notice anything unusual about it. I was beginning to wonder if Philip wasn't as straightforward as I'd imagined.

"Look closer," he smiled.

To my astonishment, hidden in the deepest recess of the window was a small navy blue box. Inside the box was a diamond ring. In front of Rob, Lydia and Cleo, he slid it on my finger.

"How did you get the right size?" I asked, appalled at my lack of romance but genuinely impressed.

"Stole a ring from your jewelry box. Hoped you wouldn't notice. Did you?"

I shook my head. It was impossible to answer. I was too busy choking back happy tears.

We agreed a long engagement would suit us all under the circumstances. No date was set, but we thought a year or so would give the family time to become fully integrated. I was only 36 and there was plenty of time if (heaven forbid) Philip felt the need to have a child from his own biological blueprint. Even though I felt sheepish telling crusty journalistic friends I was embarking on an engagement long enough to satisfy Jane Austen, it seemed the best way to go about things. This was no normal marriage. It was a union between one man, three people and a cat. All parties needed to feel comfortable.

I was just getting used to the idea of wearing an engagement ring when an important-looking envelope arrived in the post.

◆

"Cambridge must be crazy!" I said, passing Philip the letter. "They've accepted me."

He laughed, folded me in his ridiculously sinewy arms and said he always knew they would. The timing was perfect in many ways. He'd just been accepted into the Swiss business school IMD to study for an MBA (sometimes I wondered if he might be planning to drown in a sea of initials). Once I'd finished the Cambridge fellowship, the kids and I could join him in Lausanne for the rest of the year . . .

Cambridge. Switzerland. It couldn't possibly work. I'd have to leave Rob and Lydia in New Zealand for three months—and Cleo for an entire year! It was impossible. I'd write back to the university, thank them for their generosity and decline.

But Philip urged me not to turn them down. When would another opportunity like this turn up? Steve and Mum agreed with him. Mum offered to look after the children for the first month I was away, and Steve would have them for the remaining two. Cleo gazed at me steadily. Was she daring me to go or stay?

After Cambridge, Lydia would join us in Switzerland and learn French (people said it would be a breeze). Rob said he'd rather stay in his New Zealand high school and visit us during holidays. It was a wild, unrealistic plan with more hidden potential for disaster than an Angolan minefield. We decided to do it.

Cleo helped us interview people willing to rent the house while we were away. First on the doorstep was Jeff, a clean-cut accountant in a blue and white checked shirt. He seemed charming, but Cleo hissed at him and hid under a chair. An hour later Virginia, an aromatherapist, arrived in a haze of silk scarves and patchouli oil. Cleo eyeballed Virginia from a vantage point on top of the bookshelves. When Cleo insisted on claiming higher ground over someone like that it was never a good sign. Lines would be drawn in the litter box. Threats would be exchanged. A battle of wills was bound to follow. I'd already explained to her over the phone that the cat was part of the deal, in fact probably the more important part.

Virginia glowered back at Cleo and said, "One of the reasons I was attracted to aromatherapy was that cats make me sneeze. However, I've discovered that if a cat is given weekly baths in lavender oil my sneezing problem practically vanishes. Then I just have to deal with watering eyes, but homeopathy could be . . ." I let Virginia drone on as she drained her cup of peppermint tea, then thanked her for her interest.

Personally I warmed to Audrey, a flamboyantly dressed woman in search of a setting to begin her new life since her husband had run off with a massage therapist of undetermined gender. She turned pink with pleasure when I admired the magnificent necklace draped in layers over her breasts. It was a cross between one of those ribbons police stretch around crime scenes and something I'd seen hanging in my cousin's cowshed. An Italian designer piece, she said, created by a one-armed artist whose work was gaining value by the day.

Our house, she said, was perfect because there was plenty of room for her to dabble in her weekend hobby, sculpturing massive genitalia out of polystyrene, assuming we didn't mind her transforming Rob's bedroom into a studio. Fortunately, Rob wasn't home to have an opinion. As Audrey stood in Rob's doorway mentally erasing his model airplane collection and replacing it with monoliths of passion, a shadow flicked between her ankles. Audrey's reflexes were fast enough for her to snare Cleo and press her to her bosom.

"Oh, a pussy!" she boomed. "A house isn't a home without a furry friend like you!"

Cleo didn't share Audrey's enthusiasm for a bonding session. In fact, she was more interested in Audrey's necklace than Audrey. She raised a paw and patted a silver bauble inquisitively.

"I think perhaps you should put her back down," I suggested nervously.

"Nonsense! Pussy knows I adore cats, doesn't he?"

"She's a she, actually . . ."

As I tried to disengage Cleo from the necklace, she caught the bauble between her teeth and crunched. Like the first boulder in an avalanche, it tumbled to the ground. In an unstoppable flow of slow motion the bauble was then followed by a cascade of beads, gems and ribbon. Audrey shrieked. Not even the one-armed master would be capable of restoring the pile of festive rubble that now lay at her feet.

Audrey declined my offer to string the beads together again, or at least find somebody who might be able to. I grabbed an old supermarket bag and shoved what was left of the artwork into it. She was gracious enough to leave without strangling me. Or Cleo.

I was starting to feel desperate. Was nobody right for Cleo? Finally Andrea, a young doctor with green eyes and a froth of dark curls, arrived. She swore she was a cat person and would take good care of Cleo. She didn't try to seduce Cleo as others had and failed. She simply looked around the house and asked questions in an easygoing way. As Andrea stood to leave, Cleo arched her back in a sensuous curve and invited Andrea to pat her. With our cat's paw print of approval, we signed Andrea up.

I knew that as well as being capable of great affection Cleo was tough and independent, a survivor. Nevertheless, I worried. Sinking my nose into her fragrant fur, I prayed we'd see her again. The prospect of leaving the kids for three months was like chopping an arm off and putting it in the freezer. I tried to tell myself it wasn't going to be an amputation like losing Sam, but a mere putting on ice. Mum and Steve assured me the children would be fine, especially with Anne Marie's help. I knew all three of them loved Rob and Lydia, but they couldn't provide that unique combination of neuroticism and adoration that is a mother's love. They kept telling me three months would fly. Philip assured me he was going to be engrossed by his pressure-cooker MBA squeezing a two-year course into one.

Cambridge has been home to the best of Britain's grey matter for centuries. Being clever people, the inhabitants have arranged to live in one of the most picturesque towns on earth. Its thirty-one colleges, ancient and modern, are tossed loosely together around the river Cam, which can be sluggish or romantic, depending on its mood. Even on that first day in the knifelike January air, the beauty of Cambridge dragged me out of internal melodrama. The turrets of King's College Chapel pointed skywards with such delicacy they were surely fashioned by bees, not human hands.

"Miss Brown, we're expecting you," said a voice that sounded as if it came directly from God. It carried knowledge, power, authority—and belonged to the college porter.

Something about the porter reassured me I was part of his scene now and everything would be okay. After he showed me to a large, comfortable room overlooking four fruit trees, I spread photos of the children, Philip and Cleo on every available shelf. And burst into tears.

Everything about Cambridge was unfamiliar. Back home, January is one of the hottest months of the year. Even though I knew England was going to be cold, I hadn't imagined the chill would penetrate every form of clothing and footwear I owned. The English version of the sun dragged itself out of bed at half-past seven and hovered in the air like a reluctant twenty-watt bulb before collapsing into the gloom around three p.m.

Nevertheless, I adored the oldness of Cambridge. The cobblestones, the creaking colleges, the dreaminess of boy soprano voices wafting towards what must surely be heaven at Evensong in King's College Chapel (which, by the way, is nothing short of a cathedral). I loved the quirkiness of Cambridge and its adherence to rules so ancient nobody can remember why they exist. Only college Fellows are allowed to walk on the grass (though I never dared, in case I was the wrong sort of Fellow). Because most of Cambridge's rules serve no apparent practical purpose, there's a pleasant tolerance of odd behavior. If, for instance, a professor turns up at a formal dinner wearing a diving suit and mask (it was rumored one had) he was simply adhering to some tradition nobody else could recall.

Everywhere I went in Cambridge there were cats. Being hopelessly cat-sick, I tried to befriend the fat marmalade feline who sat on the brick wall behind the fruit trees. He scurried away at the sight of me.

One day I saw a black tail disappearing around the corner of an ancient church. My heart leapt in recognition. Logically, I knew it wasn't Cleo, but maybe the creature carried some of her spirit. But by the time I'd clambered over the slippery paving down the side of the church the cat had disappeared.

A smug tortoiseshell stretched himself in front of a professor's open fire and yawned. He opened one eye, licked his chops, ran a lazy paw over one ear and fell asleep. His claws snapped open and shut. His tail twitched. No doubt he was dreaming of mice.

Homesickness was such a full-time job during the first few weeks there was hardly time for research. I wrote to Philip, sent postcards and letters on tape to the children every day. Cleo made regular appearances in my dreams. One night I saw her three times the size of the Ardmore Road house. With her head resting on the chimney, she stretched her front paws around the windows and meowed. Her meow was like the roar of the Metro-Goldwyn-Mayer lion. Maybe it was her way of saying she was safe and fulfilling her duty as protector of the home. Unable to sleep, I pulled on two pairs of socks and stumbled down the stairs. The one black phone that house residents shared was mercifully free. I listened for the pulse of the phone ringing at the other end and was about to hang up when someone answered.

"Andrea?" I shouted.

"What time is it?" she mumbled in a voice heavy with sleep.

"Sorry. Have I woken you?"

"It's all right." Damn. I *had* woken her up. "I was sleeping in. It's Saturday morning. Where are you?"

"Still in the UK. I was just wondering how Cleo, I mean, *you* are getting on. Any problems with the cat, I mean house?"

"I had a rugged night," she replied. "Cleo jumped through the skylight onto my bed when I was fast asleep. It was terrifying. I thought she was a burglar."

That was the start of a series of phone calls across the globe focusing on the topic of an eccentric black cat. Andrea soon discovered Cleo's three great passions: expensive items, anything made with love, and stolen goods.

"I was heading out to work the other morning when my handbag—not the cheap copy I bought in Bangkok, the genuine Gucci one—anyway, it seemed extra heavy," she said. "Lucky I looked inside. Cleo was curled up in there! She looked all expectant, like she was sure I was taking her to work with me. She loves that bag. But honestly, how can she tell the difference between the copy and the genuine article?"

She'd always had a nose for quality. If Cleo was looking for something to sharpen her teeth on she'd favor cashmere over wool, Egyptian cotton over polyester, leather over plastic, even high-class expensive plastic.

The next phone call featured the tablecloth Andrea's mother had embroidered for her twenty-first birthday present. Andrea had arrived home one evening to find Cleo had dragged it off the table and was curled up asleep on it.

"She" s got this sixth sense," I explained apologetically. "She knows when something's been made with love."

A few weeks later Andrea complained the laces of her running shoes, left and right feet, had disappeared.

"Go into the garden and look in the ferns behind the goldfish pond," I said.

Following instructions Andrea discovered not only both shoe-laces (soggy and frayed) but several socks she" d assumed had been stolen off the clothesline by a neighborhood foot fetishist.

"I'm so sorry," I echoed across the oceans. "I didn't realize she was going to be such a handful."

Andrea was surprisingly forgiving. In fact, she" d found Cleo so interesting she" d enrolled in night classes in animal behavior.

"Cleo has classic separation anxiety," she said. "She needs lots of activities to make her more independent. I've bought her a few toys to keep her occupied. They seem to be helping, but she still prefers my shoelaces. As for jumping up on the table . . ."

"We've tried to stop her, Andrea, but she thinks she runs the joint."

"Well, I've developed the perfect solution. A water pistol."

"You squirt her?"

"Only when she's up on the table. Right up the backside. She's a fast learner."

I felt like the mother of a delinquent child receiving reports from its correctional institution. Nevertheless, Andrea was obviously fond of Cleo and it sounded like her methods were working. I wasn't going to complain if she ironed out some of our cat's quirks in our absence.

The next time we spoke Andrea told me about the personal trainer she'd hired. Roy visited the house twice a week and, according to Andrea, Cleo always knew when it was Tuesday or Thursday—a Roy Day. She waited in the front window until Apollo in a tracksuit opened the front gate. She then bounced to the front door, eager to find out what he'd brought her to play with this time—stretchy bands, balls? The moment Roy unfurled his exercise mat on the floor Cleo spread herself on it and rolled on her back, stretching her arms and legs, flicking her head side to side, watching for Roy's admiration.

"Anyone would think Roy's been hired for Cleo's fitness training," Andrea grumbled with (thank heavens) a smile in her voice, but she did confess to feeling resentful at times. Whenever Roy engaged Andrea in a particularly harrowing set of sit-ups, Cleo would upstage her by burrowing her head under the exercise mat or engaging Roy in her version of wrestling— wrapping her paws around his ankles and kicking him with her hind legs.

Upside down, her toes clinging to the Swiss ball while she attempted twenty-five push-ups, Andrea could sense Roy's attention wandering to the feline flirting with him from behind the curtains. Roy was a self-confessed dog person, but he was beginning to change his mind. He asked Andrea where he could get a cat like that. She recommended house-sitting for unusual families who'd taken off overseas.

Even though Cambridge opened fascinating new worlds to me, nothing surpassed the joy of reuniting with Lydia and Philip after three months. On the pretext of having important business in Ireland, wonderful Mary, the fashion reporter, accompanied

Lydia from New Zealand. Lydia rewarded her by throwing up orange juice on Mary's jacket as the plane flew out of Auckland.

We met at Heathrow before flying to Geneva and boarding a train that wove along the lake front. The train stopped briefly at chocolate-box villages on its way to the medieval town of Lausanne.

I promised five-year-old Lydia she'd adore her new school and would be speaking French in no time. Wrong on both counts. Apart from having a regime as rigid as the Swiss Alps, the Swiss school was a nightmare for Lydia. She couldn't understand a word anyone said. As we staggered up the vertical path to the local primary school every morning, I tried to divert her attention to rows of tulips standing to attention alongside the path, or the Alps sprinkled with icing-sugar snow across the lake. She always had a "sore tummy" by the time we reached the school gates. I hated leaving her red-faced and in tears as I abandoned her to the care of her teacher. Madame Juillard's kindness turned out to be a form of inadvertent cruelty. She spoke to the class in French, then repeated everything in English for Lydia. As a result, Lydia remained unable to communicate with her classmates.

The one subject Lydia excelled in was swimming, due to long summers spent on New Zealand beaches. The Swiss sports teacher was intrigued by the Antipodean tadpole. Despite the humiliation of a preswim shower and the insistence on a bathing cap being worn at all times, Lydia could slap out a length of the indoor pool in her deep-sea overarm. Unable to relate to the wild freedom that creates a young surfer, the teacher amused us by suggesting Lydia had a future as a synchronized swimmer.

While I was flat-out failing to meet the standards of Swiss hausfrau-hood, Philip slogged through punishing hours at business school. On one of his rare days off when we were sailing up a mountain slope in a gondola not much bigger than a vitamin pill, Philip took my hand and remarked that the skin under my engagement ring was turning a delicate shade of green. I was startled to discover he was right. Our year's betrothal was past its use-by date. He suggested if we were going to tie the knot, Switzerland was as good a place as any to do it. Besides, we both liked the idea of getting married far away from those who regarded our unusual setup as a source of gossip and amusement.

There are the Swiss Alps, chocolates, banks, watches, cheese and cuckoo clocks. While Switzerland is famous for many other things besides (including giant mountain horns and nuclear shelters for every household) it is not widely feted as a wedding destination. We were about to find out why.

◆

If there was a competition for the most difficult place on earth to get married in, Switzerland would win the prize. But then, Philip and I had a talent for doing things the hard way. We decided the land of clocks and chocolate was ideal for us to tie the knot. Someone should have warned us. As usual, we were insane.

When he wasn't studying the machinations of international business, Philip was warring with petty officials, who demanded to see and stamp every document that had our names on it (from birth certificates and proof of my divorce to Girl Guide sock-darning awards). After weeks of phoning and faxing lawyers across the globe, the Swiss officials were finally satisfied. Every scrap of paper was signed, countersigned and delivered in triplicate. But that wasn't enough. They then demanded to know how many facial moles our parents and grandparents had, at what age they had sex for the first time and which side they slept on at night. The truth is, Swiss officials don't want people getting married in their country, and they'll do everything in their power to stop it. They don't approve of holy union. It's too much paperwork. They'd rather people lived in sin.

The best thing about getting married in a foreign country is it's so inconvenient that the few guests who *do* make the effort to turn up sincerely want to be there. We arranged the wedding to take place in the September holidays, so Rob and other family members could share the occasion. I bought a cream suit and matching hat. We took a day trip across the lake to Evian to buy Lydia a French party frock with a lilac sash and stiff petticoat straight out of *The Sound of Music*.

Around forty guests turned up for the wedding. Most of them wanted to stay in our miniscule apartment. We practically had them sleeping in wardrobes. The living area was set aside for itinerant Romanians. Mum and Rob slept in Lydia's room.

Without being biased I have to say it was the best wedding I've ever been to. It was in an exquisite medieval church on the shores of Lake Geneva. Our weekend honeymoon was friendly, too. Five guests, including the bride's mother and children, accompanied us to the dreamy shores of Lake Maggiore in northern Italy. The only thing missing was a small black cat.

After the guests dispersed, Philip returned to his executive sweatshop. Golden autumn days leaked into sleety grey. Cobbled streets that had been picture-book quaint in summer faded to charcoal drawings. We never adjusted to the ferocity of European cold. No matter how thick our socks, our toes became ice.

At the end of our year in Switzerland I wasn't sad to leave. The feeling appeared to be mutual. Officials at Geneva airport decided we were such an unlikely trio we had to be terrorists. They took us aside to interrogate us. How could we possibly be married? Whose child was she, anyway? When I swore we'd packed no guns, they knew they had us. We were escorted into a room, where I was made to unpack my suitcase to reveal a weapon of minimal destruction—my umbrella.

On the way home we had a few days' stopover in New York with my old friend Lloyd. He knew all the right places to take a girl. What gay man doesn't? I made excuses to take a break from the sightseeing, sneaked into Kmart and bought a pregnancy testing kit. Back at Lloyd's I hurried upstairs past his African mask collection and shut myself in his bathroom. Holding the test stick to the light, it was hard to stop my hands trembling long enough to read the result. Hallelujah! A little plus sign appeared.

Patience

To wait is merely to consider the clouds for a while.

"Cleo is *how* old?" Rosie asked over the phone.

"Ten," I replied.

"Amazing!" said Rosie. "I never thought she'd live that long."

"Living with us, you mean?"

"Well, yes, frankly. You must be doing something right."

One of the many ways in which cats are superior to humans is their mastery of time. By making no attempt to dissect years into months, days into hours and minutes into seconds, cats avoid much misery. Free from the slavery of measuring every moment, worrying whether they are late or early, young or old, or if Christmas is six weeks away, felines appreciate the present in all its multidimensional glory. They never worry about endings or beginnings. From their paradoxical viewpoint an ending is often a beginning. The joy of basking on a window ledge can seem eternal, though if measured in human time it's diminished to a paltry eighteen minutes.

If humans could program themselves to forget time, they would savor a string of pleasures and possibilities. Regrets about the past would dissolve, alongside anxieties for the future. We'd notice the color of the sky and be liberated to seize the wonder of being alive in this moment. If we could be more like cats our lives would seem eternal.

I wasn't sure what sort of reception we'd get from Cleo. A year is a long time to be away from someone you love. There was a chance she wouldn't recognize us. No doubt she'd shifted loyalties to Andrea. That would be understandable. We'd fled while Andrea fed.

As the cab pulled up outside our front gate in Auckland I was relieved to see the house spread like a familiar smile behind the fence. Shrubs in the front garden were a little taller. Wisteria had increased its stranglehold around the veranda posts. I scanned the windows and the roof for signs of a small black cat. Nothing. Andrea, who'd moved out the day before, had assured us our cat was still alive. Maybe she'd tactfully forgotten to mention that Cleo had gone feral.

With a boulder in my chest I helped Philip and Rob unload our suitcases from the cab. The front gate opened with its familiar complaint. The wind in the bottlebrush flowers held its breath.

"Cleo!" Rob called in the man's voice that had croaked its way into his larynx.

A black shape trotted down the side of the house in our direction. I'd forgotten she was so tiny. Her pace was businesslike at first, as if she might be heading out to check for spiders in the letter box. She hesitated, pricked her ears and scowled at us. For a moment I thought she might drop her tail and scurry under the house.

"We're home, Cleo!" Lydia cried.

The cat meowed gleefully and sprinted towards us. We dropped our bags and ran to her, each of us fighting for turns to hold the purring bundle and smother her with kisses. Even though Rob and Lydia had sprouted over the past year, she remembered all four of us.

Once we were inside, the warmth of her welcome cooled. Cleo decided we needed punishment for our absence. She asked to be let outside and perched on the roof for several hours. After we'd unpacked I lured her down to ground level with a bowl of her old favorite—barbecued chicken. Halfway through her meal she looked up at me and winked as if to say *So, pregnant* again? *Can't you humans control yourselves? Oh well. Guess I can put up with a few more years being dressed up in baby clothes and wheeled around in a doll's pram.*

Early in the pregnancy I went to a specialist and begged him to anesthetize me from the neck down for the birth of my fourth child. He agreed. At the age of thirty-eight I even had a medical title—Elderly Multigravida (which, by the way, any aspiring rock band in search of a name is welcome to). To reinforce the notion I had everything to fear he showed me a chart of the increased rate of birth defects as mothers approach forty. I left his offices feeling old. Sick and old. Following his advice I underwent invasive tests, one of which brought on worrying contractions. The tests showed the baby was healthy. And a girl.

With Cleo curled on my lap one afternoon, I phoned Ginny in Wellington. Instead of laughing at my vision of a high-tech birth, all bright lights and scalpels, she put me onto a magnificent midwife, Jilleen.

The moment I opened our door to Jilleen the baby somersaulted inside me. Jilleen had the kindest brown eyes. Her small hands were crossed neatly in front of her body. I knew this was the woman who would deliver our child despite the fact that we'd never thought of ourselves as home birth people.

◆

A smudge of cloud crossed the moon. Schubert's music wrapped itself tenderly around the room. An open fire flickered shadows of Philip, Cleo and Jilleen against the wall. Time dissolved. We welcomed each muscular surge the way a surfer greets a wave, with concentration and respect. As the contraction reached its peak Jilleen taught Philip how to massage the pain away with gentle circular movements around my belly. Katharine tumbled pink and disgruntled into the world around two in the morning in her big brother's bedroom. Our support team (including Anne Marie and a local doctor) glowed with that sense of achievement seen on the faces of people who have plunged off a bridge with elastic bands attached to their ankles. Lucky for Rob, he was staying at his dad's house that night. We weren't even going to tell our sixteen-year-old son exactly where the baby had been born in case he refused to ever sleep there again. Our plans were quashed when he discovered an acupuncture needle on his bedcovers and demanded to know the truth. To my surprise he wasn't the slightest bit squeamish that his room had doubled as a delivery suite. In fact, he seemed almost proud of the fact.

Time is said to heal everything. Certainly on the surface our lives were looking good. I no longer dreaded parent-teacher interviews at Rob's school. He'd worked hard. The tone in the teachers' voices had changed. Instead of learning difficulties, they spoke of career options like medicine or engineering. His final-year marks were dazzling enough to earn him a scholarship to embark on an engineering degree at university.

I was happy, too, and grateful for the loving stability Philip brought us. Nevertheless, there was part of our lives that Rob and I tucked away and seldom talked about, certainly not in the company of others.

"Sometimes I feel as if our lives have been split in two," he said one day when the house was silent except for the mews of Cleo pacing in front of the fridge. "There was the existence we had with Sam, and the one after he died. It's almost as if we've had two separate lives."

I had to agree. Few things bridged those two worlds, apart from a handful of friends and relatives, and the small black cat Sam had chosen for us all those years ago. Even though we laughed, worked and played, our grief was still real, unresolved in many ways and buried deep inside. Concerned neither of us had undergone professional grief counseling, I sometimes embarked on "Remember when Sam . . ." stories to encourage Rob to acknowledge our previous life. We thumbed through photo albums, talked and smiled. But to say time had healed us was a lie. Although we'd encompassed the enormity of losing Sam, we were still emotional amputees. We'd lost a limb when he died. After so many years the stump was invisible to almost everyone, apart from Rob and me.

Rob sprouted into a tall, handsome young man. He was a strong swimmer and, with Philip's encouragement, a triathlete and yachtsman. While I sometimes worried about his emotional well-being his physical health was never a concern. He had an enviable ability to shrug off any virus within a day.

Watching him plunge into the surf I sometimes imagined his older brother alongside him. What would Sam look like by now? Probably a little shorter than his younger brother, but even-featured and no doubt handsome in his own way. I wondered what byways that unconventional streak might have taken Sam on. Maybe he'd have turned my hair grey dabbling in drugs and embarking on an uncertain career in filmmaking. Alternatively, he may have become a mother's dream, sailed through law school and be halfway to owning a house in the suburbs. Time-wasting fantasies were no use.

During the holidays after his first university year Rob, Philip and I were walking to the local shopping center. Rob suddenly turned pale and said he felt unwell. "Sick?" I said. "You're never sick." Rob was equally bewildered. Such a stranger to illness, he had no idea about the etiquette of throwing up in public. Instead of bending discreetly over the gutter, he spun about, showering us with his breakfast. I assumed he'd eaten a dodgy hamburger and would recover in no time. I assumed wrong.

He took to his bed and was unable to eat or drink for several days. His GP assured us it wasn't serious and wouldn't last long. But by the end of the week he was severely dehydrated and admitted to hospital, where he was diagnosed with ulcerative colitis, an inflammatory bowel condition, cause unknown. Rob's attack was diagnosed as very severe.

I sat helpless at his bedside, watching him grow weaker by the day. Once again I mustered all my life-giving power as his mother and willed him to get better. Yet again it seemed to fail. Several times I excused myself to find an alcove to weep in. The prospect of losing another son was unbearable.

A young surgeon in a green gown fresh from theater stood over the bed. If Rob didn't respond to the drugs and his already swollen colon expanded another centimeter, he said, the entire lower bowel (more than two meters long) would have to be removed. The surgeon described the operation as Big.

A tower was under construction outside Rob's hospital window. I willed time to pass, so we could move forward to a happier phase, when the building was finished and Rob (please every deity that ever existed) was well again. The more I bullied the minutes to speed into hours, the more begrudgingly they crawled. Sometimes they seemed to stop altogether, like belligerent donkeys on a mountain pass.

Rob and I reenacted his babyhood. I stroked his hair and helped him sip an unpalatable canned drink that contained essential nutrients. I tried to find ways to help him feel better. Reducing his fear was difficult when I was almost equally terrified. A rose quartz crystal on his stomach seemed to help soothe violent seizures of pain. His face always lit up when he was told someone was praying for him or sending healing energy. Rob welcomed a visit from Patrick, a psychic healer. When Patrick took his hand Rob said he felt an invisible force holding his other hand.

I stuck a photo of a mountain glowing pink in a sunset above his hospital bed. Rob looked up at it and said he'd get there someday. He'd always dreamed of taking time out to work on a ski field.

Fleets of doctors and surgeons visited Rob in the mornings. While they claimed to be using blood tests and X-rays to determine if Rob needed surgery, they seemed to rely more on how he looked and responded to them.

As they drew close to making the grim decision, I urged Rob to drag himself out of bed and walk down the corridor when the doctors were due. The effort of struggling fifty meters to the showers was enormous. Rob could hardly walk, let alone wheel the drip he was attached to. As we glided painfully past the team of doctors, their faces froze with astonishment. Rob's triumph at that moment was up there with winning an Olympic marathon.

The surgery was put on hold. Rob's condition slowly improved. We knew he was on the mend the night we found him sitting in the ward's television room.

"How do I look?" he asked Philip.

Not great, to tell the truth. Rob had lost more than twenty pounds through his ordeal. His skin glowed white against his red bathrobe, and he was still attached to a drip. Nevertheless, the return of masculine vanity was the best sign yet.

He was prescribed hefty doses of steroids for the foreseeable future and warned that his colon might eventually have to be removed. By the time he was allowed home Rob was a skeletal version of his former self. Just weeks earlier he'd been water-skiing, rising from the lake like a young Apollo. It was hard to believe all that muscle and tan could evaporate so quickly. He was too weak to walk to the parking lot. He waited on a bench outside the hospital doors while I collected the car.

We'd tidied and freshened up his bedroom at home, but more than anything he wanted to be outside. I set up a chair and blanket for him in the garden, where Cleo quickly joined him.

"I never realized the sky was such an intense blue," he said as the cat nestled into the folds of his trousers that were now several sizes too big for him.

He examined the grass, trees and flowers with the peeled-back clarity of one who has been close to death.

"The colors are so bright," he said. "The birds, the insects. I used to take them all for granted. It's a miracle. I hope I always see the world this clearly."

As soon as he was strong enough, Rob packed his ancient car to the roof and drove south. Miraculously, the car held together long enough to get him to the far end of South Island. He spent the winter skiing and making coffees in a ski field cafe near Queenstown. After that, he was ready to get back to university and finish his degree.

But his health was far from perfect. Although he suffered regular "flare-ups" the steroids ensured none were as bad as the first attack. With a stony sense of dread I noticed the steroid doses had to be increased every few months to keep his condition under control.

In case we were lapsing into an assumption that life was dull, Philip arrived home from work one evening to announce he'd had a promotion. The only complication was the job was in Melbourne, Australia.

Missing

A cat reserves the right to disappear without explanation.

My habitual terror of flying was replaced by a different neurosis—cat-in-the-hold anxiety. What if Cleo was freezing back there? Or if her carrier had been placed alongside a pit bull terrier with anger management issues? My ear was cocked for the sound of muffled meowing from the plane's rear. A pair of stewards performed the flight instructions with the flourish of chorus members from *Priscilla, Queen of the Desert*— "Should an oxygen mask appear, bat your eyelashes, swoosh that plastic tube and gyrate those hips!" Clattering trolleys, yelling babies and pilot's announcements drowned all hopes I had of hearing distress calls from Cleo.

I tried not to worry. There was a chance she wasn't even on our plane. We'd been told she might arrive up to twenty-four hours later than us.

The parched continent spread like a giant poppadom beneath us. Engines whined as we descended into Melbourne. Fear flipped into excitement and back again. As we climbed into a cab I savored the dry air and the giant blue sky. Everything about Australia was magnified, more confident and outgoing. I hoped we could burrow out a life for ourselves on its sunburnt expanse.

The girls regarded the move with almost as little enthusiasm as the convicts who'd been shipped to the country one hundred and fifty years earlier. Unlike the British penal system, we'd gone out of our way to make their transportation to Australia seem attractive. In short, we'd bribed them. Shamelessly. Katharine, who'd initially insisted on a kangaroo farm, settled for a Barbie house with a motorized elevator. Lydia was still working a deal to be driven to her new school in one of the horse-drawn carriages she'd seen trotting around the central city ("the one with red feathers on the horses' heads").

As the cab pulled up outside our rented villa in the leafy suburb of Malvern, I was still worrying about our cat. Poor old Cleo. She was probably languishing in some horrible transit prison for animals. Maybe I should have accepted Rosie's offer to adopt her. Rosie had pointed out that, at the age of fifteen, Cleo was the human equivalent of seventy-five years old. It was, she hinted, nothing short of a miracle our cat had survived this long, considering her rugged lifestyle with us. She'd implied that Cleo's vital organs might not be up to the rigors of jet travel. A short retirement in Rosie's cat menagerie was possibly a more humane option. Nevertheless, Cleo was woven into our family history as firmly as cat fur into a favorite blanket. We weren't perfect cat parents. But leaving her behind was unthinkable.

A lot had changed since our return from Switzerland five years earlier. After leaving school with a scholarship Rob completed his degree and decided to embark on an engineering career in Melbourne. Lydia was on the brink of becoming a teenager. Katharine was about to start school. My ex-husband Steve had married Amanda, and they'd produced a daughter. On a much sadder note, Mum had succumbed to bowel cancer and died after a few weeks of illness. Her suffering in the final days had been terrible to watch, yet she embraced death with great courage. As she'd withered to a shell of her former self, her spirit seemed to distill into dazzling purity, which blazed from every part of her. Harrowing as it was, I'd felt privileged to be alone with her as she heaved her last painful breath. I missed our phone conversations, her ceaseless encouragement, her refusal to regard life in its dimmest light.

Some things had stayed the same, however. Cleo was still undisputed queen of our household.

"There's something on the doorstep," said Rob.

There was a large box in the shadows of the front porch. I assumed it was a piece of junk the previous tenants had left behind. It had a mesh side. We approached tentatively. A pair of familiar green eyes glowered out from behind the wire.

"Look who's here!" said Philip.

The eyes glared back as if to say, *Well you certainly took your time!*

"Cleo! You're here already!" the girls cried in unison.

Typical of Cleo's style, she'd arrived in our new country hours ahead of the rest of us. Somewhere along the line she'd flashed a look at a quarantine officer. He'd recognized an Egyptian goddess when he saw one and given her first-class treatment.

Cleo devoured her first Australian meal in a matter of minutes. She was adapting faster than the rest of us. My first reaction was to reach for the phone to tell countless people back in New Zealand we'd arrived. They sounded warm and happy to hear from me, but I sensed we were rapidly becoming part of their history.

Calling home was the easy part. The hard bit was finding new everythings—from doctors and hairdressers to shopping centers and playgrounds. The most daunting "new" was discovering new friends. The importance of an amiable network of people struck home when I had to fill out school forms. For "Emergency Contact: i.e., friend, neighbor etc." I had no choice but to leave a blank space. We were stranded on a rock of anonymity. If we couldn't find new friends soon we'd have to invent some. I'd decided to work from home, sending columns back to newspapers and *Next* magazine in New Zealand. While I loved staying in touch with loyal readers it was a solitary occupation. Mulling over a computer screen in the suburbs was hardly going to raise my chances of meeting friends.

After keeping Cleo inside for the statutory two days I opened the back door for her. She nudged a tentative nose outside. Her whiskers twitched. She lifted an uncertain paw. Australia, with its concoction of garden smells mingled with possum fur, eucalyptus and parrot feathers, smelled different. Before I could stop her she slithered like a trout between my ankles and disappeared into a clump of bird of paradise.

"It's okay," I said to Katharine. "She's just exploring. She'll be back for dinner."

Dinnertime came and went. Not a whisker of Cleo. In all her fifteen years she'd never disappeared on us. Dusk faded. The sky turned the color of a bruise and it started to drizzle. Cleo hated rain. We called for her. No answer.

"She's probably sheltering under the house," I said, hoping it was true. "She'll turn up in the morning."

Rain hammered on the roof all night. It wasn't right. Australia was famous for drought and desert, not downpours. Soon after dawn I hurried out of bed to check doors and windows for a cat asking to be let in. Nothing. Losing our beloved Cleo would be a ghastly omen for our move to Australia. Philip left for his first day at work, a cloud of anxiety in his eyes. After breakfast, the girls and I slid into raincoats and trawled the neighborhood, calling for her. A grumpy white cat stared at us from a window. Across the road I heard a dog bark. While Cleo wasn't as resilient as she used to be, she was still tough. But what if Australian animals were tougher? If she encountered a rottweiler she might not be able to stare him down. Even though she could still run, she wasn't an elite athlete anymore.

Tucking the girls under their blankets that night, I tried to prepare them for heartache. "Cleo's had a long, exciting life," I said.

"Do you think she's dead?" Lydia asked.

"No," I said. "She doesn't *feel* dead, does she? I think she knows we still need her."

I couldn't help thinking the odds were against us. An old cat runaway in a new country had a survival chance of a thousand to one. With every hour that passed her chances were surely getting slimmer.

Next day the rain had eased. We searched the neighborhood again. My throat was sore from calling her name. We trailed through laneways and a builder's yard. We scoured a playground at the end of the street. There seemed no point investigating the busy main road just a couple of houses from our new place. If Cleo had ventured in that direction we wouldn't be seeing her again.

Heavyhearted, we turned into the gate. Now I really wished I'd been sensible enough to accept Rosie's offer to let Cleo spend her sunset years with a certified cat lover. We'd been crazy to move countries. Mentally deranged to think we had sufficient charm and energy to make new friends. Gulping back tears, I draped my arms around the girls' shoulders and croaked out one last hopeless "Cleeeeeeo!" The houses and trees of our new neighborhood responded with silence.

A shadow flickered in the basement of the house across the road, the one where we'd heard the dog barking. The shape pushed forwards and squeezed between some gardenia bushes. At first I thought it was some strange Australian animal, an urban wombat, perhaps. But it had ears and whiskers . . . and . . . to our great relief, Cleo trotted across the street into our arms. We never found out where she'd been and whether some other family had tried to lure her to their fridge. Whatever she'd been up to, she'd made a decision in our favor.

◆

Everything in Australia was bolder and more luridly colored—including the birdlife. I assumed Cleo would reassert her reign of terror over the feathered species once she knew her way around. But Australian birds aren't to be messed with. Assertive as Dame Edna on HRT, they have no intention of becoming a cat's breakfast.

Cleo was dazzled by the colors of the rainbow lorikeets, who set themselves up in our backyard pear tree. She ran her tongue over her lips, imagining the pretty toothpicks their green and red feathers would make. But they cackled derisively at the elderly black cat. They knew that if she got anywhere near them they'd claw her to pieces and fillet what was left of her with their beaks.

A couple of magpies decided to claim vengeance on behalf of the entire bird species. One afternoon I glanced out the kitchen window to see Cleo, head down, tail tucked under, running as fast as she could up the side of the house. Like a pair of spitfires the magpies were chasing her, swooping and diving and squawking with delight. I ran to the door and opened it just in time for Cleo to sprint inside to safety.

Our four walls couldn't protect us from everything, though. Just when we thought we were adjusting to our new life we struck our first day over a hundred. I'd always claimed to be a warm-weather person. A few extra notches up the thermometer would be nothing short of delightful. Having grown up in a country that welcomes every ray of warmth, I threw the windows and curtains open. Nothing like a good through-draft. Except this "through-draft" was hurtling straight off the sizzling Outback into our living room. Heat lumbered through the house like a monster. Instead of wafting through as heat was supposed to, it plonked itself in every room and expanded like a phantom until it filled every corner and reached the ceiling.

My arms and legs swelled to twice their size. My hair hung in damp streamers. My heart thudded in my ears. Paralyzed on the sofa, I could hardly move. I managed to drag a basket of laundry out to the clothesline. Our underwear practically caught fire in the wind.

We were all overwhelmed by the heat. It was worse for Cleo. Her black coat absorbed the warmth and distributed it through her body like a personal central heating system. She who liked nothing more than roasting herself by an open fire lay seemingly lifeless on her side, limbs rigor-mortis rigid, her tongue a rippling flag of surrender.

While hot days came and went, Rob's illness continued to debilitate him. The flare-ups were increasingly frequent and severe. At twenty-four, he was a qualified engineer, yet a normal working life was impossible. The extent of his debilitation struck me the day we took him for a bushwalk, or tried to: he couldn't walk much farther than the distance between two lampposts. His gastroenterologist told him the steroid levels he was taking were unsustainable. Rob agreed to see a colorectal surgeon.

I was concerned for him on many levels, including his social life. Having left his friends from school and university behind in New Zealand, he knew hardly anyone his own age in Australia. When I mentioned this to Trudy, one of the mothers at Katharine's school, she brought her niece, Chantelle, over to meet Rob one day. A beautiful young brunette, Chantelle filled the kitchen with her vibrant personality. Oddly, I felt a similar sense of recognition I'd experienced meeting Philip. I put it down to Chantelle's outgoing nature. She was just one of those people who's easy to warm to. Chantelle took Rob to a football game and introduced him to her younger brother Daniel. I could tell Rob had feelings for her, but hopes of anything other than friendship were futile. Not with massive surgery looming ahead of him.

Anxiety clawed at my insides. I hated the prospect of Rob undergoing such a radical procedure. Nobody wants their child mutilated. What if the surgery went wrong? If, on the other hand, he elected not to have the surgery the future would be even grimmer. One glimpse of his pale face, swollen from steroid intake, was enough to convince me. He was dying in front of our eyes.

◆

One morning I opened the kitchen door to find a plump baby thrush lying stunned on its back on the brick path. Cleo was losing her touch. Not so long ago she would have gone in for the kill by now. The baby thrush's eyes were bright, alarmed. Perched on the fence above, two adult birds, the parents, were creating the mayhem that had drawn me outside.

As Cleo crept forwards for the final lunge, my skin prickled with rage. How could she be so soft and loving one minute and a coldhearted destroyer of families the next? For once I had the opportunity to stop one of her ritual killings. I grabbed her and swept her into the house, slamming the door behind us.

All afternoon Cleo and I watched the adult birds flit between the fence and an overgrown camellia bush. Their shrieks were fractured with desperation. I understood their anguish as they urged their child to fight for life. At least they'd been spared the horror of seeing their child mutilated, I thought. Then again, those two little words "at least" always carried a shadow of dread with them.

Cleo was infuriated by my sentimentality. *It's nature, you fool*, she seemed to say. *You're only making things worse. Let me get it over and done with.*

Next morning, I imprisoned her indoors. The baby bird lay motionless in the same spot on the brick path. Its eyes were blank, its claws curled up in a gesture of astonishment. I gulped back tears. To my surprise the parents were still standing guard in the camellia bush, staring down at their dead child in disbelief. I'd never realized birds could feel grief for their lost children the way people do. As Sam had often said, the world of animals is more complex and beautiful than humans understand.

Witnessing the scene from a nearby window, Cleo licked her paws with regal nonchalance. I struggled to even like her at that moment.

Purr Power

A nurse cat is more devoted than her human counterpart,
though some of her methods may be unconventional.

The cause of ulcerative colitis and its terrible cousin Crohn's disease is unknown, though research continues. Why this cruel ulcerating of the bowel should occur mostly in young people aged between fifteen and thirty-five is a mystery, although I couldn't help feeling that, in Rob's case, unresolved grief over Sam had contributed. There is as yet no cure, apart from surgical removal of the bowel.

Rob didn't want a fuss. We drove to the hospital as if it were an ordinary day and we were heading into the city to have lunch. As the car hugged the curve of the river, I thought of the surgeon's hands. Today, I hoped they'd be working well. What can you say to a son who's about to undergo a massive operation that will permanently change (mutilate?) his body?

"Isn't the light beautiful on the water?"

He grunted agreement. If by some miracle the surgery was successful it would give him new life. I tried not to think of the enormity of what was about to happen. Eight feet of colon would be removed, and he'd return home with a colostomy bag. It wasn't supposed to be like this. He was born perfect. I'd used every ounce of my maternal powers to make him stay that way. My determination to heal him through sheer will had failed. If all went well there'd be a second operation two months later to remove the colostomy bag and give at least (*at least, at least*—what loathsome words they were) the appearance of physical normality.

Conversation was minimal. Toothbrush. Check. Razor. Check. Why couldn't he have the one thing that mattered? Good health. Uncheck. We caught the elevator to the eighth floor, where a small grey room was waiting for him. A crucifix on the wall was a reminder of previous young men who'd suffered more than their due. He sat in a chair that had arms but could in no way qualify as an armchair. At least the room had a view over the city.

"Chantelle will be in there," he said, pointing at a grey cube of a building. "The university."

My heart lurched. To have twenty-four-year-old male yearnings inside a body that refused to work properly seemed the ultimate cruelty. All the other patients on his floor were the wrong side of seventy.

Our silence wasn't awkward so much as textured.

"I love you," I said. The words conveyed a tiny percentage of my feelings for my beautiful, sensitive, cat-loving son.

"You can go now," he said, not moving his gaze from the window.

"Don't you want me to stay till they settle you in?"

He shook his head. "Tell Cleo I'll be home soon," he said.

My last glimpse of him as I left the ward was of a lonely figure sitting in a chair facing a window.

Outside on ground level, I crossed the street to find a small church. Wood-lined and colonial, it reminded me of the one in which I'd struggled so hard as a child to learn God's rules. I tried to pray again, but my conversation with God was one-sided as usual.

There was more solace to be found in the park outside, the giant soothing hands of branches reaching over me. It was easier to imagine God here among leaves and flowers that pulsated with life. Death and decay was woven into the beauty in ways that seemed natural and reassuring.

Gulping the oxygenated air, I thanked the Victorian minds that had decreed hospitals needed parks nearby. Grass and trees absorb human worries and help put them in perspective.

Six long hours later I fumbled in my handbag. My hand trembled and was so slippery I could barely hold the phone to my ear. The surgeon's voice was weary, matter-of-fact, with an upbeat edge.

"It went well," he said.

◆

Cleo and I nursed Rob through his recovery from the first operation, and a couple of months later, the second. As he regained strength he often draped Cleo over his stomach to let her throaty song reverberate through his wounds. While scientists have proven pets help people live longer, more research needs to be done on the healing potential of a cat's purr. It's a primeval chant, the rhythm of waves crashing on the shore. There's powerful medicine in it.

Cats are known to purr not only to express pleasure but also when they're in great pain. Some say the feline lullaby is comforting because it reminds them of when they were kittens curled in the warmth of their mother's fur. I wouldn't be surprised if someday the purr is proved to be much more than a lullaby, that the vibrations have potential to heal living tissue.

"Listen to that," he said one day. "It's a cross between a gurgle and a roar—a rurgle."

"Do you remember when you were little you said Cleo was talking to you?" I asked. "Was that real?"

"It felt real at the time."

"Does she still talk to you?" I asked, no longer concerned for his sanity. Years ago I'd accepted Rob had a special connection with Cleo that only seemed to bring good.

"In dreams, sometimes."

"What does she say?"

"She doesn't talk so much these days as show me things. Sometimes we go back to when Sam was alive. We'll run up and down the zigzag with him. It's like she's telling me everything's going to be okay."

Cleo straightened her front legs, arched her back and opened her mouth in a cavernous yawn. Appearing in Rob's dreams was just a pastime, as far as she was concerned.

I'd have willingly exchanged places with Rob to relieve him of his ordeals. Yet he shrugged when I said such things. In many ways, he said, the illness was a gift. I shivered when he talked that way. He sounded like an old man. Certainly, his experiences gave him a perspective well beyond his years.

"I've been through good times and bad times," he said. "Believe me, good's better. When you've tasted stale bread, you really appreciate the fluffy stuff fresh out of the oven."

Rob's body gradually adjusted to eating and absorbing solid food again, though he still looked like a survivor from a wartime prison camp. If, for some reason, his body refused to heal properly and he had complications I wondered if he'd have any strength left to muster a fight. Fortunately, he was young and he seemed have stores of vigor to draw on from his athletic years.

Cleo, a more conscientious nurse than I, trotted after him around the house, snuggling into his blankets and presenting him with the occasional get-well present in the form of a decapitated lizard.

Through our long days at home together, I had the blessing of getting to know Rob better. It's rare for a young man in his twenties to share his thoughts with his mother. In an unexpected way, his illness brought us closer together.

"I used to wish I had an easier life," he mused. "Some families sail through years with nothing touching them. They have no tragedies. They go on about how lucky they are. Yet sometimes it seems to me they're half alive. When something goes wrong for them, and it does for everyone sooner or later, their trauma is much worse. They've had nothing bad happen to them before. In the meantime, they think little problems, like losing a wallet, are big deals. They think it's ruined their day. They have no idea what a hard day's like. It's going to be incredibly tough for them when they find out."

He'd also developed his own version of making the most of every minute. "Through Sam I found out how quickly things can change. Because of him I've learned to appreciate each moment and try not to hold on to things. Life's more exciting and intense that way. It's like the yogurt that goes off after three days. It tastes so much better than the stuff that lasts three weeks."

My young philosopher in a dressing gown had theories to rival an Eastern mystic's. Yet deep down we both knew his dreams were the same as every other young person's. More than anything, he longed for love and happiness.

Connection

A cat who appears in a dream is no less real than one who
pads a kitchen floor.

The psychic cat is connected to the world in more ways than
we imagine. She can creep into a kitchen or, just as easily,
a dream. Waiting on her favorite window ledge, she knows
when her slaves are on their way home to her. Guardian of
unworldly powers, she beams a shield of protection over the
human household she has blessed with her presence. Sometimes
they are aware of her ability to slide between worlds. Mostly
they are not.

A couple of months later Rob was still as thin as a sapling in
winter and, as far as I could make out from an anxious mother's
perspective, not fully healed. Nevertheless, he insisted on planning
an Outback adventure with a couple of old schoolmates—"the
boys." They planned to drive through the desert to Australia's
red heart, Uluru, a journey that would take three weeks. To
say I worried was an understatement. Yet I had to accept that
Rob had no intention of having an "invalid" sticker attached to
his forehead for the rest of his days. He craved a normal young
man's life brimming with adventure, but the risks were enough
to turn a mother's heart to jelly.

I lectured the boys about the Outback being basically a vast
zoo for creatures armed for attack. From crocodiles and sharks

to snakes, spiders and ants, they're all expert killers devoid of affection for the human species. Even kangaroos can be killers, crashing inadvertently through drivers' windows at sunset.

They listened and nodded sagely. They weren't fools who'd go out of their way to get into trouble.

The only thing that concerned me more than wild animals was the danger of mechanical breakdown. Since his surgery, Rob had been urged to keep hydrated as much as possible. If their vehicle sputtered to a halt in some parched wilderness, lack of water could be a serious problem. The boys assured me they had plenty of spare water on board. Technically, they weren't boys anymore but young men well beyond the age of consent. I was left with no choice but to trust them.

"What are you worrying about?" Philip asked one night when I couldn't get to sleep. "Rob's mates are fantastic. You saw their loyalty when they visited him in hospital every day. They know what he's been through. They won't let him down."

Their beat-up Ford hardly looked ideal for journeying across the vast emptiness of central Australia. They insisted they were prepared with the latest snake-proof camping gear. Imagining them inching across barren terrain under a merciless bowl of blue sky, I wanted to beg them to stay home and do something safe and sensible—enroll in cooking classes, take dancing lessons. Anything but this. But I'd learned enough about parenthood to know there are many times when it's wiser to keep your mouth shut. I was hoping this was one of them.

◆

Three weeks later, when they were due to return, Cleo paced the hallway. She leapt to the window ledge, stared out at the street, then sprang back onto the floor to start pacing again. She was twitchy as a cobra on a desert highway. When I picked her up we exchanged electric shocks. Her ears flattened. She wriggled impatiently. I lowered her to the floor so she could pace some more.

"Don't worry, old girl," I said, talking to myself as much as the cat. "He'll be fine."

A waterfall of relief washed over me as their car, red with dust, turned into our street. With Cleo in my arms I ran outside to meet them. Rob uncoiled his considerable length from the backseat to accept with a dutiful grimace my embrace. Strange how the child who once stood on his toes to kiss his mother now bent and inclined his head to receive hers. Running an anxious eye over his entire six feet and more, I noticed his physical condition had, if anything, improved.

"How was it?" I asked.

"Fantastic!"

We persuaded the boys to stay on for a barbecue before they headed off. Basking in the glow of the coals, we watched the stars sparkle to life.

"Nothing like the night sky," Rob sighed. "Whenever things get too much all I have to do is think of the stars and all the things they look down on. Here on earth we think our little lives are so important. Even though we're an integral part of everything we're just tiny specks in the universe."

Cleo took the opportunity to lick some tomato sauce off his plate.

"I had an amazing experience in the desert," he continued. "One night when we were camping in a remote spot near Katherine Gorge I dreamt about a weird white cat. It had seven hearts and it was sitting on the edge of an inland sea."

"Was it a scary cat?" I asked.

"No. It was wise, like a teacher. And it talked to me."

"Oh no!" I smiled. "Not again! What did it say?"

"It told me I'd been protected for many years by a cat, that the cat had guided me to the right people. It said our world would continue to be racked with sadness and pain until we learn the most important lesson. To become everything we're capable of we must replace fear and greed with love—for ourselves, each other and the planet we live on.

"The white cat went on to say my cat guide had helped me find love on many levels. There was only one form of love left for it to teach me, and I was already further along that path than I realized. Once I'd discovered that love, the cat guardian's role on earth would be complete."

A shooting star scurried across the sky. I was lost for words.

"Funny thing is," Rob continued. "It was such an outlandish dream I told the boys about it the next morning. I described the shape of the lagoon and the surrounding hills. They laughed when I told them about the talking cat, of course. But then, a few hours later we visited a place that exactly matched the dream landscape I'd described. The lagoon, the hills. They were all there. If I hadn't told the boys about it in such detail earlier they'd never have believed me. An Aboriginal man introduced himself and told us about the area. He said it was a sacred healing ground. He pointed out seven tall mounds around the edge of the lagoon. For as long as anyone could remember, he said, the local people had called them cats."

From her vantage point on Rob's shoulder, Cleo surveyed every human face in the shadows of the barbecue flames and winked.

Forgiveness

To forgive is in a cat's nature—eventually.

One of the downsides of changing countries was that we no longer had access to reliable friends who thought nothing of looking after Cleo for us when we went away on holiday.

Even though we were getting to know our new neighbors, it seemed too soon to impose cat-minding duties on them. We'd never put Cleo in a cattery before. I was worried how a freedom lover like her would adapt to living in the feline equivalent of Guantanamo Bay for a week. She'd proved herself tough and versatile, though. I assumed she'd cope.

Assumption is a dangerous thing. A couple of days after we'd collected her from the cattery, her eyes streamed with gluey fluid. She went off her food and developed a cough. For the first time in her life Cleo was terribly ill.

Our neighborhood vet was plump and red-faced with a plume of silver hair. He prodded her with fingers the size of salamis.

"How old is she?" he asked, examining our precious cat as if she was something he'd scraped off his shoe.

"Sixteen."

He looked at me in disbelief.

"Are you *sure*?"

"I know exactly how old she is. She was given to us just after our older son died."

"Well, if you're certain she's *that* old . . ." He sighed. "I wouldn't hold out much hope for her. She should have died six years ago, according to the average life expectancy for a cat."

He was a tough vet. I hated his cold words. Some time in the distant past he must've had enough compassion for animals to envisage himself spending a lifetime working with them. But whatever sympathy he possessed had either dried up or, for some reason, wasn't directed at us. Maybe he shared Rosie's opinion of my cat-mothering skills. Perhaps his wife had left him for the orthodontist around the corner. I wouldn't have blamed her.

"I can't promise anything, but we could try her on a course of antibiotics, if you like."

If you like? Did the man imagine we were ready to give up on her?

"Yes, please. She's part of our family."

He seemed oblivious to the fact that Cleo had been guardian of our household for so long, she wasn't going anywhere as far as we were concerned.

"In that case, when you go home I'd prepare them for the worst."

The girls gulped back tears when I repeated what the vet had said. They both had memories of Cleo peering over the edge of their cradles. Cleo was practically a surrogate mother to them.

"It's just nature," I said, sounding more like Mum than I intended. "We were lucky to have her this long."

To our delight, Cleo's eyes cleared and her snuffle evaporated a couple of days later. In less than a week she was back to her omnivorous diet. No housefly, rubber band or sock was safe. Her coat regained its sheen. She danced across the kitchen table, climbed the curtains. Cleo was her old perky self. The vet may have considered her the walking dead, but as far as Cleo was concerned, she was still in her prime.

But she'd given us a warning. Even though she was doing a good job hiding it, old age was creaking its way into her joints. She slept more than she used to and seemed to feel the cold more readily.

In fact, she adapted to old age with aplomb worthy of a duchess. The meow that used to be so pretty and accommodating became an authoritative yowl. Cleo had seen every form of human behavior in her long life. She knew when to take a stand and when to disappear. She'd always known exactly where to find the escape routes. In her younger days, she'd barely twitched a whisker when Lydia had carried her around the house upside down. Not so long ago, she'd allowed Katharine to dress her in a hat and specially knitted gloves for Melbourne Cup Day. It had been an act of patience and affection on Cleo's part.

In acknowledgment of her advanced years we decided to make a few changes. Once past kittenhood, Cleo had always insisted on spending her nights roaming rooftops outside under the moon. Even in cold weather she'd preferred sleeping under the house, curled up around the central heating system. For the sake of her health, the girls and I agreed a change of lifestyle was required. She'd have to be an inside cat from now on. The trick was to find her a bed she approved of enough to sleep in.

Having monopolized and destroyed a dynasty of family beanbags, she was bound to adore the supersized beanbag I bought her from the pet shop. Sure, it was designed for large dogs, but there's no way Cleo would know.

Cleo had a built-in radar screen that could detect anything to do with dogs from a distance of a thousand kennel runs. The beanbag couldn't possibly have smelled doggy. It was brand new. Maybe it carried the thought remnants of its maker, who had mused over her sewing machine what kind of dog might end up sleeping on it—a dalmatian, alsatian or a plain old mutt.

So, despite countless demonstrations from us all showing how luxurious and comfortable the dog beanbag was, Cleo refused to go near it. We repositioned it in alluring sites around the house—in front of the fire, in the patch of sun on the kitchen floor. Our efforts were pointless. As far as Cleo was concerned the dog beanbag was disgusting.

Defeated, I flung it under the house for the rats (or whatever it was that chewed things under there). Maybe one bed wasn't enough. Perhaps Cleo was trying to tell us she needed options—a day bed and a night bed. Back at the pet shop (where the assistant was starting to treat me like an escapee from an asylum) we bought a fluffy pink cushion and a brown padded pouf, both designed specifically for cats.

We arranged the pink cushion between the sofas in the family room. It was treated with the disdain it deserved. During the day Cleo preferred perching on a sofa arm or, better still, on the belly of a reclining human who was trying to read. Not only did this position provide warmth and a sense of superiority, it was also an excellent opportunity to floss her teeth along the edges of the book's pages. The only bed she showed anything less than hatred for was the brown pouf. We set it up in the laundry where she grudgingly agreed to sleep at night, alongside her bowls and (the ultimate indignity) a kitty litter tray.

Holidays were problematic. We weren't willing to risk a cattery again. A live-in cat nanny was the only solution. Cleo's first cat nanny was our friend Magnolia.

Magnolia is one of the world's great cooks. Having grown up in Samoa, one of the few countries where people appreciate the beauty of bellies the size of hot-air balloons, she understands the meaning of quantity. Not only that, she has a gourmet's flair for quality. She stole her recipe for coconut cake from the angels. Her beef bourguignon would make Julia Child turn spinach-green with envy. So Cleo licked her chops approvingly when Magnolia arrived carrying extra cooking pots and bags of undisclosed ingredients.

"Don't you worry," Magnolia said, slipping an apron over her head. "Go and enjoy yourselves. We'll be absolutely fine. And you know I love cats. Not in a culinary sense, of course."

I kissed Cleo on her tiny forehead, but formal farewells were of no interest. Her focus was on Magnolia clattering a large preserving pan onto our stovetop. We worried about Cleo while we were away.

"She's such a sensitive animal," I said to Philip. "She's probably traumatized having a stranger in the house."

Every time we phoned, Magnolia said our cat was just fine. I didn't know if we should believe her. "Just fine" can mean anything from "just fine but she was attacked by magpies and had an eye pecked out" to "just fine but she hasn't eaten a thing."

"I can't talk now," Magnolia added. "We've got some bouillabaisse on the stove, haven't we, Cleo? Then I'm off to the market to get fresh prawns."

"Do you think Cleo's all right?" asked the girls.

We told them she probably was, but what would we know?

The girls talked us into going home a day early because Cleo was almost certainly pining for us. When Magnolia answered the door the fragrance of a Michelin-star galaxy wafted through our nostrils—warm and meaty with a hint of wine and truffles. A small plump animal was tucked in the crook of Magnolia's elbow. The creature had the expression of a movie star encountering fans on the way to the Academy Awards—"I see you, but you're not really there. Collect a signed photograph from my publicity team if you're desperate."

"Cleo!" we cried, all reaching out to hold her.

She hesitated for longer than was decent before allowing Magnolia to lower her into Katharine's arms.

"She likes her food," laughed Magnolia.

Cleo wriggled to be put on the floor and waddled away towards the kitchen. Not only had she grown chubby over the past two weeks, she'd become incredibly smug.

"I'm going to miss sleeping with her," Magnolia added. "She's so cute the way she snuggles between the sheets and puts her head on the pillow beside me."

There was still enough country girl left in me not to want to share a pillow with our cat, even our treasured cat goddess. And I couldn't cook like Magnolia.

I don't know if those were good enough reasons to punish us. Maybe Cleo was simply annoyed with us for going away. More likely it was a combination of crimes on our part. But she made her feelings clear enough by depositing a carefully placed turd in the middle of our bedcover.

◆

Live-in cat nannies became the norm every time we went away after that. During one of these sojourns a kitchen chair fell on Cleo's tail, leaving a permanent dent near the tip. The nanny apologized profusely. She said there'd been blood. Katharine shed tears over the damage. While the tip of Cleo's tail remained tender for the rest of her days, she didn't ask for sympathy. She wore her dented tail with the suave pride of a battle-scarred cavalry officer. Forgiveness for permanent injury was a straightforward process for her, simple as breathing.

I wished I shared her expertise in the art of forgiveness. We humans hold on to our hurt and nurse it, often to our own detriment. We're quick to assume the role of victim. Yet cats are and always have been at the receiving end of human maltreatment. During medieval times many thousands of them were hunted out and killed because it was believed they were inhabited by witches. In Paris during the sixteenth century thousands of people looked forward to fun outings witnessing the mass burning of bags full of cats. Even today, kittens are routinely dumped into sacks and drowned. Cats of all ages are tortured in experiments for the so-called advancement of science. In parts of Asia, a serving of cat meat is considered beneficial for women of a certain age.

Humanity has brought such suffering upon the domestic cat it's amazing they still tolerate any contact with us. Felines may not forget our atrocities against them. Yet, generation after generation, they continue to forgive us. Every new litter of kittens born helpless and mewing is an invitation to start again, for humans to lift their game. While our past behavior reveals the depths of the cruelty we're capable of, cats continue to expect better of us. We won't be worthy of considering ourselves fully evolved until we live up to the shine of trust and expectation in a kitten's eye.

+

I still thought about the woman driver who'd run over Sam all those years earlier. She used to haunt my mind. My anger towards her had been like fire run rampant. In those early days, whenever I read newspaper stories about parents forgiving the murderers of their children, I could only imagine they were avoiding honesty.

Time may not heal everything, but it gives perspective. Ford Escorts went out of style years before. I hardly saw them anymore, let alone blue ones. The car that killed Sam was probably an ashtray. The streets had given way to four-wheel-drives. I was finally able to accept fully that Sam's tragedy was hers as well. That January day in 1983 would be carved into her heart as deeply as it was on mine. Every time she slid behind a driver's wheel, or saw a blond boy crossing a street, she must have seen his ghost.

I was finally emotionally equipped to meet this woman, if it were ever possible. I'd tried throwing out a few lines. In a magazine interview I'd suggested I was ready. I wanted to put my arms around her, acknowledge the pain she must have endured all these years, and tell her I forgave her. Utterly.

A response arrived in the mail, but not the one I was expecting.

Dear Helen,

My wife showed me the recent article on you and she urged me to write to you as we both felt very sad after reading about the dreadfully difficult time you had following Sam's death.

I'm not sure if it will be of any comfort to you, but I came on the scene of the accident very soon after it had happened. The driver of the car was not there and I assumed she had gone for help. My companion went down the road to stop the traffic and I stayed with Sam—he was deeply unconscious and I am quite sure he did not suffer at all. I also think that he did in fact die while I was with him—before the police and ambulance people, who were, without exception very kind and thoughtful, arrived.

Eventually the police said it would be OK for me and my workmate to leave so we did. I was very distressed at what had happened, so much so that when I got home from work that night I had real difficulty in telling my wife about Sam. It seemed such a dreadful waste of a dear little boy's life—but it was no one's fault.

I thought about calling on you at that time but decided against it as I was a stranger and felt it would be an invasion of your privacy. I still don't know if that was the right thing to do, but I feel now that you would like to know Sam was not alone—hence this letter, and if it is even a small amount of comfort to you then I will be very pleased to have written it to you.

Yours sincerely

Arthur Judson
Christchurch

P.S. Have been enjoying your newspaper column for years.

I read the letter again and again. Shock coursed through me as I relived the events of that day from someone else's perspective, a stranger but a man of great heart. The letter I sent in return had no hope of expressing the depth of my gratitude to him. To have stayed alongside a dying boy would have taken courage, and to have written the letter almost as much. His letter had given me a greater sense of completion than anything I could have hoped from meeting the woman driver.

I kept the letter and treasure it to this day. Knowing Sam hadn't died alone or in great pain has gone a long way to easing my sorrow.

The world must be full of silent heroes like him, people who stay behind at accident scenes when it would be easier to leave. Risking their personal tranquillity, they give the greatest solace one person can provide another—the comfort of not dying alone. Then, like angels, they disappear without a trace.

Conversion

Beware the passionate convert. She may bore you with cat stories.

"Oh, look at the dear little kitten!" a stranger exclaimed when she saw Cleo posed sphinxlike on our front path.

"She's not a kitten," I explained. "She's actually very old."

"Really? She looks so . . . young."

If we could have bottled whatever gene Cleo had that made her look younger the older she grew, we'd have several beach houses, a yacht and a season pass to the space shuttle by now. I put a lot of it down to attitude. Hers, of course. Growing old wasn't a tragedy, as far as Cleo was concerned. She simply despised the whole process.

Menopausal women would have nothing to fear if they could see how willingly Cleo shed slinky youth to become an increasingly authoritative, essential ruler of our household. High priestess of the family, she expressed her views on everything from whether her fish had been properly mashed to how early human slaves should be forced out of bed. Anyone who hadn't risen by dawn could expect a screeching wake-up call from Cleo outside their bedroom door.

I too entered a phase where I was more inclined to air my opinions. Having long given up hope of changing the world, I felt it was still entitled to hear my views on everything from presidential politics to how blondes should never be let loose in four-wheel-drives. The only thing missing was a loudspeaker on top of my car through which I could inform other drivers and pedestrians exactly how they were endangering others, themselves and the planet in general.

Following nature's cycle, our nest was emptying out. Lydia took a year off from her university studies to teach English in Costa Rica. For a while, Rob moved to London, where he was working in a wineshop. If ever Rob and I needed proof of our powerful psychic connection all we have to do is try to call each other. Though we were on opposite sides of the earth, we'd often phone each other at exactly the same time. Even today when I call him his line's often engaged because he's trying to ring me.

"You'll never guess who I caught up with," he said one day, his voice tinged with excitement over the phone. "Chantelle. She's over here, teaching in one of those tough inner-city schools."

I felt a little sad when he mentioned she had a boyfriend. A good guy, Rob assured me, an Australian surfie, though it was hard to imagine what a wave-rider did with himself through the depths of an English winter. Not that Rob was lonely—he was living with a nurse from Queensland. Love's often a matter of timing and coincidence: while I knew Rob would always have special feelings for Chantelle, prospects of them getting together seemed increasingly thin.

Several months later I was devastated to hear that Chantelle's younger brother Daniel had died suddenly, of no apparent cause. While tragedy visits every household sooner or later, this was a terrible one for Chantelle and her family to endure. I hoped Rob might be able to help Chantelle with the overwhelming range of shock and sadness she'd be going through.

◆

As the only one left at home, thirteen-year-old Katharine became Cleo's assistant caregiver. "Look what my friends did last night!" she wailed one morning after having a group of girls over for a sleepover. "They're so mean! They painted Cleo's chest white!"

Closer inspection of the snowy fur revealed it wasn't painted but was white from natural causes.

Cleo developed a geriatric gait, moving stiffly from the hip joints, a sensation I too was becoming begrudgingly familiar with. Cleo gave up playing sock-er, though she kept an old sports sock of Rob's in her bed. She no longer sprang onto the kitchen bench. Likewise, my joints suffered a shortage of elastin. Creaking ligaments pleaded with me to give stairs a swerve if an elevator opened its tantalizing doors.

Our coats were changing, too. Teenage hairdressers felt duty-bound to instruct me how to make my thinning hair thick and glossy. ("Just massage a peanut-sized glob of this mousse into your scalp. I know it may seem expensive at one hundred and twenty-five dollars, but it'll last you a whole year.") Their older sisters lectured me about skin care. ("A cup of blueberries a day will have your skin looking like mine forever. And you'll never guess how old I am. I'm *really* old. I'm twenty-five.")

Free from the attentions of child hairdressers and beauticians, Cleo sprinkled black exclamation marks of fur over our sheets, our underwear, sometimes even our food.

Her black whiskers turned grey. I discovered an unsightly bristle sprouting from my chin.

Cleo and I had always enjoyed roasting ourselves in front of an open fire. Sitting too close nowadays made my legs resemble the surface of Mars. Cleo was even less fireproof. After ten minutes or so she had to stagger away from the inferno and lean against a cool wall to recover.

Quality was more important than we'd realized. I developed an irrational interest in the thread counts of bed linen and Italian stationery.

Our vision was no longer spectacular. An optometrist recommended reading glasses. (Who, me?) I chose the funkiest frames in the shop, green and blue metallic.

"What do you think?" I asked, showing them off to Philip and Katharine.

Their response made it clear. They were the type of reading glasses an old lady would choose in order to look funky.

Cleo developed strange blotches in her eyes, enhancing the impression she was in direct contact with other realities. I found a vet who wasn't tough and understood how precious she was. He said Cleo didn't have cataracts. The blotches were just a natural part of the aging process. Soft Vet wasn't so happy about her kidneys, though. He suggested we could fly her to Queensland for a kidney transplant, though the success rate wasn't high. (*A cat flown thousands of miles for a kidney transplant that will probably fail!* I could practically hear my mother wail from the depths of her plastic urn in the New Plymouth graveyard. *The world must be off its rocker.*)

Unwilling to embrace the less attractive aspects of growing older, I focused on body parts that, with some attention, could still look good. I discovered a nail salon run by a Vietnamese family who, I was thrilled to find out, could hardly speak a word of English. This meant they were mercifully free of small talk and unable to instruct me on methods of maintaining youthful hands and feet. As we got to know each other better, they greeted me with nods and smiles.

Around the same time Cleo's toenails started clicking like tap shoes over the floorboards. They weren't getting as much use as in her assassin days. Her claws had worn thin and were as flaky as miniature croissants. I was flattered when Cleo allowed herself to lie on her back in my lap while I attempted to trim her talons with Philip's nail clippers. Reading glasses perched on the end of my nose, I was terrified of hurting her. I hardly trusted myself with hedge clippers, let alone nail

trimmers and her tiny paws. Any clumsy mistakes were cor-
rected with swift gentle bites. After the first few attempts,
Cleo trusted me enough to actually purr during the procedure.
I was honored to take on the title of official manicurist and
(combing dry cat shampoo through her coat) beauty therapist.
In short, personal servant.

We'd spent long enough in each other's company for her
to know I had her interests at heart. We'd been through so
much together and found a kind of peace, not only with each
other, but within ourselves. Together we discovered the well-
kept secret that, give or take a few inconveniences, old cats
have more fun.

Cleo and I decided to become quirky about our eating
habits. I was afflicted with an obsession for chocolate, dark
chocolate to be precise, preferably seventy percent cocoa, made
in Switzerland and wrapped in something shiny involving
photos of mountains. Try as I might to divert my addiction
to Italian writing paper or thousand-thread-count sheets, I
could find nothing more mesmerizing than chocolate. Cleo
underwent an even more powerful food fixation. The word
"no" had never been of particular interest to our cat. She now
obliterated it from her understanding of human vocabulary. In
her mature years, however, she learnt exactly what the words
"Chicken Man" meant.

Whenever anyone announced they were off to Chicken
Man (to buy a rotisserie takeaway bird from the cheerful Asian
man's shop round the corner), Cleo trotted behind them and
waited eagerly at the door until they returned with the mouth-
watering parcel.

Cleo was circumspect about most food, though on the whole
she preferred it murdered or stolen. Chicken Man was in a
different league. One whiff of the freshly roasted flesh drove
her to salivating insanity. Anyone in charge of an unguarded

plate of chicken was at risk. Loyalties and past affections were forgotten as she embarked on chicken jihad.

We developed a routine of shutting her out of the room so we could have first choice of the meat.

"Poor Cleo!" Katharine would say, as an elegant black paw appeared under the door.

There was no "poor" about it. If the door wasn't closed properly, the paw slid down the side and pushed it open. Bones and paper napkins would fly through the air, plates clattered to the floor. It was chicken season for young and old.

Our food fixations were equally unattractive to outsiders. The only difference was, Cleo's didn't make her any fatter. In fact, she appeared to be shrinking. Her chest bones jutted out, the angles of her skull became even sharper and more prominent. With fur draped over her skeletal form, she resembled an amateur attempt at taxidermy.

That's not saying we didn't enjoy moments of friskiness. If the curtains were pulled tight enough and there was no evidence of human life within a five-hundred-meter radius, a determined anthropologist might still have caught a glimpse of me boogieing alone to the strains of Marvin Gaye.

Likewise, after a shower of rain, Cleo shimmied like a kitten up a tree trunk—until halfway up old age got the better of her and she slid unceremoniously back down.

Cleo's legs, once so tapered and streamlined, became slightly stumpy with lumps where (if she was human) knees and ankles would be. She never grumbled, though. I trudged off to the gym and lifted weights to combat back and neck pain that would never have developed if, like Cleo, I'd spent my life on all fours. The old person's fear of falling over would never have to be considered if we'd stayed firmly planted to the ground on four feet. Once again, our cat was proving herself a higher-level species.

While our bodies may have given the appearance of growing old, inside Cleo and I were growing up and getting stroppy. In the supermarket checkout line, people always used to recognize me as a pushover. Anyone from toddlers to old men knew they could sneak in front of me without consequences. But the new, stroppy me stood my ground when queue jumpers tried to nudge in front of me. I was even capable of an indignant "Excuse *me!*" I filled out complaint forms without hesitation and stopped thinking twice about hanging up on telephone marketers calling from Mumbai.

Cleo surpassed me by taking uppity to an art form. When our sight-impaired friend Penny visited with her guide dog Mishka, I placed two bowls of water on the floor—a small one for Cleo and a large one for Mishka. Cleo eyeballed the yellow labrador and claimed the large bowl for herself. Mishka shrunk to half her giant size and retreated to the small bowl.

Penny laughed and accepted my apologies for our pet's ungracious behavior. I explained that, as a kitten, Cleo had done the same thing to Rata. Nodding amiably, Penny sat on the floor. Mishka parked her rear end affectionately on her owner's lap. They made a charming vignette, a picture of owner and devoted dog. The image was too much for Cleo. She fixed Mishka with a glower that was so withering the poor animal skulked away into a corner and allowed Cleo to take over prime position on Penny's lap.

"And what happened to poor little Cleo?" Rosie asked when she phoned out of the blue one day.

"Oh, she's fine."

"In a better place," she sighed. "I always say there are sardines every day in Pussy Heaven."

"No, Rosie. I mean fine fine."

"She's *still alive!* You're joking! How old is she now?"

I was getting sick and tired of people asking us impertinent questions about age. "Twenty-three."

"But that's, let me see . . . something like one hundred and sixty-one in human years. Are you sure it's the same cat?"

"Absolutely."

"How did you do it? What have you been feeding her? What medication is she on?"

"Nothing special. How are Scruffy, Ruffy, Beethoven and Sibelius?"

An awkward silence. "Well, Scruffy disappeared, Beethoven had kidney failure. Sibelius and Ruffy went to cat heaven ten years ago. I always made sure they had the best of everything, not like your poor little Cleo. I'm surprised you remember their names. You never were a cat person, were you?"

"But I must be!" I replied. "I couldn't *not* be. Cleo wouldn't have stayed with us this long if I wasn't. Besides, we're both getting so old Cleo and I are practically the same person. No, dammit, Rosie. You're wrong. *I AM a cat person!*"

Not long after, Philip and I were at a restaurant celebrating our fourteenth wedding anniversary.

"I'll never forget that night you took us to the pizza restaurant and you beat Rob at that game filling in the squares."

"It was snakes and ladders, wasn't it?" he said, sipping his champagne.

"It was filling in squares. You nearly blew it that night. Not letting a boy win. I was going to send you packing."

"Were you?" he replied with a twinkle. "I'll always remember Cleo bouncing around the house like she owned the place."

"She *did* own it. Not many people would have taken us on the way you did, you know", I said, changing the subject. "A solo mum eight years older with two kids."

Rob had once said having Philip in our lives was like winning Lotto. I'd been in awe of Philip's love and commitment to all three of our children, never once making a distinction between Katharine, his biological daughter, and the other two. Their love for him in return was equally deep and seamless. I was fortunate to have spent so many years with such a rare, open-hearted man.

"Not work again, is it?" I said as he took his bleeping mobile phone from his pocket.

"It's Kath," he replied, his face grave as he listened to her distraught staccato.

"We'd better go. Cleo's having some sort of fit."

Tough Vet, Soft Vet

Chicken Man each day keeps the vet away.

By the time we arrived back home Cleo was her normal self again.

"It was so scary!" said Katharine, still flushed with shock. "She made a horrible growl, then she fell over and twitched. Her whole body seized up. She must've been in so much pain."

Listening calmly to the report, Cleo licked her paw. *I don't know what you're making such a fuss about,* she seemed to say. *It was just a little hiccup.*

After breakfast next morning, Cleo succumbed to another dreadful fit. I ran to the phone and called Soft Vet. His honey-voiced receptionist said he wouldn't be available until later in the day.

"But we need to see someone *now!*" I said.

"In that case you'll have to try another vet," she replied sharply.

For a Soft Vet he had a pretty hard-hearted receptionist. The only other vet who knew anything of Cleo's history was dreaded Tough Vet.

"If you bundle her in a blanket and bring her over he'll see her now," said Tough Vet's nurse.

As I carried Cleo to the vet's clinic, she revived enough to take an interest in the traffic and the sky. She purred lightly as I clutched her to my chest. Maybe a simple pill would do the

276

trick. On the other hand, I wasn't a fool. She was twenty-three and a half years old.

We loathed everything about Tough Vet's surgery. We didn't like the anesthetic smell of the waiting room or the bags of pet food piled in the corner like headstones. Cleo particularly disapproved of the big black labrador, its pink tongue dripping obscenely from its mouth. It was impossible to ignore the blue plastic bucket over his head. I knew exactly what Cleo was thinking: *How typical of a dog to allow itself to be shoved into such a demeaning fashion accessory.*

Tough Vet appeared from an operating room and beckoned us in. Cleo stood defiantly on the stainless-steel table while he poked and prodded parts no lady likes to share with a stranger. Kidney failure and thyroid malfunction was his diagnosis.

"How long do you want to drag this out for?" he asked, his voice drained of expression.

I heard his words and understood what they meant, but couldn't summon up any kind of answer.

"I can put her down now if you like."

Now? Immediately? The shock must've shown on my face.

"All right, I'll keep her here a few hours for observation so your family can get used to the idea," he said. "Phone me at five o'clock."

I was about to snatch Cleo back and run home with her. But the prospect of helplessly witnessing her fits all day was unbearable. Heading out his door, I hated Tough Vet with every muscle in my heart—until he called out to me.

"You can leave her blanket with me."

He'd understood that our ancient animal would be more comfortable with a piece of home to snuggle into. Maybe Tough Vet wasn't such a monster after all.

Back home, I pulled the old towels and rugs off our furniture as a reminder of how much prettier and cleaner life was going to be without a dribbling, fur-shedding old cat. Glancing at Cleo's bed in the laundry, I considered dumping the stinky thing in the outside bin—but couldn't quite do it.

No way was she going to vanish up Tough Vet's chimney. A daphne bush by the front gate would be her gravestone, if she had to have one at all.

Philip arrived home early from work to make the five o'clock call. Tough Vet invited us to pay a visit. Not a good sign. Katharine stayed home resolutely watching TV as we headed out on our morbid mission.

Tough Vet was friendlier this time. I thought it must be his "putting animals down" mode.

"She hasn't had a fit all day," he said. "She hasn't eaten anything, but her vital signs are good and her heart's strong. She's in remarkably good condition for her age."

The light in his eye said it all. Even in her decrepit state, Cleo had charmed him with her determination to defy the feline life expectancy chart on his wall.

Wrapping her in the blue blanket, he handed her back with some pills to stimulate her appetite. "Oh, and if you really want to get her eating again, there's an excellent takeaway chicken shop across the road," he added. "I don't know what he puts in them, but one whiff of that stuff and it drives all the cats crazy."

I guess a visit to Chicken Man each day keeps the vet away. Cleo purred all the way home.

I draped the old towels and rugs back over the furniture and shook her smelly bed. We were on borrowed time, but one thing Sam's death taught me is time is only ever on loan. Life can change irrevocably for any one of us at any moment. Awareness of that is what made me scan my dressing table every time I went out in case for some reason I never returned. Even though I wasn't a tidy person I didn't want to go down in history as a shockingly messy one.

I phoned Rob in Britain to update him on Cleo's latest drama.

"I've just been trying to call you, but the line was busy," he said.

"That's because *I* was calling *you*," I said, delaying the Cleo news as long as possible. "What did you want to talk to me about?"

"I can't face another English winter. People live like moles here, in the dark and underground most of the time. I've been offered an engineering job in Melbourne. It sounds great. I'll be home for Christmas."

✦

Not long after Rob's return a surprise visitor turned up on the doorstep. He was a tall dark-haired young man, with looks that were a blend of Brad Pitt and Johnny Depp. I scanned the movie-star jawline, the well-defined brow. But it wasn't until I looked into his eyes that I recognized him.

Baby-faced Jason from Rob's boyhood zigzag days had morphed into a fine adult. To receive a visit from Ginny's son was an unexpected compliment. He planted kisses on each of my cheeks, leaving me momentarily dazed. This man Jason was a far cry from the brown-haired boy with almond eyes and an impish smile. Last time I'd seen him he hadn't been much taller than my waist. I was touched his memories had been warm enough for him to turn up in person so many years later.

"Don't tell me Cleo's still alive!" he said.

"Only just," I replied. I called Rob and arranged to meet him at a cafe near his work with our surprise guest. Rob took less than a second to recognize his old friend. I basked in the glory of dining with two young men with rock-star looks. So this was how it felt to go out with two adult sons. If Sam had lived I wondered how many times we would've got together like this. Would it have felt so warm and tinged with almost unbearable sadness? Maybe there'd be no sorrow at all, just a vague pattern of irritations and assumptions families can grind themselves into.

"Do you know what my strongest memory is?" Jason asked, perusing the wine list.

"*Digging that hole!*" the boys said in unison.

I must've looked blank.

"Remember that wild bit of land below your front gate? Rob and I decided to dig a hole there. We dug for years, and it never seemed to get any deeper."

A vision of two small boys hacking into clay under the tree ferns suddenly sharpened.

"That's right," I said. "You had spades and a pickax. You probably shouldn't have been allowed that pickax. I'd be sued these days."

"That's the whole point," Jason said. "It felt manly and dangerous. Do you remember the day we found a rusty old wire mattress? We spread it over the hole and turned it into a trampoline for a while. Then we got bored with that. We took it away and went back to digging."

Even now sometimes, Rob said he wondered why the hole never seemed to get any deeper. If his adult self could return to the scene he'd finish the job in an afternoon.

"Maybe you were digging it too wide?" I said. "How deep did you want it anyway?"

"Decent-sized hole deep," Jason replied.

I felt vaguely guilty the boys' memories weren't of me teaching them Mandarin or Gregorian chants. If Jason had inherited half of Ginny's brains—she'd just finished a doctorate in midwifery—he'd have been more than capable. On the other hand, maybe letting them dig had a hand in making them into the philosophers they'd grown into.

It was hard to believe that somewhere underneath their easy manners and red-wine-drinking maturity were the same little boys who'd lived on the zigzag. Watching them I was reminded of the miraculous renewal of the Australian bush after a fire. Against the blackened outline of taller trees, banksias and wattles create fresh new undergrowth. Similarly, the boys had sprung into strong, handsome young men. During the devastation of those zigzag days I'd underestimated the resilience of nature.

Renewal

To the paradoxical cat, an ending is sometimes a beginning.

It's easy to fall in love with a kitten. Everything about its furry softness says hold me, cuddle me. In its middle years a cat can be admired for its gleaming coat and sleek athleticism. But an old cat is an acquired taste. She dribbles on cushions and uses vomiting as a form of peaceful protest. People who live with old cats make allowances. Even those who have never suffered a moment of house pride are compelled to cover furniture with old towels and blankets.

Cleo's fur thinned and carried the odor of an Egyptian tomb. She had to think several times before forcing her arthritic joints to jump onto a sofa. When strangers visited I occasionally imagined distaste flashing across their faces as she teetered to greet them. Our geriatric feline was no longer a great beauty, yet our love for her grew deeper with the knowledge time was running out.

The right side of her face swelled up so spectacularly she couldn't open one eye. I wrapped her in her blanket and carried her back to Tough Vet. We'd changed our minds about him since our last visit.

"Hmmm," he said grimly. "A tooth abscess. I could operate and remove her teeth, but she's so weak I doubt she'd survive the surgery."

He recommended the obvious, gently this time, while running a hand over her back.

"I know what it's like when an animal's been part of a family for a long time," he said.

He sent us home to mull it over. If Cleo was a person she would have been forced to have a "natural" death like the one Mum had endured. I'd seen how, as disease takes hold, the victim enters a grey realm of pain that makes death a welcome visitor. Maybe it's nature's way of making the process ultimately acceptable. Given the choice, I wouldn't want to suffer what Mum went through. Fortunately, Cleo's animal status ensured she wouldn't have to. Death is one of the few areas where animals are granted superior rights.

Katharine, her face a waterfall of tears, readily agreed this was the right thing. Philip helped us wrap Cleo in her blanket for the last time to take her to Tough Vet, whom I'd decided wasn't tough at all.

"It's time, old girl," he said, slipping a tiny needle into the back of her paw. The movement was so gentle she didn't flinch. As we said our good-byes, Cleo curled in the shape of a crescent moon. Her head drooped. She was suddenly gone.

The vet put her in an opaque plastic bag and we carried her home inside the blanket.

Philip began to dig a hole under the daphne bush in the front garden. The spade hit the ground with soft, regular thuds. He wasn't in the mood for talking. Reading the back of his head as he swung the spade, I could tell he was upset—not in the tears-on-television way that's become grindingly fashionable for both sexes. His was a restrained, dignified grief, the sort men were famous for until they were told it was bad for their health.

I wanted to make him put down the spade and just hold him for a while, but it would only drag things out. Men are better off doing things. Besides, there were my own useless tears to deal with.

After what seemed a very long time, he stopped and rested on the spade. We both stared down at the hole. It was deeper than it probably needed to be, but this is a man who always went the extra mile for his family. And Cleo was an integral part of that.

"I don't suppose we want to bury her in the blanket," he said.

Unwrapping the blanket he slid Cleo's lifeless form from the vet's plastic bag onto the soil. He bent and kissed her head before lowering her into the hole.

"She's been with this family longer than I have," he sighed.

Birds sang a requiem as, spade by spade, the earth covered her body.

◆

Some cultures prefer to bury their relatives in their gardens. I was beginning to understand why. Every morning I said hello to Cleo on my way to the letter box. The gardener looked alarmed when I told him not to dig too deep around the daphne bush. Our precious cat didn't need disturbing.

Cleo presided over our family through nearly twenty-four years. She helped heal wounds I thought we'd never recover from. Maybe her work was complete now, the healing was done, and we could get along without her. Except she left us with a different kind of sorrow. I suddenly understood the logic of ancient Egyptians shaving their eyebrows when a family cat died.

People asked when we were getting a new cat. They spoke as if one cat would lead to another. A friend took me to a pet shop. We watched a bunch of kittens tumbling about in an enclosure. They were mostly tortoiseshell. Adorable. Some were locked in a play fight, rolling around in a bundle of fur. Others dozed. Cute, so cute. A small grey kitten climbed the wire mesh, hitching himself paw by paw above our heads. A group of shoppers gathered around the cage, the expressions on their faces tender as a Leonardo da Vinci portrait. Among them was a disheveled man I'd noticed out on the street earlier. He'd looked angry and so withdrawn people had stepped sideways to avoid him. The layers of aggression he'd been carrying around disintegrated when he saw the kittens. His unshaven jaw softened into a smile. Leaning against the wire he gazed at them with pure benevolence. Now he was watching the grey kitten, who'd suddenly realized he couldn't get back down as easily as he'd climbed up. He glanced anxiously down at the floor, then back up at the wire. He couldn't climb any higher. There was no choice. The kitten performed an impressive backwards flip and landed safely back on ground level. The man laughed. Maybe the kitten reminded him of himself, climbing for the heavens only to land with a thump back on earth.

"Can we take one home?" a teenager asked his mother. He, too, was enthralled. If he persuaded her to take a kitten that day it had a noble task ahead. The young man was mentally disabled.

A sad woman pointed at a pretty tortoiseshell. Maybe her house was empty, just waiting for the pad of velvet paws.

Every kitten in the enclosure had a purpose to fulfill, human hearts to heal, lessons to teach about the true nature of love. There wasn't one I didn't want to scoop up and hold warm and soft against my chest. But I wasn't going to take one home that day.

Cats aren't something to be "got." They turn up in people's lives when they're needed, and with a purpose that probably won't be understood to begin with. I certainly hadn't wanted a kitten so soon after Sam's death. Not consciously, anyway. Life is a contrary business. Sometimes what you think you don't want and what you need are the same thing. Cleo's cuddles, her fun, her uppity behavior, were exactly what we needed to take our minds off monumental sadness and remind us what joy there is in living and breathing. She taught us to loosen up, laugh and toughen up when necessary.

Guardian of our household, Cleo watched over every step of our journey. She stayed with us for as long as we needed her—which turned out a decade or two longer than expected. Whether she'd been sent to us by Sam or the Egyptian cat goddess, she bestowed her healing powers on us with more generosity than could be asked of any creature.

Once we started trusting life again magical things seemed to unfold. Wonderful people like Ginny, Jason, Anne Marie and Philip turned up at exactly the right times. Cleo supervised every encounter, sometimes giving the impression she'd actually arranged them. I'll always be grateful to these people and many more who helped us recover from the loss of Sam. Not that I'll ever confidently say we've recovered. We've changed, grown. Sam, his life and death, will always be part of us.

Anger ultimately gave way to forgiveness and, years later, the enormous relief of learning Sam hadn't died alone and frightened. I discovered Superman is real, after all. He's the hero who stops at accident scenes and does what he can for victims. For us his name was Arthur Judson.

＊

For years I'd avoided returning to the zigzag in Wellington. With typical sensitivity, Ginny understood and never pressed me to visit her. We'd arranged reunions in Australia or other parts of New Zealand, anywhere that served good sauvignon, really. But curiosity eventually got the better of me. As the rental car ground up the hill towards Wadestown I prepared for gut-wrenching replays. Rounding the first hook bend, then the second, I noticed there was still a stretch of public land, a mini park, overlooking the harbor. I'd once dreamt of erecting a sculpture there in Sam's memory, but concrete and stainless steel lack warmth. There are better ways to honor a lost child.

The road straightened, narrowed and became steeper as it rose towards the footbridge, still hanging across the cutting like a gallows. As the car sped underneath, I absorbed a rush of impressions. The steps down from the bridge, the edge of the footpath where Sam had turned to his brother all those years ago and said, "Be quiet." The harsh surface of the asphalt where his blood had spilt. My chest jarred. What was the point of putting myself through all this?

The houses on our old street seemed more brightly painted, the gardens better maintained since we'd left. At the end of the road I was astonished to find the zigzag had disappeared. Ginny had mentioned the neighbors had clubbed together to pay for a bulldozer to create drive-on access for all the houses, but I hadn't imagined anything this dramatic. The old zigzag with its twists and turns had been replaced by a full-on driveway plunging straight down the hill. I stood at the top of the zigzag that was now a road and looked down on the city. It sprawled farther up the hills these days. There were several new high-rise office blocks. Wind jagged up from the south.

"Bubbles, darling?" asked a familiar voice. Ginny and I wrapped arms around each other. Laughter lines and streaks of grey through her hair had only intensified her beauty. Leopard-skin tights and wild earrings had succumbed to a flowing skirt and silk shirt that wouldn't have looked out of place on the streets of Milan.

Together we walked down the driveway over what once would have been one zig and a zag to Ginny's place. I deliberately avoided turning towards our old bungalow. A single glimpse had potential to unleash an army of demons. The jungle that used to surround the Desilva's had gone, but their house sat serene as ever. A champagne cork popped as Ginny explained how she and Rick had looked at apartments in town, but nothing could surpass the convenience and outlook of this house.

Nodding, I took in the surroundings. Ginny's taste in interior design had moved on from eighties chic to European understatement. Having lived there nearly thirty years, Ginny confessed she and Rick were the neighborhood establishment now. The Butlers had moved ten years ago. Mrs. Sommerville had gone to the great staff room in the sky.

"And our old house?" I asked tentatively.

"A footballer and his girlfriend lived there for a while," said Ginny. "Someone wanted to renovate it, but they gave up. It's been tenanted ever since. There's a good view from upstairs, remember?"

I followed her tentatively up the staircase, safe in the knowledge that if I broke down Ginny of all people would know what to do. She pulled a curtain aside and beckoned me towards the window. Our old bungalow was barely recognizable. The front garden with its path lined with forget-me-nots had been obliterated, along with the boys' digging patch, to make way for a concrete slab wide enough to park two cars alongside each other. Sensible, yes. No more rain-soaked treks carrying groceries to the front door. Not that it resembled our front door anymore. The dark paneling had been painted white, along with the mock-Tudor beams that had once given the place "character." Someone had decided to rid the place of its ghosts by throwing buckets of white paint over it. The house seemed narrower, chastened. Rob's bedroom window where Cleo used to sit was the same shape, the roof pitched at the same angle, but it wasn't our house anymore. Like the zigzag and everything else in the neighborhood, it had moved on.

I'd been steeling myself for flashbacks on this visit. Instead, looking down on the old house with Ginny, I experienced an unexpected sensation of lightness and peace. A circle had completed itself. Our life on the zigzag was faded as an old photograph. Nothing but a memory. The only thing that mattered was the lives we had now.

+

Even after Cleo died she continued to leave physical reminders of her presence. Unmistakable black hairs were scattered through our sheets and clothes. There was frozen cat food in the back of the freezer. Hauling Cleo's rejected dog bed out from under the house, I had an urge to call Rob. His line was busy, of course.

"Were you trying to call me?" I asked when I finally got through.

"No, I was talking to someone."

"Who?"

"Chantelle. She's back in Australia."

"Oh, that's lovely! With her boyfriend?"

"She's broken up with him."

The bond of friendship between Rob and Chantelle had deepened with the death of her brother. Sam's loss was so much a part of him that Rob was able to understand a lot of Chantelle's pain. They both now belonged to the nameless club of people who have lost brothers. Within a year they were living together, engaged to be married and discussing what type of kitten they'd like to add to their household. Intense research was carried out over the Internet. A British Blue, perhaps, or maybe even a Siamese.

When they stayed a night at the house of Chantelle's Aunt Trudy, who'd introduced them nearly ten years earlier, the resident Burmese insisted on sleeping on their bed.

"No way am I living with a pedigreed kitten," Rob said next day. "That cat spent the whole night talking to me, telling me to get out of his bed."

"What *is* it with you and cats?" I said.

"Dunno. Guess it's a Cleo thing."

I smiled, remembering six-year-old Rob cradling his brand-new kitten, how she'd helped him sleep alone in his bedroom for the first time without Sam, "spoken" to him through his dreams and helped him develop friendships. Watching over him for nearly a quarter of a century, Cleo our cat goddess had presided over countless birthday parties and nursed Rob through illness. From her resting place under the daphne bush, she was still exerting her influence.

If and when Rob and Chantelle do acquire a cat, Rob says, it'll have to be an ordinary mog. I wouldn't be surprised if it turns out to be a crossbreed with just a whisker of Abyssinian.

The Beginning

Acknowledgments

Every kitten belongs to a litter. Likewise, Cleo's story would never have been born without help from many wonderful people. I'd like to thank Catherine Drayton at InkWell and Amy Pyle, Laurie Parkin, Michaela Hamilton, and the magnificent team at Citadel for embracing Cleo with such enthusiasm. Thanks, too, to Louise Thurtell and Jude McGee in Sydney, who believed in our cat story from the beginning. They provided me with unwavering support through various forms of self-doubt and an unexpected health hiccup while I was writing the book.

A purr to U.S. friends Helen Trammell, Faith Kaiser and Sarah Heineken, who discovered my stories on the Internet and sent generous reassurance that people laugh and cry about the same things whatever part of the world they live in.

Huge thanks to Roderick and Gillian Deane, who encouraged me to write about Cleo in the first place. And to Douglas Drury for providing soothing lunches during what seemed, to a superficial 500-word-story journalist, long months of writing. Julie Wentworth, the world's best yoga teacher, deserves a salute for her flowers and phone calls, which arrived just when they were needed. As does Sarah Wood for regular laughs over cups of coffee, along with Heather and Mano Thevathasan for countless acts of kindness. Big hugs to my sister Mary for her loving care during my recovery.

Thanks from the depths of my heart to Philip, Rob, Lydia, Katharine, Chantelle and Steve for allowing me to share my version of our story with the world. Given the chance to write from their personal perspectives, there's no doubt each tale would unfold differently. Their trust and generosity is boundless. An extra high five goes to Philip and Katharine for taking over cooking, shopping and laundry duties, and to Lydia for her heavenly massages.

The deepest bow is for Cleo, who loved us with all her heart for so long.

www.helenbrown.com